Nova Gibson is a leading expert on narcissistic abuse recovery in Australia. She is the director and founder of Brighter Outlook Narcissistic Abuse Counselling Service in Brisbane, where she is also the primary counsellor.

In this book, she brings the expertise gained from her research into narcissistic abuse and years of experience in helping thousands of clients as well as personal experience.

Before opening her practice in 2012, Nova gained extensive experience working in child safety in the government sector, and with individuals, couples and families experiencing crisis and trauma. She has a Bachelor of Social Science in Behavioural Science and Counselling and at the time of writing is studying for her Bachelor of Human Services in order to better identify abusive relationships.

Nova has a substantial global audience and has helped thousands of people from around the world with one-on-one professional support and her popular online Q&A and narcissistic abuse recovery sessions.

Visit www.brighteroutlooknarcissisticabusecounselling.com.au
Facebook: Nova Gibson Narcissistic Abuse Expert
Instagram: @novas_narcissistabuse_recovery
TikTok: @novasnarcrecovery

fake love

NOVA GIBSON

HarperCollins*Publishers*

HarperCollins*Publishers*
Australia • Brazil • Canada • France • Germany • Holland • India
Italy • Japan • Mexico • New Zealand • Poland • Spain • Sweden
Switzerland • United Kingdom • United States of America

HarperCollins acknowledges the Traditional Custodians
of the land upon which we live and work, and pays respect
to Elders past and present.

First published on Gadigal Country in Australia in 2023
by HarperCollins*Publishers* Australia Pty Limited
ABN 36 009 913 517
harpercollins.com.au

A catalogue record for this book is available from the National Library of Australia

ISBN 978 1 4607 6433 6 (paperback)
ISBN 978 1 4607 1635 9 (ebook)
ISBN 978 1 4607 4917 3 (international audio book)

Cover design by HarperCollins Design Studio
Author photo: Nova Gibson
Typeset in Bembo Std by Kelli Lonergan

Printed and bound by CPI Group (UK) Ltd, Croydon, CR0 4YY

*Dedicated to the memory of my late father, Neil Gibson.
If not for you, Dad, and your unconditional love and
reassurance that I could achieve anything my heart desired,
I may never have written this book.*

Contents

AUTHOR'S NOTE

To illustrate recurrent patterns of narcissistic abuse and the effects such abuse has on victims, I've used the story of 'Sofie'. Sofie is not a real name; indeed she's not just one person: her story is an amalgam of the experiences of many real people. Also, the character Justin (and any other narcissistic abuser, male or female, described in this book) is not a real person but a fictional one, again drawn upon from multiple experiences shared with me over many years' professional experience, and the reader should not consider that any character described in this book is in fact an identifiable person engaging in abusive conduct.

FOREWORD

I'd like to tell you that my intimate knowledge of narcissistic abuse is purely the result of years of professional experience and the clutch of letters after my name, but that's not the case. The dynamics of this insidious, covert form of psychological torment were not learned on the job, nor did I become an expert through my university studies. Rather, it comes from personally experiencing just how easy it is to be pulled into the narcissist's charming web – and how hard it is to break free. So I bring that lived truth as well professional expertise to my counselling sessions – and to this book.

I first became passionate about supporting victims and survivors of narcissistic abuse after my own experience. Nothing could have prepared me for the crazy-making and pain of these toxic relationships. I tried to seek support but found none in the places you'd expect. I found myself feeling patronised by experienced psychologists who blamed me, the victim, for being co-dependent. This did not sit well with me at all so, like many victims of narcissistic abuse, I turned to private online support groups and forums for victims of narcissistic abuse, as well as videos shared online by other victims and experts in the area. It was in these safe spaces that I finally found validation and support.

So it was that in the course of my own search for aid and assistance I discovered that victims of narcissistic abuse were crying out for effective support worldwide. My substantial international online following is an indication of just how widespread the lack of compassionate, practical, professional advice for these victims is.

After I'd done the work to heal my own trauma, I made it my mission to help victims understand *their* abuse, find a way to break the toxic cycle that kept them going back, and heal. I know it feels as if you will never be happy again at times, and that life cannot get any worse, but I am your living proof not only that you will one day be happy again, but that you will thrive!

Every day people contact me from all over the world seeking support in their narcissistic abuse recovery. This type of abuse can happen to anyone, but core wounds from child abuse or previous relationship trauma will make you even more vulnerable. A mental health professional is not immune to the insidious trauma bond that takes place in these appalling situations, and clinical psychologists, social workers, medical doctors and psychiatrists who are themselves struggling with their inability to leave an abusive relationship have all asked for help from me as the go-to expert on narcissistic abuse.

It's a form of abuse so hidden from view that friends and loved ones, let alone health professionals, just don't 'see' it or know how to deal with it. My beautiful clients, who often come to me after other mental health professionals have been unable to help them, frequently tell me of their relief at finally finding someone who 'gets it'.

As a counsellor who specialises in narcissistic abuse recovery I have supported over 4000 victims of undiagnosed narcissists to leave their abuser, heal once the relationship has ended, and go on to lead happy and fulfilled lives.

If you are reading this book, then you are, or have been, in a relationship with a narcissist – or you know someone who has. And you *know* you deserve more! I have written this book for you.

INTRODUCTION

One day, Sofie woke up and realised that her soulmate had turned into someone she didn't recognise. The person who remained hated her. He also appeared to dislike one of their three children, and made no attempt to hide his preference for their eldest child. Their youngest child, their son, was simply invisible to him, and no longer even tried to gain his father's attention, let alone affection. It was distressing to watch her children, who were in constant competition with each other, become resentful of each other.

It seemed that as a wife and mother Sofie couldn't do anything right anymore. Why did he change? Who was this person who made her feel so ugly and worthless and couldn't seem to love his own children? What could she do? She wanted her soulmate back. She wanted him to tell her how to get back to their former blissful bubble. But he wouldn't. She wanted him to realise how much his younger children loved him, and for him to give them the 'love' that he showed their eldest child. But again, he wouldn't. Yet she couldn't leave him. Sofie thought that if she just tried harder, one day her soulmate would return.

Such is the reasoning of every victim of narcissistic abuse.

Narcissistic personality disorder, or NPD, is at the extreme end of the spectrum of what's known as narcissism or 'self-love' and it can have a devastating effect on people who love the narcissist.

However, there are few scientific studies on narcissism, and relatively little is known about NPD – despite the prevalence of narcissistic traits in general society – simply because narcissists don't believe there's anything wrong, so don't seek treatment. Consequently, it's virtually impossible to get accurate statistics on the prevalence of NPD in Australia or the rest of the world. The statistics that are available vary, suggesting that between 0.5 and 1 per cent of the population are diagnosed with NPD. However, these statistics must be wildly inaccurate, given that the likelihood of someone being diagnosed with NPD is minimal and most often limited to instances when psychological evaluation is court-ordered.

Not only do these statistics grossly minimise the prevalence of toxic narcissists in our society, they don't provide accurate insight into the abusers' gender. But people with this disorder do have characteristic traits.

People with NPD use emotional abuse, or coercive control, to control and denigrate their victim. And that *can* be quantified. According to a report released by the Australian Bureau of Statistics in 2022, 2.2 million women and 1.4 million men aged 15 or older have experienced partner emotional abuse. That's one in four women and one in six men.

Not all narcissists are physically violent, but narcissism is a strong risk factor for physical violence. When the narcissist's sense of superiority and entitlement is threatened their behaviour may escalate quickly from psychological/emotional abuse to physical abuse in an episode of narcissistic rage. The physical abuse is not always as obvious as punching and hitting, but can also involve restraints and intimidating behaviours such as yelling directly into their victim's ear.

The Personal Safety Survey conducted by the ABS defines emotional partner abuse as occurring 'when a person is subjected to behaviours that are aimed at preventing or controlling their behaviour, causing them emotional harm or fear'.

Sound familiar?

To illustrate why you may have become a victim of such abuse, how you were hooked by your narcissistic abuser, and why you stayed when the abuse became impossible to ignore, I've used the story of 'Sofie'. Sofie is not a real name; indeed she's not just one person: her story is an amalgam of the experiences of many real people. Most victims of narcissistic abuse will suffer a cluster of the behaviours discussed in Sofie's story, so many of these may chime with your own experience. As you'll see in Sofie's story, I've characterised her as a client who came to see me, and as someone who was discarded by the narcissist (rather than someone who left the relationship), as this allowed me to analyse the experience of narcissistic abuse with more depth and breadth.

This book is not intended to be used as a textbook or a 'how to' step-by-step guide. Rather, it is a companion and handbook for victims and survivors of narcissistic abuse trying to make sense of the abuse they are experiencing or have experienced in the past. So I've kept it informal and chatty – I want to engage, not intimidate!

I've used Sofie's story to illustrate the many stages of narcissistic abuse, from the initial 'pink cloud' of the love bombing stage through the processes of devaluation, discard and beyond, as well as other common strategies employed by narcissists. I look at life after the initial shock of the discard: divorce, how to heal yourself, and the long-term effect on any children of the relationship as they become adults. I also answer common questions victims ask, such as 'Why did I stay?'

So you might want to read *Fake Love* cover to cover or prefer to dip into chapters that are most relevant to you right now – and perhaps return to other chapters at other stages of your journey.

I have chosen a woman's story, but narcissistic abuse is *not* gender-specific. Female narcissists create just as much damage in the lives of their victims. If you are a man who needs this book, your story may differ from Sofie's because of obvious gendered societal and environmental influences. However, as Chapter 11, Boys Don't Cry, shows through two stories of male victims of NPD, the predictable tactics and cycles of the narcissist and the incomprehensible, intentional nature of the abuse are the same.

Sofie's story helps to explain the tactics the narcissist uses to hook you, tactics that fly under the radar of even the most intelligent and strongest of people. Finally, and most importantly, Sofie's story will demonstrate that the abuse you endured was *not your fault*.

It will help you to understand that the love a narcissist offers is fake, hence the title of my book. It will help you to armour up so that, should another narcissist dare to enter your life, you'll never become a victim of this abuse again.

This book will provide you with answers to questions you may have asked yourself time and time again. Not just from the start of your intense love affair, such as *How did I get so lucky?* and *What did I do to deserve this incredible chemistry and soulmate connection?* but those that might have started prickling at the edge of your mind as the relationship progressed, such as *Why can I never please them no matter how hard I try?* And *Why is nothing I do ever good enough?*

It will help answer the questions going round and round in your head when your once kind, caring partner becomes cruel and dismissive - and worse - and who now seems to despise everything they once purported to love about you. Who sabotages any chance of happiness in your life and who constantly confuses you with words and actions that reflect their dislike and hatred for you most days but their undying 'love' on others.

At the start, the feelings you have for each other are intense. You spend every second you can with them. They say they want to take care of you. They tell you that all they can see in their future is the two of you together, and you feel the same way. Your head is in a whirl. It's going so fast, but relationships like this only happen once in a lifetime, right? You take your seat on the roller-coaster and you hold on tight to the love of your life. You will be together forever.

Or so you think.

CHAPTER ONE

Fake love: When the mask falls off

When Sofie walked into my office, she looked like a woman who bore the weight of the world on her shoulders. Her eyes had a hollowness that I had seen many times before. Her life was, as she described it, 'a train wreck'. She was visibly traumatised and hypervigilant – permanently alert to danger – and her body would be responding by providing a constant, exhausting stream of adrenaline and cortisol.

As she sat down and the tears began to flow, I felt her pain. The excruciating pain of feeling nearly 'dead' without the familiar chaotic environment she had come to be dependent on. The fear of never again experiencing the comfort of being in the physical and psychological space that had become both her prison and sanctuary. The agony of knowing that someone else may have taken her place, while she staggered around wondering to herself: 'How did I get to this place where I don't know who I am anymore? And why can't I stop thinking about someone who made me feel worse about myself than any other person in my life before?'

Sofie came to me after her husband, Justin, had left her and immediately moved in with his girlfriend, Rachel. She suspected her ex-husband of being a narcissist. I believed her.

I've worked with thousands of victims of narcissistic abuse throughout my career, and Sofie's story is a textbook case, and her husband Justin had all the classic traits of what's known as a 'covert narcissist'. For this reason, I decided to centre her story in this book in the hope and expectation that you might recognise yourself in her and her experience, and feel less alone.

To understand Sofie's trauma we must first understand what narcissistic personality disorder is, and what narcissistic abuse is.

Narcissistic personality disorder

When narcissism is so extreme that it impacts negatively on all relationships, and these ego driven, exploitative traits are consistent over space and time, this is known as narcissistic personality disorder or NPD.

The American Psychiatric Association's *Diagnostic and Statistical Manual of Mental Disorders*, Fifth Edition (DSM-5), 2013, defines NPD as the presence of at least five of the following criteria in a variety of contexts:

+ A grandiose sense of self importance
+ A preoccupation with fantasies of unlimited success, power, brilliance, beauty or ideal love
+ A belief that they are special and unique and can only be understood

by, or should associate with, other special or high-status people or institutions

+ A need for excessive admiration
+ A sense of entitlement
+ Interpersonally exploitative behaviour (using and manipulating people for personal gain)
+ A lack of empathy
+ Envy of others or a belief that others are envious of them
+ A demonstration of arrogant and haughty behaviours or attitudes.

CAUSES OF NPD

The exact cause of NPD is not known, but much research centres on risk factors such as genetics, environmental influences in early childhood such as the relationship between the child and their primary care giver (their parent), childhood trauma/abuse, and/or an overindulgent environment where exploitative behaviours are role modelled, encouraged and rewarded. The abusive actions of the individual with NPD, which are designed to protect the weak, true self, become a skill that is honed as the individual grows older and becomes more adept in abusing with successive relationships. While their manipulative behaviours are largely inflicted with malice upon their victim (they are intentional), it stands to reason that these ongoing, consistent behaviours become second nature to the abuser, where the distinction between intentional behaviour and automatic responses may become blurred.

COVERT NARCISSISTS

In many years of helping the victims of narcissistic abusers I have noticed that most pathological narcissists are what is known as 'covert narcissists': they hide their tendency well while infiltrating your life. Their victims do not see them coming because they aren't loud and arrogant; in fact, they are the complete opposite. Many are quiet, anxious and forever the victim – a 'victim' who engages in passive-aggressive behaviours such as fake tears and the use of past trauma to justify their abuse of you. This might sound like 'I abuse you because I was abused.' Many victims describe their abuser as shy and introverted, with their loud, aggressive side only coming out behind closed doors. In at least 70 per cent of the thousands of cases I've dealt with, the behaviour described by my clients exhibits clear traits of covert narcissism. This is how they were able to infiltrate the lives of their victims so easily.

OVERT NARCISSISTS

There is a societal misconception that you can easily see a narcissist coming because they are flamboyant and their regular behaviours include vanity, such as constantly admiring themself in mirrors, being loud and obnoxious, and bragging about themselves to all and sundry. That they seek to be the centre of attention in public and love having the spotlight on themselves. This is an 'overt' narcissist. While overt narcissists may be less common, both types are dangerous in that they lack compassion, or empathy, for others and will cause devastation in the lives of their victim.

Whether they are covert or overt, the narcissist will at first present themselves as the perfect mate. They will mesmerise you by mirroring all your best qualities back to you and wooing you with grandiose gestures of love and commitment. This stage is called the 'idealisation' or 'love bombing' phase and at this time a psychological and physical dependence develops due to the rush of feel-good hormones such as oxytocin. The dopamine receptors are all being hit at once and it is these feelings you will literally crave, like a drug addict chasing that initial high. Unknowingly, you will then adjust your tolerance for abuse to higher and higher thresholds in order to get a 'fix' of those feel-good hormones.

Once the narcissist knows you're hooked, the devaluation stage begins, as the narcissist does not have to pretend to be nice anymore and can be who they really are: a predator, devoid of empathy, who uses others as vehicles to boost and maintain their ego. To succeed in this quest, you must be 'less than' them in every way and therefore their mission is to destroy all that is 'good' or 'better' in you. To this end, they will push you away and pull you back in a cycle that ends with you the victim ultimately being discarded – only to be replaced immediately by an 'exciting' new target.

The continuous roller-coaster of abuse followed by intermittent periods of kindness produces a powerful trauma bond, or addiction to their abuser, and the victim struggles to understand why they cannot leave someone they know on a logical level is so abusive. It is especially hard for victims to stay away when the source of their addiction keeps drawing them back in to see if they'll accept another round of abuse. (This is called the 'hoovering stage' after the vacuum cleaner of that name.)

DIAGNOSING NPD

Many of my clients are anxious about categorising their partner as a pathological narcissist when they do not have a diagnosis from a professional, and they wonder if their partner can change. With more in-depth discussion, I usually discover that the powerful trauma bond with their abuser has led to the victim minimising the abuse and searching for a way to keep their abuser (who they are, by this point, addicted to) in their lives. In essence, I discover that their partner in all likelihood *is* a narcissist. I explore this trauma bond further in Chapter 4. If any of this sounds familiar, then I ask you to trust your instincts. The reality is that the likelihood of NPD being diagnosed anywhere other than a courtroom setting, where it is mandatory, is almost zero. Narcissists do not think there is anything wrong with them, and it is everyone around them who finds themselves in therapy.

Your ability to trust your judgement was compromised by a toxic person who benefited from your lack of confidence. Now is the time to start trusting your intuition. The diagnosis of NPD, or any diagnosis, is a label that is given to a set of traits or symptoms so that a treatment may be applied. But you will never hear of a narcissist walking into a therapist's office and asking to be treated for their narcissism. And as I explained in the introduction, this means it's very difficult to find reliable and credible statistics on the prevalence of NPD in society and, more importantly, the resounding destruction of people's lives that the disorder inflicts.

With a lack of willing subjects to participate in clinical studies comes a lack of research and consequently a lack of truly informed clinicians to help the victims. My belief is that pathological narcissism is common and, like a cancer that spreads undetected until it's too late, is incurable. The victims, however, are everywhere and it is the victims who become the experts in their own trauma. This is why, when they tell me they were abused by a narcissist, I believe them. It is highly likely that many of my clients will have been abused by someone who would be diagnosed with narcissistic personality disorder. However, as mentioned earlier, a diagnosis of such is unlikely, so when talking about narcissists in this book I will be referring to 'pathological narcissists'.

Let's circle back. You – yes, *you* – are the expert in your trauma. *You* have done your research and have discovered this person meets at least five of the criteria. *You* are aware that your abuser is demonstrating consistent and repeated patterns of abusive behaviour over time, and that these are not the isolated incidents of an 'unpleasant' person prone to bad manners. If you don't feel comfortable labelling your partner with NPD then I suggest forgetting the label and asking yourself whether this person's behaviour is toxic, and whether you feel emotionally safe and secure with them.

If the answer is no, your job is not to wait for a diagnosis, nor is it your job to try to fix them. Your job is to leave. Nobody has the right to abuse you and you can re-evaluate from a safe distance of no contact, where your confidence and ability to trust yourself will grow stronger.

Whether my clients are not yet confident enough to trust their judgement, despite the evidence they've accumulated, or if they are resolute in knowing they have indeed been abused by a narcissist, my support is the same. I will help them to validate their trauma, to help them understand why they stayed, and support them with strategies to escape or stay away from their abuser and to begin their healing journey. I will *never* provide anyone who has been abused with strategies to 'risk manage' the abuse, or to appease their abuser so they stop abusing.

Again, once you recognise that that your partner is demonstrating consistent and repeated patterns of abusive behaviour over time, and that these are not isolated incidents, your job is not to stay and try and fix them. *Your job is to leave.*

Narcissistic abuse

Most victims have trouble articulating the exact nature of the abuse they've suffered because of the covert and insidious nature of the abuse, and of course the lack of understanding in society by even well-meaning mental health professionals. The common symptoms that my clients report include:

+ Being hypervigilant or on constant alert (which they tend to describe as 'walking on eggshells')
+ Being unable to trust their own judgement (also known as 'second-guessing themselves')
+ Being unable to trust others
+ Having difficulty making simple decisions
+ Physical symptoms that may include headaches and insomnia
+ Feelings of anxiety
+ Fear that any success will be sabotaged (which can result in self-sabotage and isolation)
+ Symptoms of post-traumatic stress disorder
+ Feeling numb or in shock.

The term that is commonly accepted by experts in narcissistic abuse recovery to describe the symptoms a victim experiences is narcissistic victim syndrome (NVS), which is not currently recognised as a diagnosis in the DSM-5. (It is, however, recognised by many narcissistic abuse recovery experts who acknowledge the severe and long-term destructive impact such abuse can have on a victim's mental health.) This reflects the lack of support and understanding in the professional world. As a victim of narcissistic abuse, you are more likely to be diagnosed with post-traumatic stress disorder (PTSD) or complex post-traumatic stress disorder (CPTSD) by a professional because of the ongoing symptoms and behaviours resulting from your trauma.

Therefore, to help with your understanding of what narcissistic abuse is, I will provide you with *my* definition. This definition is based on my own personal experience, and the experiences of the thousands of victims and survivors of narcissistic abuse that I have counselled.

I define narcissistic abuse as the psychological and emotional abuse of another individual with the intent of stripping that individual of a sense of identity, a sense of self-worth, their self-esteem, their dreams and their goals in order to make them dependent upon their abuser. In a nutshell, the narcissist seeks to dismantle and erode their victim's personality and create a new one that will consistently boost the narcissist's ego.

This is achieved by creating an environment of immense confusion where the victim is conditioned to blame themselves for the abuse. The victim is conditioned to 'tolerate' the abuse through the use of intermittent 'nice' treatment, which provides relief and distracts from the abuse. Using these manipulative techniques and more, the narcissist distorts their victim's reality to such an extent they no longer trust themselves to make simple decisions.

To the narcissist, a divided mind is a conquered mind. And who does the victim turn to for reassurance as to what their reality is? The very person who distorted their perceptions in the first place. Their abuser.

Narcissistic supply

The narcissist needs to make their victim as dependent upon them as possible in order to gain maximum 'narcissistic supply'. Narcissistic supply is found in the attention a narcissist seeks, which can be either positive (admiration, adoration), or negative (fear, contempt). In essence, it doesn't matter whether you're loving them or hating them, the narcissist is soaking up the supply that comes from your attention regardless. The only thing that matters to them is that they are occupying your thoughts constantly. Just as we all need oxygen to survive, the narcissist cannot exist as the resilient persona they have created without this supply. This is what sustains them. To be without it is to be alone with their true self, and that is a place they will avoid at all costs because it's a form of vulnerability. To be vulnerable is, in the narcissist's mind, to be weak and pathetic, and it is simply too painful for the narcissist to confront the shame that comes with perceived weakness. Their quest for narcissistic supply is insatiable and at the expense of anyone and anything.

The true self vs the false self

It is impossible for a narcissist to take responsibility for their toxic behaviour. Taking responsibility for their behaviour would suggest they have flaws, and this threatens their mask of superiority — a defensive facade which must be sustained at all costs so the weak, wounded, true self is not exposed. To that end, all real or imagined criticism that presents the narcissist with their own weaknesses is rebuked and the offender raged against and punished.

This was distressing and confusing for Sofie when she had done nothing except ask her partner to allow her to express her feelings. Very early on, she developed ways to make the punishments bearable by apportioning blame to herself, thus minimising the severity of the abuse. She reasoned that Justin was right: she probably *was* oversensitive and she didn't give him nearly enough credit for putting a roof over the family's heads. After all, he did work hard to provide for them, so why shouldn't he be allowed to go out after work and relax for a few hours without being pestered about where he went and with whom?

Sofie worried that perhaps she had created this situation because she had not felt like being intimate with Justin lately, and she regularly thought of ways she could make him happy again and bring back her soulmate, and so reignite her desire for him. She was sure if she just tried hard enough, the amazing person who'd treated her like a princess would return and they would live happily ever after. This was the explanation that made the most sense to her, as believing that this person who made her feel so alive and loved could also be the same person who made her feel so worthless was too overwhelming to contemplate. That would mean she didn't really know her soulmate at all and that the relationship was a toxic charade. For Sofie, it was easier for her to believe that the golden times she'd experienced in the beginning would one day return for good.

You might be wondering: how did Sofie allow herself to become so attached to, and dependent on, Justin? Why did she develop these strategies to overlook the abuse and stay with someone who treated her so badly? These are logical questions. But Sofie had been effectively brainwashed to the extent that she didn't trust her own judgement when it came to her husband, and she believed she needed him. The groundwork for the powerful bond between victim and abuser, which is so difficult for outsiders to understand, is laid by the narcissist in the love bombing stage.

For Sofie, it all started after she met her soulmate.

IN SUMMARY

- Narcissistic personality disorder, or NPD, is at the extreme end of the spectrum of what's known as narcissism or 'self-love', but it is almost impossible to diagnose as the narcissist doesn't believe there is anything wrong with them.
- The narcissist wears a mask of superiority, a defensive facade which must be sustained at all costs so the weak, wounded, true self is not exposed.
- The narcissist requires constant narcissistic supply or attention, whether positive or negative, to make their victim as dependent on them as possible.

CHAPTER TWO

The love bombing stage

Sofie was just 20 years old when she met her abuser. She'd had a tumultuous childhood as a result of being raised by what she now recognises as a narcissistic mother and an enabling father, and all the dynamics that are part of that environment. She never felt good enough for her mother no matter how hard she tried, and her childhood was painful to recall. Her memories were in stark contrast to the image of the 'perfect' family her mother conveyed to outsiders. Sofie couldn't wait to leave home, managing to do so when she was 18 and a year into her university studies.

When Sofie started to date she had a couple of short, failed relationships before deciding to try her hand at online dating. After a few weeks of chatting with a couple of men who seemed nice but certainly didn't rock her world, a man that she was very attracted to finally swiped right. Once they'd connected, they talked on the phone and messaged incessantly for five days. Sofie thought about him every spare minute. She hadn't even met him in person yet but the chemistry was already palpable. Her heart would skip a beat and she would grin every time she received a notification that he had messaged. Finally, they met in person. This genuine, kind, funny man was now a reality, and her attraction to him deepened. They talked and laughed all night and it felt completely right to leave the restaurant and go back to his place where their connection was consummated.

From that moment on, Sofie and her new beau, Justin, spent nearly every waking moment together. She felt giddy with happiness.

The 'happy' hormones continued to pulse through Sofie's body constantly in response to Justin's romantic behaviour. He continually told her how beautiful she was, how amazing her skin was – even saying that her breath smelt like roses first thing in the morning. (She knew he might be stretching it with this one, but it was so nice that he wanted to make her feel good about herself.) Justin had placed her on a metaphorical pedestal and made her feel like a goddess.

After just two weeks of knowing each other, Justin told Sofie he was in love with her, and it felt right to her to say it back. Then he asked her to move in with him and she agreed instantly. Why waste time when she knew she'd met her soulmate?

Sofie was being love bombed. This is a strategy the narcissist engages in to ensnare their victims quickly by providing an environment that makes their target feel desirable, confident and loved. Strategies the narcissist employs are grandiose in nature and intense, with the victim being bombarded with messages and gestures that pull at their heartstrings. These may include extravagant statements of passion and desire reminiscent of a romance novel or Hallmark greeting card, poetry and music, generous gifts and holidays, and constant messages implying a future together.

Many victims describe their feelings in this initial love bombing stage as euphoric, as if they were on a pink cloud of happiness, and say they had never felt so desired by another person. The intensity of these feelings is extremely important in the narcissistic cycle of abuse because it's these 'good' feelings the victim will remember when they inevitably come to a screeching halt. It is this euphoria that will trump all manner of abuse and set the victim up for an incredibly high tolerance for abuse, believing the pink cloud will return at any time.

As Justin did to Sofie, the narcissist will love bomb their target to entrap them very quickly and secure them as a constant source of narcissistic supply. They will go to incredible lengths in this stage, and victims describe a whirlwind romance that swept them off their feet. These grandiose strategies are also used by the narcissist to refute their internal shame. They must be bigger and better than everyone else to reflect the false persona that says: 'I am superior and omnipotent.'

This stage happens so quickly the victim is unable to think clearly and make rational choices, and this of course is part of the narcissist's plan. The narcissist will often say those magic words 'I love you' in a matter of days or weeks after meeting their victim, and declare it's a soulmate connection unlike any other relationship they've ever been in. The reason they do this is simple: they need to hook their target before the target sees the true identity of the person they are dealing with. Would you have stayed if your abuser revealed themselves immediately? Of course not. The person you meet in the beginning is the actor convincing you they are the person of your dreams. The intensity of the 'soulmate connection' means that any confusing behaviour by the narcissist at this time that does not align with the victim's perception of their perfect soulmate (a red flag) will normally be overlooked, and rationalised away.

Mirroring

Before she moved in with Justin, Sofie looked forward to Justin's daily 'good morning princess' and 'sweet dreams' texts. Their phone conversations would last for hours. He was such an amazing listener, seeming to hang on every word she said. It felt wonderful to be with someone who allowed her to express herself freely and didn't judge her. Justin listened intently as she told of her problematic relationship with her family, as well as problems she had experienced in previous intimate relationships. In return, Justin confided in her about his last relationship, which he'd ended after his partner cheated on him. He'd been crushed by the experience, he told her, and added that his ex had recently started stalking him when she found out that he was casually dating someone else, telling him she was still in love with him and wanted him back. He despised cheaters, he declared to Sofie, and couldn't understand how anyone could betray someone who loved them so much. Sofie felt for him, and the trust in her he showed by sharing these intimate details made her feel deeply connected to him.

When it comes to a narcissist and everything you discover you have in common with them, there are never any coincidences. One of the reasons you feel so connected to this person is that in the very beginning they are mirroring you. You are actually falling for all the amazing qualities that belong to *you*, because they are reflecting them back to you. And how amazing does it feel to have someone who practically hangs on every word you say? Someone is listening to your feelings and allowing you to talk about your innermost secrets and past traumas without judgement. It feels good, and the narcissist knows it.

I always tell my clients that listening is a skill that develops, and sometimes we all stumble in this department when our emotions are heightened. The narcissist's skill in listening, however, is unparalleled at the start when they are gathering data. The reality is they are listening very intently to assess you as a candidate for narcissistic supply. They are picking up on your likes, dislikes and past experiences – and then, hey presto! They become the yin to your yang. They become your soulmate, because you've unknowingly given them all the data they needed.

Sadly, you have also provided them with enough ammo to obliterate your heart at a later date. They especially love to hear how you have been hurt by previous partners. The narcissist does not want to be outshone in the power stakes, so they listen to what your ex did to hurt you, and they will likely repeat that behaviour when the time comes, only they will make it hurt twice as much. The information you provided in confidence will sit in the memory bank of the narcissist until the time comes when you need to be 'punished', when it will unceremoniously be pulled from their arsenal and used as a weapon against you.

Future faking

After a whirlwind three months during which Sofie became accustomed to living on her own personal cloud nine, Justin asked her to marry him. She was elated, and eagerly accepted. Four months later, they were married. Sofie and Justin had gone from first meeting to marriage in just seven months. Sofie was 'high' on the fumes of the love bombing she had experienced up until this point.

Just two months after the wedding, Sofie fell pregnant with their first child, a daughter. Two years after having her daughter she gave birth to another daughter, and two years after that she gave birth to their son.

Justin urged Sofie to stay at home with their children to give them the best possible start, assuring her that he would always take care of them and they would want for nothing. So Sofie put her own ambitions for a career as a teacher on hold, feeling grateful that she could devote these early years to her family. She felt privileged to have such a caring, hardworking husband and they agreed she would pick her studies back up when the children were older.

'Future faking' is a strategy that narcissists use to manipulate you into thinking they are invested in a future with you, and it begins very early in the love bombing phase. The narcissist will paint a picture of a glorious future they believe possible in a life with you, which appeals to their target's dreams of meeting 'the one' and settling down. They will appear to innocently drop comments such as 'I think you would make the most amazing wife' or 'Let's make plans to go on a holiday next year', or 'My mother would love me to settle down with someone like you', or they might talk about buying a home they could imagine living in with someone just like you.

Future faking is about cementing the unsuspecting target in the present by talking about plans that most of the time the narcissist has no intentions of keeping. These future plans suggest to the victim that this person they've just met is interested in more than just a short-term fling, and they become even more desirable. The narcissist knows exactly what will pull at your heartstrings, as they made a point of manipulating this information out of you during the love bombing phase, and will use your heart's desires to reel you in with promises to make your dreams come true.

In Sofie's case, Justin presented her with an ideal version of family life in which she could devote herself to their three young children and give them what she'd lacked in her own childhood while he supported them financially.

By the time the victim becomes aware the narcissist's promises have not, and are not likely to, come to fruition, it is too late. The victim is completely enmeshed with the narcissist and trying to reconcile the narcissist's words with their actions. The narcissist is very skilled in shifting around the timeline for when these promises will become a reality, so the victim stays hooked, then eventually develops their own skills to rationalise the narcissist's lies.

Future faking will be used to devalue the victim continuously throughout the relationship. The narcissist will get the victim's hopes up by promising them something very important to them, and then deliberately fail to follow through. Watching the victim's excitement grow as their special day gets closer means greater narcissistic supply when their dream is ripped away from them. The victim will learn not to look forward to anything, as anything that is potentially enjoyable is always paired with disappointment. The narcissist is conditioning their victim to not ask for anything, and to be grateful for very little.

* * *

The mask worn by the narcissist is designed for you especially, and they will only drop that mask when they know you are hooked. As sure as the sun will come up tomorrow, that mask must drop because it is an extremely arduous task to pretend you are someone you're not, especially when the narcissist is the one deserving all the attention (in their mind). It takes a lot of effort and commitment to love bomb someone, and as soon as they know they have landed their prey they can relax and become who they really are. The love bombing phase is unsustainable because the narcissist is only interested in the end goal, and that is for you to reflect back to them just how amazing they are. As gravity suggests, what goes up must come down, and when the mask drops the true self is revealed, and that is when you will be punished for your knowledge of that true self.

During the love bombing/idealising phase you will of course be reflecting back to the narcissist what a loving, compassionate person they are because this is what you're seeing, and this is what you perceive about them. In turn, you are perceived by the narcissist to be 'all good', and a suitable conduit to match their grandiose view of themselves. When the mask drops, and the narcissist starts to reveal their true self, you of course will react as any normal human being would do. You have just seen your prince or princess shapeshift into a monster so you will react negatively. It's at this time that you are deemed as 'all bad'. There is no grey area for the narcissist. Healthy people are still able to love you and maintain a positive connection despite any flaws you may have. Once the narcissist perceives criticism from you, however, you are viewed as worthless, and from then on will be treated as such. It is an inevitable lose–lose situation for victims because you are set up to react and then punished for doing so. This strategy of set-up and destroy will be used strategically on numerous occasions for the entire relationship.

IN SUMMARY

- The first stage of narcissistic abuse, 'love bombing' lays the groundwork for the powerful bond between victim and abuser. To the victim it can feel like a 'pink cloud of happiness'.
- The narcissist will mirror the victim's own qualities back to them as part of the love bombing process.
- Using phrases that imply the narcissist is envisaging a future together is another tactic of love bombing.

CHAPTER 3

The devaluation stage

Over time, Sofie realised that Justin had a quick and explosive temper, but she noticed it only seemed to be with her. He had turned into a bully who made her feel worthless. He would hold grudges, too. If she made even a small 'mistake', he'd never let her forget about it.

With everyone else, Justin exuded charisma and was ready to lend a helping hand. But with her he was always impatient and she could never please him. Whenever she thought she had pleased him, he would shift the goalposts: he'd asked for something different or he hadn't asked her to do anything at all.

Sofie's answer to managing the changes in his behaviour was to attribute his irritation with her as part and parcel of having young children and a stressful job. However, her resentment started to build as Justin not only refused to own his appalling behaviour, but managed to twist it so that everything was *her* fault.

Perhaps counselling was the answer: a marriage guidance expert could surely tell them what had gone wrong and how they could get back that soulmate connection. She'd be able to describe his behaviour to the therapist and explain how badly it affected her. Sofie thought that Justin would have to listen and believe the counsellor rather than 'blow up'. She even allowed him to choose the counsellor.

Before the meeting, Sofie spent hours researching Justin's behaviour in order to be thoroughly prepared, and one day she came across the term 'narcissist'. That was Sofie's lightbulb moment. Despite her new lack of confidence in her own judgement, she realised that Justin met the criteria for all nine traits of narcissistic personality disorder. His sense of self-importance and self-entitlement; his belief that he was special, unique and superior to others; his need for attention and admiration; his envy of others and belief that everyone envied him; his need to be in control; and of course his complete lack of empathy and remorse. Sofie became angry at herself for not noticing the red flags sooner but was comforted that at least she could now define what had been happening to her: narcissistic abuse. She also discovered that Justin fitted into the category of 'covert narcissist'.

Sofie's response was completely normal for a victim who, perhaps for the first time, was having their trauma validated. Justin's narcissism explained everything. He was full of self-importance and had a grandiose belief (or 'delusions' as Sofie called them) that he was more powerful than, and superior to, everyone else. He thought he was special; that everyone wanted to be him. In his eyes, anyone who didn't think he was amazing simply misunderstood him. He hated it when someone had something that made them look better than him. He would have to either outdo them or discard them. He had an enormous sense of entitlement and no hesitation in using people to get what he felt he deserved. He was arrogant and devoid of empathy, which he routinely demonstrated by destroying Sofie emotionally without remorse, then asking her what she was making for dinner as if nothing had happened. Justin was a textbook narcissist.

It would be natural to assume that Sofie would have started making plans to leave Justin once she discovered that he was never going to change and he was incapable of truly loving her. An inability to love other people is one of the key characteristics of pathological narcissists. But if you're reading this because of your own toxic connection to a narcissist, you've probably guessed that this information alone wasn't enough to sever the invisible ties Sofie had with her abuser.

When you have your own 'light bulb' moment that you are dealing with a narcissist, there are some important rules to remember – rules that Sofie was unaware of.

The 5 golden rules when dealing with a narcissist

1. NEVER TELL THEM THEY'RE A NARCISSIST

Never tell them you know. Keep that card close to your chest.

Regrettably, before the first counselling session, Sofie informed Justin of her findings. She thought she had something they could work with: a diagnosis. She wanted him to know that she would do everything she could to help him with his 'problem' – they would work through it together.

Sofie had hoped that Justin would feel liberated once he finally understood why he felt and behaved as he did and that most of their issues as a couple stemmed from his narcissism. She hoped that the counsellor could 'fix' him, even though she'd read that people with this disorder do not change, since changing would mean admitting to having a problem.

When Sofie showed Justin how his behaviour correlated with the traits of narcissistic personality disorder, he read the information in silence. He didn't mention it again until their first counselling session.

Justin had indeed listened to Sofie's concerns, but instead of agreeing with her, at the session he told the counsellor it was not he who had all the attributes of a full-blown narcissist, it was Sofie. He had also researched the topic and succeeded in painting himself as the victim of Sofie's abuse. He completely changed the narrative, portraying Sofie as a villain. Justin ensured he was the one to bring up certain situations he knew Sofie would want to discuss. But in his version of events, the roles were reversed every time.

He told the counsellor about his concern for Sofie's mental health; that she couldn't control her outbursts even when the children were around. He came across as a caring man who was willing to stand by his partner despite her many faults. Sofie told me that she broke down in the counsellor's office as Justin spun these fictional accounts of their life together. The counselling session went rapidly downhill from there (from Sofie's perspective, at least) as, consumed by anger and frustration, she yelled at Justin and called him a liar. It became apparent that the counsellor empathised with Justin after she asked Sofie to see her separately to address her problems that were impacting on the relationship.

2. NEVER GO TO A COUNSELLING SESSION WITH THE NARCISSIST

Narcissists only ever go to counselling to manipulate the counsellor, to seek narcissistic supply in the form of someone's undivided attention, and to use the counsellor's office to further abuse you. Only this time, they have a mental health professional backing them up.

The narcissist will portray themselves as your victim and bait you into a reaction to support their claims. If you've told them you believe they're a narcissist, you've also armed them with damaging weapons to use against you.

The fact is that the issues that Sofie was experiencing in her relationship were not relationship issues; they were issues of abuse. As such, Sofie should never have been attending counselling with her abuser, but as an individual needing the knowledge and skills to escape the abuse. She already had the strength to break free, she just couldn't see it because her abuser benefited from her lack of self-belief.

The relationship subsequently continued, and Sofie was diagnosed by her doctor with anxiety and depression for which she was prescribed medication. Afterwards, Justin would use the fact that she was 'on pills' to undermine her any time she disagreed with him.

3. MAINTAIN A SUPPORT SYSTEM, EVEN IF YOU HAVE TO HIDE IT

Justin would regularly call Sofie 'crazy', tell her she was bipolar (even though this was untrue) and claim that many other people ('everyone') agreed with him, including Sofie's own friends and family. These comments meant Sofie felt betrayed and she stopped calling on them for support. Her friends had already started dropping away because Justin was rude to them. The charismatic mask Justin wore when he was around 'outsiders' would slip if it seemed as if they saw through him, and he would take steps to isolate Sofie from those people. This is part of the reason why Sofie stayed with someone who abused her for so long.

Sofie rationalised that this wasn't such a bad thing because Justin had told her many times he thought her friends were bad for her and didn't have her best interests at heart like he did. With practically no-one left in her life for support, Sofie felt she had to try even harder to make her relationship work with Justin as he was all she had. And of course, she loved him. The thought of losing him was unbearable.

4. YOU FORGETTING TO DO SOMETHING OR CHANGING YOUR MIND IS *NOT* THE SAME AS THEIR PATHOLOGICAL LYING

Sofie recalled a time she came home from a shopping trip with the children. She was met with Justin's stony silence, something she was used to but could never pinpoint a reason for. When she asked, Justin told her that a friend had seen her at Target, yet she had told Justin she was going shopping at Kmart. He told her she was a hypocrite for calling him a liar when she was a liar herself. There was no way of making him understand that she'd simply changed her mind about where to shop. She had told him one thing then done another. In his mind this was a betrayal of trust.

Another time she'd stayed up late watching a movie in the lounge room and fallen asleep on the couch, only taking herself to bed at 2 am when she woke. In the morning he accused her of lying because she'd told him she would be in bed straight after the movie. Her punishment was the silent treatment for two weeks, two nights of which Justin didn't come home without explanation. Sofie knew not to question him. She already knew he would say that she had no right to ask him anything when she had lied to him.

The punishment for failing to adhere to Justin's expectations ranged from small things, like refusing to eat the meals she cooked and presenting her with clothes or dishes she had washed that were in his view 'still dirty', to removing access to electrical appliances he believed were too costly to run such as the dishwasher, cancelling her credit card, and denying her access to a vehicle in lieu of public transport because petrol was 'so expensive'.

Sofie became expert at 'walking on eggshells' as the years went by.

5. OPEN A SECRET 'RUNNING AWAY' ACCOUNT

Within the realms of being safe, start thinking about your independence, and your capacity to leave when you are ready. Sofie's expenditure was closely monitored so this would have been incredibly difficult for her, but if you are able to, open up your own account and start depositing small amounts of money that your abuser won't miss. If your abuser gives you a cash allowance to live on, put little bits away. If you have to produce receipts for what you have purchased, you can always purchase an item and then take it back for a cash refund.

One day Sofie mustered up the courage to apply for a job as a teller at the local store which had perfect hours for a mum with school-aged children. (She had long since given up the idea of going back to university as Justin had made her feel so guilty every time she raised it.) But when Justin found out, he told her the job was not worth it and she wouldn't earn enough to justify the time spent away from her family duties. Why did she want to work anyway when she had a beautiful roof over her head, and all the bills were paid for? Why should he and the children suffer because she was bored? But Sofie dug her heels in and kept her interview appointment.

The night before her interview, Sofie was watching television when Justin – who hadn't spoken to her in a week as punishment – came in and accused her of cheating on him. He had seen a man regularly 'liking' her posts on Facebook. Looking at the man's profile, he'd discovered he was single, and, after some further digging, on a dating site. Sofie realised he was referring to an old school friend she'd befriended online. She spent the next four hours deleting all men off her account and trying to convince Justin of her innocence. The argument went on all night, with Justin waking her demanding answers every time she managed to fall asleep. Sofie barely slept that night, and, after taking a look at her swollen, tear-streaked face in the mirror the next morning, called the interviewer and cancelled.

After 14 years of loyalty to her husband, Sofie had been accused of cheating. It was at this time that she noted her anxiety was at an all-time high and she suffered a panic attack in the middle of a shopping centre while picking up some groceries. Light-headed, hyperventilating and terrified, she was too scared to drive home and called Justin to come and get her. Instead of expressing relief she was okay, however, he verbally attacked her for calling him away from work.

That was the moment Sofie decided enough was enough. She left the relationship and took the children with her to stay with her mother.

Hoovered (the first time)

At her mother's house, Sofie rocketed from one emotional extreme to another. The first night she felt strong and indignant, but by the third night of no contact from Justin she was an absolute wreck, checking her phone every two seconds to see if he'd called. Sofie described this time without him to me as torture. She couldn't eat or sleep; all she could think about was him. Who was he with? What was he doing? Maybe it *was* her fault and she just needed to do better. Yes, he could be incredibly nasty, but it was only some of the time. Mostly he was nice to her, and she knew her anxiety made her hard to live with.

On the third night, Justin finally texted her. What he wrote reminded her of the early days when he'd called her his 'princess'. He expressed his love for her and spoke of the amazing life and family they had built together. Sending her the song they had danced to on their wedding night, he reminded her of the wonderful moments they'd experienced together at the beginning. He'd been going through a lot of stress at work, he said, and she had this way of pushing all his buttons. They had too much to lose; throwing it all away wasn't the answer. Besides, they had to think of the children: putting them through a divorce would be selfish. He realised they both had issues they needed to work on; she wasn't perfect either. He suggested they try counselling again to work on their 'communication issues'.

Sofie felt huge relief when Justin finally got in touch. What she didn't know then, however, was that Justin had also contacted her mother expressing concerns about Sofie's mental health. He told her mother of Sofie's anxiety issues and explosive outbursts.

All her mother saw was Justin's desire to help and care for her 'needy' daughter. Sofie's mother convinced her to go home, and Sofie returned to the cycle of narcissistic abuse that was her life.

For the next three months, life seemed wonderful. Justin was more patient and there were no arguments. He even took her out to dinner and allowed her to buy a new dress for the night. Slowly but surely, however, things started to unravel, with Sofie never being able to please him and the emotional and verbal abuse getting worse. Sofie could now see what was behind Justin's toxic behaviour. But she didn't realise she'd developed some effective coping mechanisms to survive the abuse, such as minimising, rationalising and sometimes even defending the abuse.

Sofie immersed herself in her children – now teenagers – and abandoned all hope of changing things. This was her life and she needed to accept it.

It had been a long time since Justin had left his phone lying around, his computer open or any of his social media accounts unlocked, but one night after a bout of binge drinking he did just that. Sofie noticed he'd left his inbox open on his computer and there was an email from Rachel, the woman he'd been messaging a few years earlier who Justin had quickly explained away as 'no one', a business contact. She opened the email and its attachment. Nothing could have prepared her for what she saw. Endless nude and semi-nude photos of Rachel, and messages that could only be described as sexting in which they described what they wanted to do to each other next time they were together. As Justin slept in their marital bed, Sofie sat down to process the extent of the betrayal.

Sofie's initial suspicions had been correct. Justin and his 'business contact' were having an intimate relationship. They had been seeing each other for years, and his 'work trips' over the years were, in fact, liaisons with her. In the emails he expressed his love for Rachel, and they talked to each other about their loveless marriages. He told her he was going to divorce Sofie one day, but he was worried about her mental state and he needed to stay with her for now because of the children. After reading nearly three years worth of emails Sofie grabbed the computer, shook Justin awake and told him she knew everything. She had the evidence in black and white – and a few colour pics to boot.

A non-narcissist who has been caught cheating, having been presented with reams of incriminating evidence, might confess and apologise. Justin, however, raged against Sofie for invading his privacy. He flatly denied the affair: he claimed he'd simply been trying to be a friend to this woman whose husband was very abusive towards her. He'd only told her his own marriage was in trouble so she would feel comfortable with him. He couldn't help it if she'd sent him those photos – he didn't even look at them! And he'd been about to cut off communication with her anyway.

Then Justin shifted the blame to Sofie: yelling about her 'mental health issues' and how he was only talking to someone else because she was so cold and distant and wouldn't be intimate with him. Maybe if she took better care of herself, did some exercise occasionally and lost some weight, he wouldn't have to look at other women. She wasn't the same woman he'd married; it wasn't fair that she had let herself go so much. Other people agreed with him, he told her. Other people constantly asked him about the negative changes they saw in Sofie. He emphatically denied cheating, but said that he'd have been completely within his rights to cheat, because she had changed so much.

The next day Justin moved out, saying he couldn't be with someone who didn't trust him and was so insecure. Barely a week later, Sofie discovered he'd moved in with Rachel, who'd happened to leave her husband that same week. And Justin's reply to Sofie's frantic texts wanting answers and closure? 'Well, if I'm going to be accused of it, I may as well do it.'

* * *

To you and me, Justin was clearly a toxic abuser. So why did she stay so long? Why did she continue to 'allow' him to treat her so badly? Just like the frog that is boiled alive when it can't feel the water around it going from cold to tepid to hot, Sofie stayed because the abuse increased gradually and insidiously, and by the time she realised just how bad it was, it was too late. She was addicted and was powerless to escape.

The textbook techniques of devaluing

Once you are perceived as imperfect by the narcissist, the devaluing process must, and will, begin. When Sofie started to question Justin about his toxic behaviour, she was inadvertently telling him she knew he was wearing a mask. She was also telling him that she could see *behind* that mask, and she now had the power to expose the shame-ridden true self that Justin had buried a long time ago.

In order to create balance and repair his wounded ego, Justin's mission became one of destroying all that was 'good' about Sofie so he could again feel powerful and superior to her. The irony here was that all the things he said he loved about her in the beginning became targets for his disdain. In the beginning, Sofie remembered him telling her that he loved her singing around the house and that she was so open and friendly, and that he loved her friends. By the end, she was being berated and ridiculed whenever she opened her mouth to sing, she was now no longer friendly but 'desperate' and 'flirtatious', and he despised everyone she knew.

The narcissist's need for attention and to feel special is insatiable, and in that quest they become bored very quickly. Couple this with the fact that narcissists see other people as vessels of narcissistic supply – only valuable if they meet their needs – and you have the perfect recipe for the love bomb, devalue and discard cycle. Each new target is objectified, and just as a shiny new car becomes old, tiresome and not worth the effort of fixing, so too does each victim. The narcissist then gets rid of the old model and gets a new one, moving on without looking back.

To be devalued, tossed away and replaced without an ounce of remorse or empathy is soul-destroying for the victim. Who does that? The narcissist does, because they are devoid of those qualities. To a narcissist, empathy and remorse are weaknesses that only make you vulnerable to attack from others. Caring about the feelings of others and putting the needs of others first also make you vulnerable to attack. If you don't care about anyone else, they can't hurt you.

Empathy is a trait that most of us take for granted in other people. It is difficult to imagine someone being devoid of empathy. Empathy is what makes us human. It's what stops us from committing atrocious acts against others because we can put ourselves in someone else's shoes. But imagine someone in an adult's body, with an adult's intelligence, but without caring how they hurt others. This is what you have been living with. This adult is also very capable of telling right from wrong; they know what they are doing. The biggest clue you will have is their ability to change their behaviour at the drop of a hat, depending on who's watching. Because they know their behaviour is wrong (but they just don't care), they will come up with a way to justify their abuse. The victim is told they deserve the abuse, as when Sofie was told that it was because she put on weight, or perhaps you questioned their behaviour (in other words you were calling them a liar). A lack of empathy and remorse not only makes the devaluing phase feel justified to the narcissist, but makes it feel thoroughly enjoyable.

The narcissist will find fault in everything about you and anything you do when devaluing you. In their mind *you* lied. *You* pretended you were the perfect partner in the beginning but then *you* stopped worshipping them. They are the one who is left with a broken person, who is nothing like the perfect being they first met.

The narcissist's actions in finding constant fault with you are not just based on punishment, however. They are about getting you to continually try to please them. But to them, where would the fun be if you actually succeeded, completing every task they asked of you with an A plus? The harsh reality is that when you embark on any activity to please the narcissist they are setting you up to fail. They will constantly shift the goalposts with comments like 'I never asked you to do that' or 'You didn't do it right.' The victim's confidence is shattered every time but just like the boiling frog, the victim is becoming acclimatised to their environment and tries even harder to please.

There are numerous strategies the narcissist can use to devalue you during which they lie, blame shift, deny and distort. I have listed some of the textbook techniques they may use to abuse you in this stage.

COERCIVE CONTROL

Soon after they were married, Sofie started to notice changes in Justin. Confusing changes that indicated a side to him Sofie hadn't seen before. He became extremely controlling. At first, it felt good that he always wanted to know what she was doing, and that he cared about the types of clothes she wore and the way she looked. She was flattered when he told her that she didn't need to wear make-up when she went out because she was pretty enough without it. But it soon became obvious that he just didn't want other people looking at her.

His 'caring' ways began to feel suffocating, however, when she had to account for every moment of her day and who she was with at all times.

One day she went out wearing make-up and red lipstick because she felt like a change. When Justin saw her, he exploded with rage, telling her that she looked like a slut. Then he left for a week. She had no idea where he went and she didn't ask for fear of igniting his anger again. Never again did she let him see her with make-up on.

Coercive control and narcissistic abuse go hand in hand. The narcissist needs to control their victim to feel powerful, and the best way to maintain dominance over another person is through coercion. They use fear to control you. In all the devaluing strategies such as isolation, sabotage and gaslighting, the narcissist engages in coercion to confuse their victim and have them comply with their demands.

The way the controlling strategies are implemented, especially in the early days of the relationship, impact the victim's ability to see this type of behaviour as abusive. When the narcissist is first testing their victim's boundaries, they will have seemingly innocent requests, such as wanting to pick you up from work each day. This request is implemented under the guise of caring and the victim thinks they have a loving partner who cares about them so much they are happy to make this 'sacrifice' of time each day.

The narcissist realises you've accepted this behaviour so they step up the control a notch by always wanting to know who you are talking to on the phone. The narcissist tells their victim they should have no secrets because they love each other. Soon after that they may ask you not to wear make-up because you are 'prettier without it', or perhaps your clothes will not be to their liking and they would like to help you shop for them. Once again it's because they 'care' about you so much.

The victim learns much later that the real motivation for these types of requests is that the narcissist didn't want others looking at you, and they didn't want you to feel attractive when you were out without them. It might be a different story, however, when the narcissist is with you. If you are holding on to the arm of the narcissist while out and about, you may be able to dress as provocatively or as demurely as you please, depending on the narcissist's taste. Your job is to prop up the narcissist's ego so the narcissist feels special and/or envied.

The victim is also learning, or being conditioned to believe, that caring and control are the same thing. Someone who cares for you controls you. The victim reasons that the narcissist must care about them a lot, because they are so concerned with what they are doing. In the beginning it is actually flattering to have someone 'care' about you so much. The behaviours start in small ways, and before the victim knows it, they are handing their passwords for their social media over to the narcissist.

The behaviour has escalated to a point where the victim feels trapped, harassed and stalked. They have no idea how it got to this point, because the coercive control was so gradual, and because it felt good in the beginning. It felt good that this person wanted to spend so much time with them; was so interested in their life. The victim was unable to distinguish between caring behaviour and controlling behaviour until it was too late, and they can't talk to their own mother on the phone without the narcissist wanting to know the exact content of the conversation. In the end, the victim is timing their calls for when the narcissist is not around. In the end, they are whispering to their mother to call them back later, and telling the controlling narcissist it was just a salesperson on the phone. The victim has learned coping mechanisms and behaviours to survive the abuse that they still can't define as abuse.

Another reason that victims fail to define these patterns of controlling behaviour as abuse is that they have said yes. There was no gun to their head; no threat of violence. They said yes when they could have said no. What was not obvious to them again was how gradually and 'small' the punishments started off if they said no.

Perhaps in the beginning the narcissist sulked a little if their victim denied them sex. They made the victim feel guilty and and was 'hurt' that the victim wasn't considering their needs. The victim feels compelled to give in to the sexual request because it felt terrible to have the narcissist upset with them. Slowly but surely the punishments ramp up until the victim realises it is easier to do what the narcissist wants them to do because the silent treatment, harassment, humiliation, intimidation, alluding to abandonment and so on are just too much to bear. It is far easier to submit to the sometimes degrading and humiliating requests, and get their 'chore' out the way for another day.

FINANCIAL CONTROL

Justin had complete control over the family finances. He told Sofie repeatedly that he didn't enjoy looking after the finances, but he wanted to take this burden from her, and she agreed with him, believing his claims that she wasn't very good with budgeting. (I pointed out to Sofie that she must have excellent budgeting skills to feed a family of five on the pittance he gave her.) She was given a small weekly allowance for groceries and had an emergency credit card with a limited maximum spend. She rarely used the credit card as she had learned that the 'discussion' about her expenditure every time the statement came in and the efforts to justify her spending were exhausting.

Sofie even had to present Justin with the grocery receipt every time she went shopping and justify items that he felt were unnecessary. However, if she questioned him about a new car, motorbike or computer he'd bought for himself, those items were always 'necessary' and 'deserved' (usually because he 'worked so hard'). Whenever Sofie asked for anything for herself, whether it be new furniture, a holiday or money for clothes, she was chastised like a child and told they couldn't afford it.

Justin kept his income and their financial situation from Sofie so he could use the supposed state of their finances to his advantage and she would have no comeback.

She reasoned that it wasn't a bad thing he was so concerned with budgeting. At least he wasn't gambling all the money away at the casino, right?

Narcissists want to have complete power and control over their victim, and one of the perfect weapons to do this is money. By controlling money and resources, they make their victim dependent on them, and they will use this to punish or reward as they see fit. If you are 'good' they may even give you a little more money to buy groceries the next week. Conversely, if they feel you've overspent, they may withhold money as a punishment until you 'learn' better spending habits.

The idea is to demean and humiliate their victim and let them know who's boss. Without access to money, the victim feels trapped and isolated, and is constantly subjected to the humiliating experience of having to explain every cent they spend. To a narcissist, money equals power, and you are to be completely powerless in this relationship. With free access to this type of power, you might leave, and the narcissist wants to make that as difficult as possible.

In order to gain complete control over you, the narcissist must first gain your trust. When Sofie fell pregnant with her first child she was assured that he would take complete care of her after they made the joint decision that she would stay at home with the children. It was subsequently decided that Justin would 'look after' the finances to take the burden from Sofie. In other words, the financial abuse began under the guise of caring. Sofie trusted Justin and was made to believe this was the best decision for her family. Her condoning of this decision, and her belief that it was made to protect her, paved the way for an insidious slippery slope into complete financial helplessness.

Like many victims, Sofie had no idea how much her husband was earning and was always left utterly confused every time she asked. What she did know was that every time she asked, the business was not doing well, so she should be grateful for what he gave her. So it was even more confusing when he would lash out on extravagant gifts for himself while telling her they were on a tight budget. The narcissist *wants* you to be confused, and they want you to beg. This gives them a great deal of narcissistic supply when you argue the unfairness of the situation, and in watching you struggle to please them by making do with your rations.

When financial dependence becomes a way of life for victims, it's often hard for them to think of it as abuse. It becomes their 'normal' and the abuse only becomes apparent when they can compare it with a more healthy and equitable relationship. Like Sofie, victims will be made to justify their expenditure and will suffer crushing anxiety when credit card and bank statements come in. They will be made to sit down with the narcissist and pore over grocery receipts to see how they could have done better. The narcissist may even deny their victim a credit card 'for their own good', as they have manipulated them into thinking they are terrible with money. These actions are demoralising for the victim and reinforce their lack of confidence and low self-worth.

The narcissist will also often put assets such as the family business solely in their name. Money may also be placed in an account in their name only so the victim can never draw out money without the narcissist's permission.

MANUFACTURED CONFLICT

Justin would always say he hated drama, Sofie said, and yet it seemed to follow him everywhere.

Sofie told me of numerous times when a peaceful moment would be shattered by Justin shouting at her for not cleaning the shower properly or failing to iron a shirt he needed. Out of nowhere, an argument would begin as Sofie defended herself, then Justin would leave the house for hours because she was so argumentative.

The 'I hate drama' is a textbook line used by narcissists to deflect and confuse their victim.

The narcissist's constant boredom results in never-ending conflict in the relationship. The devaluing process continues as the narcissist intentionally incites arguments and ruins special events or celebrations by creating drama. Without drama they become anxious because there is no attention on them and they are then alone with their true self, so they must continually manufacture chaos.

It's an even bigger win when the passive-aggressive nature of their actions has you participating in the drama by defending and explaining yourself.

ISOLATION

It's difficult to think of a world without social media these days, but Sofie spent most of her married life without it. Sofie decided to shut it down. She felt guilty when she was on it, she wanted to be a better wife and spend more time with her husband, and she wanted to show Justin that she was loyal and cared about his feelings. She thought it was her decision to take herself off it, but it was the controlling strategies that Justin engaged in – such as the silent treatment, staying out at night because she 'didn't care about him', or threatening to leave her (abandonment) – that ensured that he got what he wanted: Sofie taking ownership of the decision to close down her social media accounts.

Social media took the attention away from Justin; he was jealous of the time she was talking to others, and he was worried about the influence of others online. Sofie may have made the final decision to shut down all social media, but Justin had coerced that decision with great skill, and was responsible for those actions as sure as he had pushed the buttons himself. Another area of potential support had been successfully closed off to Sofie.

It's hard to get someone to do what you want when there are others telling that person to do the opposite. You will have much more success if you are able to isolate them, and this is exactly the premise the narcissist works from. Justin used many strategies to cut Sofie off from any support system that might influence her and encourage her to leave. When a victim is cut off from the outside world and repeatedly bombarded with influential messages from their abuser, you have the equivalent of a cult leader manipulating a vulnerable target to do their bidding, increasing their power and dominance over that person.

It is also important for the narcissist to isolate you from family and friends as much as possible, as they are potentially the greatest support system you will have. The narcissist will get the victim to do the 'dirty work' by saying no to invitations and not responding to phone calls, thus causing them to begin to think that they caused the isolation themselves. The narcissist is then able to further devalue the victim by saying things like 'Even your friends don't want to be around you', or perhaps 'Your own mother told me she thinks you have problems because you ignore her.' The victim thinks that everyone they once loved is against them and they are isolated further, spending most of their time with the narcissist.

The narcissist will often use absolute terms such as the word 'all' to increase the power of the coercive control, for example, phrases like 'All your friends think you're a loser. They don't know why I stay with you'. The victim feels incredibly alone, which increases their dependence on the narcissist.

To manipulate the victim into 'choosing' to be isolated, the narcissist will often put forth very plausible arguments under the guise of caring and respect for the relationship. They might say things like 'These are our personal issues, so we don't discuss them with others.' And 'It's disrespectful to talk about me to others.'

Justin would suggest the notion that Sofie's friends did not really care about her, and when they stopped calling her it appeared that Justin was right. With the level of conditioning that had taken place to coerce Sofie's behaviours, she was unable to discern that they had stopped calling because Justin had set it up that way.

Victims may also find themselves letting go of anything they had been passionate about, such as hobbies and physical activities. Once again, they are led to believe that it was their decision. In fact, their life was made so difficult by the narcissist when they spent any time on themselves, they had no other choice. Sofie told me about a time she decided to join the gym. Justin complained so much about the time it took away from the family that she started going at 6 am. He found fault with that, too, saying it interfered with the children's morning routine, so Sofie gave it up.

There are many other ways the narcissist isolates their victim: taking away their phone, their car and their access to money (removing access to credit cards any time they displease the narcissist); convincing them to physically move far away from any support; making them financially dependent; getting them pregnant so they are unable to work – just to name a few. All strategies are designed to prevent the victim from realising the truth of what is happening to them, and preventing them from getting away and taking their power back.

TRIANGULATION

Another manipulative strategy the narcissist uses to keep their victim confused and trying harder in the relationship is triangulation. This occurs when the narcissist brings a third party into the relationship, either real or perceived, to make themselves feel more superior, and often just to enjoy the drama that ensues. The narcissist will strive to keep the other people apart so they don't find out the truth of what's happening, and the narcissist becomes the point of contact for the other parties. They need to keep you apart so you cannot compare notes.

Justin triangulated Sofie with Rachel to stir up feelings of insecurity and jealousy in Sofie. Of course, Sofie was told by Justin that she was 'crazy' for her normal reactions. The emotions that Sofie exhibited reflected to Justin his power and desirability.

The narcissist commonly tells their primary source of supply whom they are devaluing (Sofie) that they are imagining things while simultaneously providing clear evidence of their betrayals. The secondary source (Rachel) will see the frantic reactions of the primary source and reason that the narcissist must be pretty incredible to incite such feelings. Usually, the secondary source has been told that it is over between the narcissist and their spouse, and the spouse is either 'crazy' or still in love with them. The secondary source feels lucky that the narcissist 'chose' them. They feel they have won the prize.

It also spurs them to try harder to please the narcissist as they would never dream of putting their newfound love through that same torture. The narcissist might go to the secondary source and cry on their shoulder, implying that they are done with their 'crazy' ex-partner, someone they'd given everything to. They need someone to love them for themselves. The secondary source feels sorry for the narcissist, who is portraying themselves as the victim, and the relationship is cemented even further.

Meanwhile, the narcissist now has two sources of narcissistic supply as they soak up the negative energy from the primary source and the positive energy from the secondary source. Justin had become a hot commodity: his desirability had increased a thousandfold. His status had elevated and he would continue to enjoy the perceived rivalry that he'd intentionally created. The narcissist can also keep this going indefinitely by changing the positions on the triangle of the two 'opponents'.

Justin also used triangulation when attending counselling with Sofie. With masterful skill he manipulated the unsuspecting counsellor onside to revictimise Sofie, who once again was made out to be the villain rather than the victim.

Quite simply, triangulation involves tactics of divide and conquer. The narcissist remains the 'go-to' person that each party confides in so they have total control over the narrative and can sit back and enjoy the drama they've created.

TRIANGULATION WITHIN THE FAMILY

Sofie had all the normal dramas went hand in hand with raising teenagers, but there was also an intense sibling rivalry between the three children that went beyond what she considered normal, and she noted that Justin was often the driving force behind this rivalry. Justin had always favoured their oldest child; in his eyes she could do no wrong. On the other hand, their second child, who was more like Sofie, could do no right but was always looking to please her father. It particularly upset Sofie when Justin took a far keener interest in their eldest's schoolwork than in that of their other children. Their eldest daughter was academic, like him, and he would spend significant amounts of time helping her with her homework as well as bragging about her excellence in maths and science.

However, he regularly told their younger daughter he had no time to help with her schoolwork and her look of hurt would pain Sofie. Justin had no interest in art or drama, their younger daughter's passions, and was dismissive of her achievements in these areas.

Sofie felt powerless to improve the situation: any comments she made to Justin seemed to exacerbate his behaviour. It was almost as if Justin and their eldest child had formed an alliance against her and she had very little authority left to parent her child, as anything she said or did was overridden by Justin.

Triangulation can be used in any relationship, a classic one being that of the golden child/scapegoat child dynamic. Justin had clearly assigned the role of 'golden child' to his oldest child, Taylor, and this was used to create rivalry with her younger sister and insecurities in their mother. Triangulation strategies that Justin used regularly included baiting Sofie to react in frustration then taking the children out and buying them something special. This elevated his status in their minds and devalued Sofie's status. He was intentionally trying to create a wedge between mother and children to hurt Sofie without any regard for how this would impact on the children's emotional welfare. Without knowing it, they were all pitted against each other, each blaming the others and oblivious to the manipulations of their father and husband.

SABOTAGE

Sofie once arranged a birthday party for Justin after he'd said that no-one had ever cared enough to do this. She was devastated when he ruined the day by telling her that he'd never even wanted a party and it was a waste of money. Come to think of it, she realised, he'd ruined every special occasion Sofie could remember, and she couldn't think of a single birthday party, Christmas holiday or vacation without drama or conflict.

The narcissist will sabotage any chance of you being happy. If the narcissist is not the centre of attention, they are in withdrawal from their drug, that drug being narcissistic supply. If there is something going on in your life that is meaningful and important, the narcissist feels rejected, and will actively seek to bring the focus back onto themselves. This might be an important job interview, an exam you need to study for, or a special event you're organising. As Justin did to Sofie, they may keep you awake at night by starting an argument. Sleep deprivation is not only a great way to sabotage any day that is special to you, but it is also just a generally good way to destablise you. Without sleep you cannot function properly in any aspect of your life, you will have more failures (which the narcissist will enjoy), and you will be more likely to react to them with volatility, providing potent narcissistic supply when police or other family members become involved.

They may pretend to be sick themselves, or simply create drama that takes your attention away from an important task and puts it back on the narcissist. To them, your lack of attention equates to betrayal, and they justify their behaviour because you are 'selfish'. They will even sabotage their own birthday if they see that it is bringing you joy. Justin did this to Sofie when she was trying to do something special for him. Even though the party was for him, it was something she was enjoying and therefore became a selfish act rather than a loving one in Justin's mind.

The narcissist will regularly sabotage holidays, Christmas and any type of celebration or peaceful occasion by creating drama and conflict out of nothing. They will leave you behind at a holiday destination, where you have no idea where to go, or perhaps you have no money. They will tell you to get out of the car and leave you behind somewhere. This is done to punish you for a made-up indiscretion, to ensure that the holiday does not end well. Of course, you will be blamed for this chaos, and the blame shifting in these instances is extremely frustrating and infuriating, but the victim's distress at trying to work out how they are going to get out of their situation overrides their ability to think about how they were manipulated. They experience such relief when the narcissist returns that they would rather not bring up the reasons for the 'argument'.

Happy occasions mean happy people, and the narcissist does not have the resources to feel this genuine bliss. They become uncomfortable when there is peace, and envious of people who can feel this way. You will never be on the same emotional playing field as the narcissist. If you are happy, they are anxious and/or angry and they will do whatever it takes to reverse roles. The drama they create naturally causes you to be angry and upset and, as they see your frustration escalate, their mood improves. You are then blamed for the sudden end to the holiday and the narcissist is happy. If you are on holidays with children or friends, the narcissist may manipulate the situation to appear that it was your fault, and you will be blamed by these other people as well.

The sabotage applies not only to happy events but to distressing events as well, such as the loss of a parent, or when you are sick or trying to provide support to someone else who is sick. On any occasion when you need support yourself, or you are receiving attention from others, the narcissist will do something to make themselves the centre of your attention. In a relationship with a narcissist you are not allowed to have needs. Distracting you from these lifechanging moments also serves to keep the narcissist in your memory by associating them with those important dates for years to come. For example, the narcissist in your life instigates chaos on the day of your mother's funeral. On every anniversary of her death, what will you be thinking of? Will you be thinking of the special memories you shared with loved ones at her funeral, or will you be thinking about the narcissist, and what they did to destroy the day?

GASLIGHTING

Sofie recalled a time Justin had flown into a rage when she'd confronted him about private Facebook messages she'd seen on his phone from a woman he knew through work, Rachel. The messages showed a level of intimacy that Sofie was shocked by. Sofie had questioned Justin about his relationship with Rachel a year earlier when he'd been working late with her on company projects. At the time, Justin had assured Sofie that they were 'just friends' and told her to stop being paranoid and insecure. So, although she was devastated to find they were still in regular touch and apparently close, she felt vindicated by this evidence, which she promptly presented to Justin. But not only did Justin deny that any intimate connection existed, he also flipped the blame onto Sofie for being so 'insecure, paranoid and untrusting' that she felt the need to spy on his phone. He declared that it was she who owed *him* an apology and that he did not know if he could be with someone who was so jealous.

As he had done so many times before, Justin was gaslighting Sofie, causing her to question her judgement and her perception of his behaviour. Yes, she had snooped. How could he trust her? It was no wonder he had a PIN on his phone and she wasn't allowed to touch it.

It must be her anxiety that was causing her to act so irrationally, she told herself. Maybe she should make an appointment with her doctor to have the dosage of her medications changed. If she didn't get her act together, she was going to lose him.

Sofie had developed several coping mechanisms to survive this abuse, and one of the most effective was blaming herself and ignoring her gut instinct.

Gaslighting is a manipulative technique the narcissist uses to distort the victim's reality. This type of brainwashing causes enormous confusion for the victim as they are convinced by their abuser that what they have seen, heard or understood is not true. The narcissist will use this technique consistently to gain control of their victim, and as their victim continues to doubt themselves, they are slowly conditioned to ignore their instincts. The narcissist will provide an alternative reality with such conviction and adamance that the victim reasons there must be some validity to what they are saying. The victim's confidence to make decisions is eroded as they are continually told their perceptions are wrong, and they look to their abuser for their truth. This leads to feelings of low self-worth, hopelessness, and a loss of identity for the victim, making them a perfect target to exploit.

The term comes from the 1944 film *Gaslight*. In this movie the wife is manipulated into thinking she is going crazy by her husband. Things go missing, gaslights unaccountably dim and brighten. The husband convinces his wife she is imagining things and that she must be suffering from hallucinations. In another instance, the husband tells his wife that his watch chain is missing, and then proceeds to find it in her handbag. It is at this point the wife becomes hysterical in front of guests. The husband now has an audience to support the theory that she is indeed unstable. As a result, the wife started to believe that there is something wrong with her, and she becomes paranoid and reliant on her husband to dictate her reality. The husband's desire to convince his wife she was going crazy was even more despicable because it was done under the guise of care and concern.

A common way that narcissists gaslight is to trivialise and ridicule your emotions. They may use phrases such as 'you're too sensitive', 'you're overreacting', 'I was only joking', 'you're crazy', 'you're paranoid', 'you just need to get over it', 'you're jealous/insecure', 'you have mental health issues' and 'everyone agrees with me'. These phrases are used to distort the victim's perceptions, even in the face of black–and–white evidence the victim may present. This enables the narcissist to avoid accountability for any wrongdoing and the blame is shifted back onto the victim as being the one at fault. Gradually, the victim is conditioned to minimise the emotions they are entitled to feel, as Sofie did when she found the clearly provocative interactions with Rachel. The reality was that she had caught him cheating, but she was manipulated into believing the act of betrayal was hers as she had invaded his privacy.

Gaslighting strategies also include outright lying, denying and sabotage. Early in the relationship, Justin had told Sofie that he hated cheaters. Imagine how confused Sofie must have been when the person who deplored such behaviour was actually guilty of it. By laying the groundwork for his supposed integrity during the love bombing stage, Sofie's ability to reason against conflicting information would have been weakened. It was easier for her to rationalise that Justin and this person were just friends. Another classic example of gaslighting was when Sofie was led to believe that having a party for Justin would be something special and meaningful for him. Instead, she was berated, and told he didn't want a party and it was a waste of money. The gaslighting continued when Sofie's innocent shopping somewhere other than first intended was deemed malicious lies. Sofie was manipulated into believing that her 'lies' were comparable to Justin's outright betrayals, and that her actions were hypocritical.

Gaslighting someone causes them to feel confused and delusional as they try to reconcile what they are seeing and hearing with what they are being told. As happened in the movie *Gaslight*, narcissists will even shift objects around, hide or steal something – then tell you how careless you are for losing it. If you feel the need to record conversations and play them back to the narcissist to prove you're not crazy, you are probably being gaslighted.

When gaslighting you, the narcissist may put you in a dangerous situation where you could be harmed, then come to your rescue. They will also expect your gratitude for saving you from the dangerous situation that they created. This is maddening for the victim, whose ability to discern what is real has been compromised. Ever try to find your car keys, phone or the like, and the narcissist finds it in a place you *know* you didn't leave it? How silly did you feel and how righteous did the narcissist appear? Now, they had not only an excuse to 'joke' about your bad memory, but also a scoreboard where you owed them and must be grateful.

The narcissist will tell you they said something you have no memory of, or on the flip side they will be adamant that you didn't tell them about something when you know you did. Not only does this serve to confuse the victim but it provides a generous delivery of narcissistic supply as the victim proceeds to defend themselves to prove their point. In essence, the narcissist wants you to surrender your reality to them, and gaslighting is the perfect weapon to ensure this happens.

PROJECTION

A narcissist spends their lifetime creating and maintaining a grandiose image that reflects their belief they are superior to everyone around them. The persona they create masks their true self, which is 'weak', vulnerable and shame-ridden. The narcissist will never take ownership of the deep insecurities associated with these traits, as they conflict with the grandiose view of themselves. They will externalise anything about them that seems like a fault, and like a spotlight they will shine it on you where it will be attacked and disowned. This is projection.

How many times did the narcissist accuse you of doing something or saying something and you wondered why on earth they would think that? Or they accused you of doing something you were pretty sure they were doing themselves? When the narcissist accuses you out of the blue of doing something such as cheating, or they call you selfish or deceptive, you should take it as a confession. They are giving you an insight into what they are doing or thinking about doing. They are describing themselves when they call you names, and when they verbally attack you, they are attacking the very qualities they hate about themselves. Projection once again makes the victim feel crazy as they struggle to find a reason for the narcissist's accusations.

Justin regularly projected his insecurities and toxic behaviour onto Sofie. By using Sofie as a 'dumping ground' for all that he deemed weak or broken in himself, he was able to purge himself and restore his grandiose image. This occurred when Sofie found the messages that proved he was cheating. He denied and distorted the truth and accused Sofie of deception. It happened again when Justin's envy relating to her time talking to friends on social media was projected onto her, and she became the recipient of his self-centred emotions.

An acronym we regularly use in narcissistic abuse recovery to explain the narcissist's act of projecting is DARVO. This stands for 'deny, attack and reverse victim and offender'. This describes Justin's actions to a T: he would deny any wrongdoing, fly into a narcissistic rage because his ego was wounded, and then accuse Sofie of the very thing he was doing himself. The roles of victim and offender were reversed.

NARCISSISTIC RAGE

Sofie described numerous occasions when Justin would fly into an uncontrollable rage over tiny things. Sofie would try to defend herself verbally, but she admitted to feeling frightened during these times, especially when he'd come very close to her and scream in her face, or even punch the wall behind her.

She remembers him regularly wrenching a baby or toddler away from her if he could see their child was enjoying themselves with her. It would irritate him, and he would make the child give their attention to him. To avoid an argument, Sofie would ignore his behaviour and turn her attention elsewhere.

His aggression was at its peak when he was driving. If he was angry at her, he would speed dangerously, drive recklessly, unexpectedly slam on the brakes or threaten to run off the road. All of this led to panic attacks. But because he never hit her, she never believed it was abuse. 'Everyone argues,' was what she told herself, and she told me she didn't have it nearly as bad as some other people who were physically abused and didn't live in a beautiful house like she did, who weren't allowed access to a credit card like she was, or 'allowed' to get their nails done. I noted that Sofie referred to the place where she spent most of her time as a house and not a home, and the erosion of her boundaries and self-worth in the face of Justin's controlling behaviour.

Watching their partner fly into an uncontrollable rage with no justification can be a terrifying experience for the victim. It is often during these times, when the abuse is overt, that the victim starts to think there might be something wrong with their loved one.

If the narcissist experiences a narcissistic injury, or their ego is wounded, it conflicts with the perfect image perpetuated by the false self: an image that reflects how amazing they are. The victim might have had an achievement of some sort, which made the narcissist feel inadequate, or perhaps they just weren't paying the narcissist enough attention. The victim might have caught the narcissist doing something wrong or criticised them in some way. Any of these actions, whether real or perceived, will ignite the narcissist's shame and make them feel vulnerable and weak. The false mask they wear must be protected at all costs and the one responsible for exposing the weakling behind the mask must be severely punished.

Sofie remembered Justin coming within inches of her face and screaming in her ear, and verbal assaults in which she was called hideous names and her motherhood attacked. She remembered him positioning himself so she was blocked in the bedroom, and she had no choice but to listen to his ranting. The degree of anger seemed to be an extreme response to the minor infraction he said he was angry about.

Narcissistic rage is not always visible as it was in these cases. It can also be extremely passive aggressive. If a victim does something to offend the narcissist, the narcissist may decide to punish them in a way that is much more deceptive – by creating chaos behind their back. For example, they might undertake a smear campaign, in which the narcissist seeks to tarnish the victim's name, isolate them and destroy their reputation. See Chapter 6 for more about smear campaigns.

WORD SALAD

Sofie and Justin had endless arguments that went round in circles until Sofie couldn't even remember her point and would end up apologising for small 'mistakes' that she'd made days, weeks, months or even years earlier (such as leaving the car low on fuel). During these arguments, she simply could not follow Justin's logic or understand that he just didn't care about the impact of his behaviour on her self-esteem and on their relationship. When thinking about these confusing and nonsensical arguments in our sessions, Sofie recalled that he'd never sincerely apologised for being wrong. Every time Sofie pointed out that his actions were inappropriate or hurtful, he would find a way to deflect the blame back on to her and she would be the one at fault.

Occasionally Sofie would risk Justin's wrath to defend herself when he denied culpability for something he had intentionally done to hurt her. Fighting back and yelling at him in pure frustration was out of character for her and she'd be stricken with guilt and remorse for days afterwards. Every time she retaliated like this, Justin would stop yelling and cursing, become eerily quiet, smirk at her and call her crazy or bipolar. This would further incense her and she'd start to shake and cry uncontrollably. Once, Justin got his phone out and filmed her like this.

He always seemed to incite these reactions when the children were present. Then he'd make a show of 'cheering them up' after having to witness Mum's emotional outburst, taking them out for ice cream or to buy a new toy. At the time, Sofie simply could not see the manipulation that had taken place and blamed herself for upsetting the children. Justin, of course, reinforced this notion by telling her that he and the children 'accepted her apology' for her behaviour.

Eventually, Sofie simply stopped standing up for herself. It was too exhausting and she knew it would only ever end badly for her. The 'good' Justin would only come out for fleeting moments here and there, but that would just confuse her more. Sofie dismissed the niggling theory that there was a 'good' and a 'bad' Justin as ridiculous: there must be a logical reason why she had, in his mind, gone from a woman who 'hung the moon and stars' for him to a broken-down wreck whom he despised.

When we engage in discussion with someone, the idea is that it should be space of equality for both parties. You sit down to discuss the issue at hand and even if you don't come to an agreement, you know that you were able to get your point across, that the other person heard and understood you, and vice versa.

When the narcissist senses they are under attack, however — perhaps you are trying to make them accountable for something — they will engage in circular conversation and reasoning to distort and deflect the conversation away from the issue of importance to you. For example, you may have approached them to talk about their lack of respect towards you when they were clearly flirting with someone. Instead of addressing that, they may bring up an occasion from years ago when you hurt their feelings. You are diverted into debating this topic instead, the discussion about the current flirtatious behaviour is forgotten, and you end up apologising for that past 'indiscretion'. The discussion winds up being a win–lose with the narcissist coming out on top. The debate is confusing and makes no sense to you.

By engaging in this 'word salad', the narcissist avoids responsibility again, protecting their flawless image. The outcome also conditions you to avoid talking about your feelings to the narcissist, as these conversations are just too frustrating.

THE SILENT TREATMENT, STONEWALLING AND GHOSTING

One of the factors that made it so difficult for Sofie to recognise that her abuse was horrific and deliberate was her husband's unpredictable affections, which yo-yoed from one extreme to the other. He would seem to treat her respectfully but at any moment that 'nice' respect would be withdrawn to punish her for very small 'mistakes'. It was at these times that Sofie realised she would do almost anything to make the punishments – such as the silent treatment and disappearances for days at a time – stop. The times when she was starved of communication were often so painful that Sofie would beg Justin to return, and she would accept him back without expecting an apology for his behaviour. He would return as if nothing had happened, and the cycle would continue. In essence, he had conditioned her to not hold him accountable for any of his actions, which meant he could do as he pleased and get away with it.

Anyone who has been the recipient of stonewalling, ghosting or the silent treatment from a significant other will tell you that it is torturous. To have someone completely cut off communication with you, to leave for days or weeks without telling you where they are going, and pretend they don't see you or hear you, can leave you feeling worthless, confused, rejected and lost. It is an extreme form of emotional and psychological abuse the narcissist uses to punish you and regain control.

Justin punished Sofie with the silent treatment for giving her attention to social media rather than him. After raging at Sofie for invading his privacy, he again gave her the silent treatment, after which he returned as though nothing had happened. The silent treatment feels so painful for the victim that they allow their abuser back with no apology or demand for changed behaviour, just to put an end to the torture. The relief the victim feels because the silent treatment has ended far outweighs any need for justice, and the initial argument is swept under the carpet.

The narcissist knows exactly how their victim will be feeling, and the length of the silent treatment will be in proportion to how much they want to hurt you. It usually starts with a short and swift withdrawal then gradually increases so eventually the narcissist can disappear for weeks with no consequences. Sofie became conditioned to know which behaviours would result in the silent treatment and avoided that pain at all costs. As a result, Justin could get away with just about anything.

SEX AS A WEAPON

Justin also became controlling in the bedroom. In the early days, Sofie had loved to make love to her husband, but within just a few weeks of getting married it had become a daily chore that she hated. Now, she had to fake enjoyment or be punished. Justin made this very clear one night when he told her coldly that she wasn't 'into it' enough for him, and threatened to show the naked pictures he had coerced her into posing for to all his friends if she didn't please him. He would also punish her with the passive aggressive behaviours that made her flinch and feel sick with dread – slamming the fridge door, loudly 'placing' his dishes on the kitchen bench for her to attend to, or crashing the front door shut so hard it broke the lock.

To the narcissist, sex is not an act of intimacy. Sex is simply another way the narcissist uses people to fulfill their own selfish needs. It is a weapon they will use to control and manipulate you. It will be given in abundance to set the initial hooks in the love bombing period – and to reel you back in should you start to pull away later. Once they have you dependent on the 'intimacy' they have created in your mind, they are then able to withhold it to punish you at the correct time. In the beginning, the narcissist makes you believe they love every crevice of your body, and love nothing better than feeling your skin against theirs. When the time comes to devalue you, they will reject you, tell you that you don't turn them on anymore, or perhaps they might say they just don't feel like having sex as much as they used to.

Whatever their strategy, the withholding of 'intimacy' will make you feel worthless, and you will wonder what you did wrong. 'Why don't they desire me anymore?' This is exactly what they want you to feel so you will try harder to please. It is at this time, when the victim is devastated and confused about why their partner is pulling away from them, that the narcissist can coerce them into engaging in degrading acts they know the victim is uncomfortable with. They will use guilt to manipulate you into doing things to 'make them happy'. You have been gaslighted into believing you have been failing in this department and are eager to try anything to make them happy. They may request threesomes, or ask you to engage in humiliating acts, watch porn with them, or allow photos or videos to be taken during the act. They are skilled in the art of coercion, and afterwards, if you bring it to their attention how humiliated you felt at that time, they will say you're crazy. You could have said no. No-one was forcing you to do it. You said yes.

Sex is just another way for the narcissist to exert their control over you. For many victims it becomes just another chore they must complete each day, to fulfill their duties as a partner, and to avoid any punishment that would result from saying no, such as abandonment, with the narcissist implying they will find someone else.

It is painful when you realise the sexual chemistry and intimacy you felt with the narcissist was all one-sided. Intimacy requires a connection of the soul and a desire to make the other person feel as special as you feel. When you are feeling these intimate connections with the narcissist, you are experiencing the equivalent of a tradesman showing you the tricks of their trade. They have spent a great deal of time perfecting their skills to become what their victims want. To hook you in they need to make you feel special, and they need you to remember this feeling forever. They want you to crave it when they pull it away from you, and it will shatter you when you think of someone else receiving that kind of 'love'. Once you're hooked on the feeling, the narcissist sets about enacting their hidden agenda, which is to make it all about them. Their highly developed sense of entitlement will now ensure that you provide sex whenever the narcissist feels like it.

It will never be about *your* needs. Only the narcissist's needs are important. This doesn't always mean that you will never be pleasured, however. On the contrary, the narcissist derives a great deal of ego-boosting supply from their ability to give pleasure. Being able to perform in this area increases their desirability. They like to view themselves as the best, who can outdo any previous partners you've had. If this is your experience, remember it was *never* about you and your needs. It was all about the narcissist's delusional belief that they are a highly skilled lover. Whether they guilt you into pleasuring them only, or they want you to moan with pleasure so they're reminded of their sexual 'expertise', sex is now your duty. Expect to be punished if you don't perform on demand.

All of the devaluation strategies mentioned here, which are underpinned by coercive control, ensure that the victim is completely dependent on their abuser in every way. The victim's ability to define their situation as abusive is limited as they have been gaslighted for so long, and they have been conditioned to believe that love and control are the same thing. The upshot of this is that many victims choose to stay with their abuser who 'loves' them.

IN SUMMARY

- Once you are perceived as imperfect by the narcissist, the devaluing process must, and will, begin.
- In order to create balance and repair their wounded ego, the narcissist must feel powerful and superior to their victim by finding fault in everything about them.
- They use techniques such as coercive control, gaslighting and manufactured drama including arguments that the victim can never win.

CHAPTER FOUR

Why did I stay?

If you're reading this book, then at some stage you may have been judged by others – even blamed – for staying so long with your abuser. 'What is wrong with you?', 'Can't you see what a loser they are?', 'Why don't you just leave?' are all phrases you might have had thrown at you.

Or maybe it was the opposite: no-one else could see what you experienced behind closed doors so they think you must have exaggerated the abuse – to them the narcissist seems charming and respectful.

Either way, it seems you are doomed. And if you yourself don't understand why you stayed, it's easy to think you must be impaired in some way; you deserved it; it was your fault; or perhaps the abuse wasn't as bad as you thought.

None of these statements is true. The abuse was not your fault. There is nothing wrong with your intelligence. You are not weak, and the abuse was every bit as vile as you remember. Only people who are ignorant and naive about the insidious dynamics of narcissistic abuse engage in such victim-blaming statements. Unfortunately, such comments all too often come from well-intentioned friends and relatives who become frustrated watching their loved one seemingly 'choose' the abuser. What they don't realise is that victims know exactly how to leave. They know that they should go and they're well aware that there are support services available. What the victim most often doesn't understand and needs vast amounts of support with is 'Why did I stay? Why do I keep going back?'

Most victims describe mixed feelings when they finally have that lightbulb moment: that explanation for the trauma they endured in the relationship with their abuser. The word 'narcissist' is raised by a supportive friend, or they start researching the behaviour of the toxic person and find Google telling them they may be in a relationship with a narcissist. But this kind of research in itself is a huge red flag that you may be in a toxic relationship – people in healthy relationships don't feel the need to research their loved one's behaviour.

The victim continues to research and it all starts to make sense. It's a huge relief to finally have a label for it. They watch video after video on YouTube and soak up every bit of information they can find on narcissism and narcissistic abuse. This is completely normal. You are having your trauma validated. You have just stumbled upon a key that will release you from the prison of not knowing. The fog starts to clear and you realise that for so long you were in the fight of your life without knowing the rules of engagement.

Sofie described feeling almost elated when she learned about narcissistic abuse and realised that she wasn't going 'crazy' as she had been told so many times by Justin. As happens with most victims, Sofie also felt despair, sadness and horror as the reality of what had been done to her became clear, and she understood that Justin's love for her was fake.

What was not so clear was her future, when even with all the information she possessed, she still missed the man she thought she knew. She felt as if she was chained to him no matter what she did because she just couldn't get him out of her head. He had betrayed her in so many ways and brought her to what felt like the brink of insanity, yet she just couldn't stop thinking about the 'illusion' of the man she fell in love with.

Trauma bonding

Even after Justin left, Sofie reasoned to herself that she must be still in love with him because she just couldn't stop thinking about him, and the thought of him being with another woman was still excruciating for her. The conflict between her rational brain and her feelings for him made her feel even crazier and (in her words) she truly started to 'act crazy'. She found herself blocking and then unblocking him and stalking his social media with a fake account. Wearing sunglasses, she would drive past his work and his home just to catch a glimpse of him, and once she even looked at the mail in his letterbox. She felt so irrational when she was doing these things and she tried to talk herself out of doing them, but her anxiety would build until she finally gave in.

Sofie was trauma bonded to Justin. She was as dependent on Justin as the heroin addict is to their supplier. And, just as a heroin addict will virtually crawl on their hands and knees for a few crumbs of their drug to end the pain of withdrawal, so too did Sofie. Sofie was in withdrawal from that which she had become physically and psychologically addicted to. Her thoughts were consumed with Justin, the source of her addiction, not because it felt good to be with him, but because it felt so painful to be without him.

Trauma bonding, which is sometimes known as Stockholm syndrome, is extremely difficult to break. It occurs when a victim forms a very powerful attachment to their abuser as a result of the cyclical nature of abusive treatment, where there is a real or perceived danger, followed by intermittent periods of minimal acts of kindness. The victim is isolated from the influence of others in an environment of perceived highs and extreme lows. The unhealthy attachment flies in the face of any kind of logic to the outside world, and more importantly to the victim themselves, because they just can't seem to break that attachment, even in the face of obvious abuse. Victims will often liken the relationship to being on a roller-coaster, where the intense emotions feel like passion and chemistry. However, being with a narcissist is not like the movies, when the couple comes together in the end and lives happily after a turbulent beginning. The intensity in these relationships is based on toxicity and unpredictability, and never ends well.

Once the victim is hooked in the initial idealisation phase, the abuser creates situations of terror and despair for the victim, then proceeds to be kind to the victim and treat them respectfully. The victim experiences utter relief that the abuse has ended, and the 'nice' treatment feels amazing, not because it *is* amazing, but because the terror has ended. In other words, the abuser creates the wound in their victim and then becomes a hero for healing the wound. The victim is conditioned to look to their abuser as being the only one capable of making them feel better. As Sofie reflected on the 'nice' treatment that followed the rounds of abuse, she was able to realise it wasn't so nice at all. These crumbs of niceness simply felt so good because of the stark contrast between the good treatment and the bad. The bad times made her feel so incredibly low that she perceived very small acts of 'kindness' as though she were being treated like a princess. Her threshold for being treated well was as low as it could be.

STOCKHOLM SYNDROME

To explain why you stayed with your abuser it's helpful to consider what the victims went through in the bank heist in Stockholm, Sweden, from which the term 'Stockholm Syndrome' was coined.

In 1973, a bank robbery occurred at the Norrmalmstorg Square in Stockholm. Four hostages were taken. Can you imagine the terror those hostages experienced? Their captor and his accomplice had guns, and threatened to shoot the hostages if their demands were not met by the negotiators. During the six days the hostage situation went on, the hostages were isolated from the outside world with only each other and their captors for company. During this time the captors would provide small comforts to their victims, and talk to them about their own lives, and all the wrongs that had been done to them. The victims got to know their captors and began to 'humanise' them. Their captors became 'real people' who had lives and stories of their own. As they got to know them, they started to feel sorry for their captors and even appeared to protect them.

The six days were extremely intense for the victims as terror flooded them when the captors did not get their demands met by the negotiators, followed by relief when the abuse ended.

Now let's look at the reality of what happened here. The four victims were abused/terrorised when they were taken hostage by their captor. Due to the isolation from the outside world, the captors had free rein to manipulate their victims' perceptions and distort their reality, resulting in an alliance between hostage and captor. The roller-coaster of emotions would have produced extreme chemical changes in the bodies of the hostages as they cycled from terror/hypervigilance to relief when each period of danger ended. A chemical roller-coaster is extremely addictive and is craved when the 'flatline' of normality returns. The terrible wrong that was done to the hostages was minimised by them because of how incredibly good it felt when their abuser was kind to them. In essence, the perfect storm was created to brainwash the victims into thinking they were not being abused.

TRAUMA BONDING IS AN ADDICTION

The reason it feels like you are losing a limb when your abuser ghosts you or discards you is because you are trauma bonded or addicted to your abuser. Physically, psychologically, emotionally and biochemically. Imagine being in a constant state of push/pull, I want you/I don't want you, and all the hormones that are continually needed to survive a life of walking on eggshells.

Now think of what happens to your body when the never-ending drama and continual ups and downs are gone: you crash. It's the equivalent of a heroin addict having their drugs flushed away, and even before the physical withdrawals begin, they are panicking, wondering how they're going to survive without the substance that dictates their existence. This is why you dwell on your abuser. What do you think a heroin addict thinks about day and night in the beginning of withdrawal? They think about heroin. The withdrawal is terrible and they crave relief from the pain. The addicted brain minimises the severity of the destructive nature of the drug, and they reason that it would be okay to have just one more hit because they can now control it instead of it controlling them.

It is this same mindset that has you dismissing your rational thoughts which tell you this person is toxic and returning to your abuser because they are 'not that bad'. Every time you have any kind of contact with the narcissist it is the equivalent of the heroin addict putting the needle in their arm after being in withdrawal. Many abuse victims liken their irrational dependency on their abuser to a drug addiction. In fact, many former drug addicts I have spoken to describe the pain of being without their abuser as worse than their drug withdrawal. This is the reason you feel as if you are suffering a hideous withdrawal every time you are given the silent treatment, are abandoned or try to go no-contact. It's because you *are* in withdrawal.

A drug addict is rewarded with major highs of increased dopamine levels just as the victim is in the love bombing stage. Reward for behaviour means 'do it again'. Of course, as many drug addicts will tell you, the initial high is never obtained again, as the more they have of it, the more the brain develops a tolerance for it. Eventually, addicts need the drug just to feel normal.

Does this sound like when your logical brain was screaming at you that this person was abusive, but you just couldn't stay away? Sofie described an actual sense of relief in learning about the chemical dependency that had taken place inside her without her knowledge – so it wasn't because she was weak or stupid. She learned that when she was being love bombed, there were all sorts of changes taking place in her body. 'Happy' hormones such as oxytocin, or 'the love hormone' as it is sometimes known, were flowing in abundance and her dopamine receptors were seemingly all being hit at once. In short, biochemical changes had taken place. The continued release of dopamine during the love bombing phase felt good. The reward system in her brain had been activated and this pleasurable feeling would now drive her actions as she continually sought out that initial 'high'.

It is one thing to know that a dependency on naturally occurring chemicals took place, but what do you do when the actual source of your addiction is a person? A person who much of the time is actively ensuring you don't break that addiction by placing themselves back inside your head in any way they can? If it was alcohol she was addicted to, then Sofie could at least admit some fault, in that she picked up that first drink, and she continued to drink to the point of dependency knowing it was bad for her. But this was different. It all happened under her level of awareness. She did not choose this in any way, and yet she was continually thrown into the push/pull cycle of withdrawal and then relief from the withdrawal pains when her abuser threw her some breadcrumbs of the love bombing stage. For her this was exactly like a drug addiction. And Justin was the drug dealer who would never let a paying client get clean.

Many trauma-bonded victims who are in withdrawal from their drug (the narcissist) believe they must love their abuser. Sofie told me over and over that she wished she could stop loving Justin and get him out of her head. She supported her notion of love by telling me that much of the time he was 'nice' to her and he was only abusive some of the time.

If you believe that you still 'love' your abuser or that your abuser still loves you when they are attempting to regain control of you, ask yourself: 'What percentage of time is it okay for this person to abuse me?' Is it 10 per cent? Twenty per cent? Maybe even 50 per cent?

It should be zero. It should *always* be zero. Ask yourself too: 'What is my version of love? Can I love someone who treats me so terribly? Can my abuser love me when they treat me so terribly?' The answer is no. Love is just a word unless it is backed up with consistent patterns of behaviour that reflect respect, compassion, empathy and kindness. 'I love you' are three of the most manipulative words in the English language when used by the narcissist, because the narcissist knows the value that normal people place on them. No, you do *not* love someone who abuses you, and someone who abuses you does *not* love you. The painful truth is that the intensity of your feelings when you are without the narcissist is not love. It is withdrawal.

INTERMITTENT REINFORCEMENT

Several factors come in to play to strengthen the trauma bond. One powerful manipulative tactic the narcissist uses is an intermittent reinforcement schedule. To explain this theory, I'm going to talk about rats.

In the 1950s, psychologist B.F. Skinner designed an experiment using a box he called the Skinner box. With this box, he wanted to prove that behaviour could be shaped or changed by reward or punishment. The box was designed with a lever that would release a pellet of food to a rat inside the box every time it pressed on the lever. The rat very quickly learned that it would be fed every time it hit the lever. But soon the rat stopped pressing on the lever until it was hungry again. Once it was established the rats knew what to expect, the experiment was adjusted so that there was no fixed relationship between hitting the lever and being rewarded. The pellet might drop after pressing on the lever twice, then not for 20 or even more presses. When the rats realised that they couldn't predict when they would be rewarded they appeared to panic and kept pressing and pressing frantically.

What this experiment showed was that once a behaviour is established, the most powerful way to get someone or something to repeat that behaviour is to make the reward intermittent. In other words, when a person doesn't know when the reward they crave is coming, they will hang in there for long periods of time, knowing that eventually they will be rewarded for their effort.

This is exactly the technique that Justin used to keep Sofie trapped, even in the face of historical abuse. She never knew when those breadcrumbs of kindness were coming, which made the eventual payoff even more tantalising. In her abuser's mind, this meant he could continue the abusive behaviour, knowing that she would remain trapped indefinitely in anticipation of the unpredictable reward of his company, or simply a day when he was not abusing her.

Cognitive dissonance

Cognitive dissonance occurs when we have two conflicting thoughts or beliefs, which causes us discomfort. The word 'cognitive' relates to thinking and the acquisition of information, and 'dissonance' relates to incompatibility, inconsistency or disagreement. Cognitive dissonance goes hand in hand with trauma bonding and emotional abuse, as both rely on the conflicting information the victim is receiving from their abuser. Gaslighting is a classic strategy used by the narcissist to create cognitive dissonance in their victims. When the victim has two beliefs that conflict with each other, it produces feelings of confusion, self-doubt and a lack of self-trust. In other words, it feels bad.

In the relationship with Justin, Sofie would have experienced cognitive dissonance on a regular basis when Justin's behaviour changed abruptly or his actions did not match his words. A classic example of this would have been when the love bombing phase ended and the devaluing phase began. How confusing for Sofie to be treated like a queen one day and like his arch enemy the next. Another example would have been when Justin denounced everything about Sofie that he professed to love in the beginning, including her singing.

When we are in survival mode, our brain does what it needs to do to protect us so we can survive that trauma. It will come up with all kinds of coping mechanisms to bring our body back to a state of equilibrium and equip us for survival. In an abusive relationship, the discrepancy in the information received by the victim creates feelings of unease, so the brain kicks in by taking the path of least resistance and getting rid of the thought that feels bad.

In order to do that, however, you need to make the other thought totally believable. The victim achieves this by changing their perceptions of their abuser's behaviour to something that was unintentional, misunderstood or not abusive at all. For example:

+ They will rationalise the behaviour away: 'He changed his mind about birthday parties because he was getting older. I was selfish for not thinking about this.'
+ They will minimise the behaviour: 'He came home late from work. So what? He should be allowed to relax because he works hard.'
+ They will deny the abuse: 'He's not having an affair. He's just friends with that woman.'

+ They will sometimes even defend the abuse: 'I put on lots of weight, so he had good reason to cheat.' Note that in this situation, Sofie blamed herself for the abuse, which supported her belief that she deserved the abuse.

These were all strategies that Sofie incorporated to reduce her mental anguish when Justin was lying and manipulating her. By creating cognitive dissonance in the mind of someone who is continually striving to return to the idealising phase, the narcissist ensures the invisible chain between victim and abuser remains intact.

Financial abuse

Because they have been conditioned to hand their power over to the narcissist, the unusual situation of complete financial dependence on the narcissist only becomes apparent to most victims when they try to leave. Consequently, like a long-term convict who is scared to leave jail where they at least know they will get three meals a day and a roof over their head, the victim becomes institutionalised and stays with their abuser. This is even more likely if they have children, as they cannot conceive of a life in which they will be able to support their children without the narcissist. They have nothing and cannot even afford to hire a lawyer. Even if they could find a lawyer to act pro bono, the narcissist would litigate them endlessly, having all the family resources to themselves. It seems a lost cause and the victim resorts to a 'better the devil you know' mindset and stays.

This is exactly what the narcissist wants. They want complete control while you are with them, and if you leave, you will leave with nothing.

The FOG (fear, obligation and guilt)

Why did the narcissist target you? They targeted you because of all the attractive qualities present in you that *they* are devoid of. You are an empath, and as an empath you are full of compassion for others. Your kind and giving nature was naturally attractive to the narcissist, who sensed your willingness to put the needs of others above your own. It is the perfect union as far as the narcissist is concerned. Their only desire is to fill the insatiable void inside them by draining the 'goodness' from others. However, it is impossible for you to see just how one-sided the relationship is when you are conditioned to feel it is your duty to prioritise the needs of the narcissist. The haze of fear, obligation and guilt (FOG) has blinded you to this fact.

When you are in a relationship with a narcissist, you are in a constant state of fear of being punished or abandoned. The narcissist knows they have you hooked (addicted), and the notion that you are replaceable will be continually reinforced, whether passively or overtly. This is 'crazy-making' for the victim and ensures their boundaries are non-existent as they strive to please the narcissist. The narcissist is entertained by knowing the victim fears losing them, so they continue to shift the goalposts, and the victim fails again and again, so keeps trying. The victim ultimately loses their sense of self in the toxic relationship and fears not being able to survive on their own.

The narcissist conditions the victim to feel obligated to meet their needs by reminding them of how much they have done for them. A toxic parent might say something like: 'I brought you into this world and gave you life!' A toxic, abusive partner might say something like: 'You live in a beautiful house and don't have to work. You should be grateful!' The victim feels confused because these statements are true, yet they subconsciously know these things should be given freely in a loving relationship. The victim is conditioned further to endure the abuse because they are indebted to their abuser.

No matter what you do, you will never be able to please the narcissist and you will feel guilty for failing. If you stick to the grocery budget they've given you, they will tell you there is not enough food in the house. If you ask for help with something they will tell you that you're lazy and to do it yourself, but if you take on that task without asking for help and don't do it correctly, you will be criticised for that, as well. You will never be good enough no matter what you do. The narcissist wants you to feel deflated no matter how much you try to please them, so you never feel worthy of a life without them.

Your core wounds

Just as a wolf senses their next meal is close by the smell of blood in the air, so too does the predatory narcissist sense when a vulnerable target appears. The narcissist exposes the victim's wounds and reflects them back to the victim, who may not even be aware of their existence. It is these wounds that keep many victims hanging in there in the relationship, trying to please their abuser in an environment that feels safe and familiar. It is these subconscious wounds that put you in the path of the toxic people who benefit from you having no boundaries, and steer you away from the unfamiliarity of unconditional love.

CORE WOUNDS RESULTING FROM CHILDHOOD TRAUMA

Sofie told me about her problematic relationship with her narcissistic mother who made her feel worthless for never being good enough. She always felt as if she was in competition with her mother and she had no idea why. She just never seemed to be able to make her happy. She never felt like her mother wanted her as a young child and she would be left for long periods of time with her grandmother. Sofie came to realise that she had several core wounds buried deep within her as a result of her childhood. She came to realise that she harboured a deep sense of abandonment, betrayal and rejection by the person who was supposed to look after her and make her feel secure.

If you grew up in an environment that was chaotic, unpredictable and abusive, then your idea of what constitutes a healthy, loving relationship is going to be very much tainted by what you were conditioned to believe is normal. We come into this world as a blank slate upon which our primary carers will write, and the way we view others will be dictated by them by about the age of 12 months. By this age, you have developed an attachment style that permeates your view of relationships into adulthood, reflecting feelings of either security, anxiety or avoidance.

A secure attachment style is developed when a baby is having their needs met and always knows their carer will return to nurture them. An anxious attachment is formed when the carer's presence is unpredictable, as are their emotions. Sometimes that carer may be nurturing and other times they may be unavailable. The baby will therefore be scared to let the carer leave them, as they cannot predict when they will return. An avoidant attachment style is developed when the carer is not responsive at all and the baby learns that crying will get them nowhere as no-one is coming to help them.

Our brains continue to grow until the age of around 25, so imagine the information we're absorbing in the primary years of our lives with a parent or parents who provide inconsistent, conditional or non-existent love.

Imagine it was your mother, the most important female role model in your life, who always put her own needs above yours. If you came to her with a problem, she would tell you to work it out for yourself as she was too busy, or would tell you were useless and never good enough. Even if you proudly brought home a report full of As and just one B grade, you'd be shamed for not getting all As. Imagine trying to talk to her about important life issues, like boy- or girlfriends or your first period (if you were a girl), and she was simply uninterested. Imagine if your mother appeared to be annoyed when you accomplished something wonderful, and it seemed as if she was jealous.

You would have learned to dumb yourself down, to never be proud of yourself because that was selfish, and that your needs were not important at all. You would have learned that no matter how much you tried, the goalposts would always be shifted so you would never feel good enough. You would have absorbed your parent's version of love, which meant that love would always be conditional upon you meeting their needs. You would have learned that love and abuse go hand in hand.

Now, let's throw into the mix a very common life-changing event: your parents divorce. Imagine you're either completely abandoned by one parent, or your parents selfishly use the children as pawns to hurt each other. Let's also add overt physical and/or sexual abuse when a person of trust betrays you in the worst possible way. What does your child-brain do with this information? Perhaps it processes the information to mean: 'This is what people want from me. This gets people to be nice to me', and a precedent for promiscuity in a quest for love is established. Consider, too, a family in which domestic violence prevails, where children are taught either how to abuse their victim or how to tolerate violence. Because once again, abuse and love go hand in hand.

These toxic and faulty views on life, love and relationships set us up for failure as adults. If the most important person in your life forbids you to have boundaries to protect yourself, then that lays the foundation for every relationship in your life.

This is why you might find yourself in one toxic relationship after the other. This is why you might now look around and realise there were numerous other toxic 'friends', colleagues and others in your life who were all using you as a doormat to wipe their feet on. They sense your lack of boundaries, and they sense your core wounds, and with the precision of a surgeon they will reopen those wounds and present them to you.

If this is your story, the toxic person in your life is familiar. These toxic relationships are familiar. They meet your standard of 'normal'. Without realising, you veer away from healthy relationships. You will find something wrong in a healthy person. You might say to yourself they're too short or their nose is too big, but what your subconscious is really screaming at you is that they're *not toxic*. There are no goalposts to outrun with this person: they're showing you respect. There's no drama; no roller-coaster to climb aboard. They're boring. So where do you find yourself? In that familiar environment where you don't get your needs met and you must work hard for any breadcrumbs of love. You find yourself with the mirror image of that parent or carer who didn't do right by you; who failed you. But this time you're not a child anymore. This person isn't going to walk away from you because you will do anything, put up with any treatment, to keep them from rejecting you.

Children

Victims of narcissistic abuse who have children will often suffer terrible feelings of guilt while they are with the narcissist, due to not being emotionally available for their children. They are unable to recognise that their 'failure' to nurture their children as they would like results from a lack of emotional and physical resources, with most of their energy being devoted towards surviving their trauma. They feel emotionally depleted, beaten down, anxious and depressed. If they manage to escape or are discarded, they again suffer the agony of trying to nurture their children with the same lack of emotional resources, only now with no money and perhaps no home.

This is why many victims stay with their abuser. They reason to themselves that at least they have a roof over their heads, and some money, and the children can stay in their schools and their chosen extracurricular activities like sport. The victim doesn't want their children to be deprived, so they sacrifice and stay with their abuser. The abuser who controls the finances reinforces that only a 'bad parent' would take the children out of their home and split up a family. Once again, the victim has been conditioned to believe that everything they do has a selfish agenda.

In a relationship with a narcissist, it is not always the biological children who keep the victim tied to the abuser. There is a good reason the narcissist introduces their children to the new supply very quickly. Justin's children met Rachel just two weeks after he left Sofie. He ensured they spent time together as a family and she was always there at pick-ups and drop-offs. For a non-disordered person, it would probably feel odd to have a love interest throw their children at you so early in the relationship. But remember how manipulative the narcissist is. Justin would have told Rachel how deprived the children were because they had such a terrible mother, and he would have told Rachel how wonderful she was with his children and how much they loved her. He would have organised numerous 'family' occasions for the four of them to cement the bond, and to imply that he was invested in a future with her. Any bemusement on Rachel's part would have evaporated very quickly as a result of the whirlwind events that made her feel like an integral part of the children's lives.

This loving bond was intentionally manufactured between Rachel and the children. The bond will be used against Rachel whenever she displeases the narcissist. They are *his* children. They are his *property*. She will be abused if she disciplines them; she will be abused if she doesn't discipline them. He will triangulate the children with her when he is bored and pit them against her. He will threaten to leave her and tell her that she will never see his children again. He will make sure the bond between her and the children is non-existent to keep her trying harder to please, or he will ensure that she adores those children so he can break her heart into a million pieces when he rips them away from her.

Alternatively, you may bring children from a previous relationship into the new one with the narcissist. The narcissist misses no chances when it comes to creating a weapon to use against you at a future time. Many narcissists will work hard to form a deep bond with your children. They take them everywhere and have plenty of one-on-one time with engaging conversations. Your children grow to love this person and respect them. Then the axe falls, wiping from your face the smile that was put there by watching your children fall in love with your soulmate. The narcissist triangulates you with your own children. The narcissist may insidiously provoke you into an argument in which you are the only visible one reacting. The children are pitted against you for being unjustly mean to this person they love. You stay in the relationship for fear your children would hate you for leaving.

Your confidence is shattered

The narcissist wants you to remain vulnerable so they keep control of you. To ensure you remain vulnerable they must destroy your confidence, as a confident person may have the power to leave the relationship. When your confidence to complete even minor tasks on your own is diminished, your dependence on the narcissist increases, and contemplating how you will survive without them can be a terrifying thought. They will destroy any semblance of self-esteem you possess and it will be done with such stealth that you'll have no idea how you came to be that shell of a person. I am constantly asked by my clients: 'How did I get here? I used to be such a confident person, and now I barely have the confidence to order a pizza let alone hold down a job and support myself.' Through all the strategies listed above, the narcissist ensures their grandiose view of themselves is propped up by pushing you down. Very simply, they need to destroy you to feel better about themselves, and to make sure you feel unable to survive without them. The narcissist is unable to regulate their own self-esteem and this task is given to you, which you accomplish by handing every ounce of your power over to them.

One confidence-buster that I don't believe gets enough attention relates to driving — something I hear many stories about. Driving is something victims once took for granted. But once that confidence has gone, everyone believes they are the only one this is happening to, and they are embarrassed because they can't do something as simple as drive. Maybe the narcissist is right: maybe there is something profoundly wrong with them. They get behind the wheel and experience their first major panic attack. It's terrifying. They then become scared to drive again in case they have another one. It's now not just the fear of driving, but the fear of having another panic attack, losing control and maybe injuring themselves or someone else. Let's look closely at those words, 'losing control'.

During the relationship with the narcissist, you felt completely powerless and your confidence was eroded. So when you get behind the wheel of a car suddenly you have a lot of power, and you don't know what to do with it. You have to be in control: you're in charge of a lethal weapon and you could hurt other people, including your passengers if you're not careful. Suddenly you're in the grip of a panic attack. Why?

Victims may especially struggle with driving on the highway, or going over bridges, across railway tracks or through tunnels. In these situations, you're trapped. You have so much responsibility. What if something happens? You won't know what to do! You can't get off the highway: there's no exit! Your anxiety peaks, and the fear of being that out of control again prevents you wanting to drive. You may also have had your abuser sitting beside you many times telling you what a hopeless driver you are. Or perhaps they would always be the driver and would intentionally terrorise you on the road with their dangerous and erratic driving and threats of causing an accident.

For many victims, driving equates to a degree of freedom. When this is taken away, they become even more dependent on their abuser. It's one more thing they believe is wrong with them, and the narcissist has one more thing they can brag to others about, because they must drive you around. If this is another reason you are not able to leave your abuser, please get help. A good cognitive behavioural therapist can work with you to overcome your fears and get you back to driving.

* * *

The narcissist wants you to be miserable to punish you for failing to remain the flawless being they met in the beginning. At the same time, they need you, because the narcissistic supply they receive from you as their primary source is potent. They have put a lot of time and effort into destroying your confidence and self-esteem and you're not going anywhere. When your ability to trust yourself becomes non-existent, and you have been conditioned to believe that it was your fault, when you look to your abuser to define your reality, when you don't believe that anyone else will love you because you're not worthy of love, where are you going to go? And that's the way the narcissist wants you: believing you're not going to survive without them.

IN SUMMARY

- Trauma bonding, when a victim forms a very powerful attachment to their abuser, is a key reason victims stay with their abuser.

- Unrecognised core wounds stemming from childhood trauma may contribute to a victim being attracted to and staying in the relationship.

- Other reasons include shattered confidence; the 'fog' of fear, obligation and guilt; and the need for financial security for themselves and their children.

CHAPTER FIVE

Discarded

The loneliness, fear and anger Sofie felt when Justin left was indescribable. Her whole world had been turned upside down and she had no idea how she was going to survive on her own. The anger she felt was directed not only at Justin but at herself: even after everything that had happened she still missed him. How could she miss a monster who could simply discard her and the children like yesterday's rubbish? She cried uncontrollably, her weight plummeted, her hair began to fall out and she couldn't sleep.

She had a mortgage, children to support and no means with which to do that. She started to receive notices of arrears for household utilities such as the electricity and internet connection, and the children needed uniforms and books for the new school term. Sofie needed to be strong, but she was a crumpled mess. Worst of all, she was emotionally unavailable to her children, something that caused her the most shame and guilt of all.

After no word from Justin for days, Sofie finally received a text from him telling her that he wanted to do what was 'right' for her and the children. He wanted the split to be as amicable as possible and in the best interests of the children. He bore no ill-will to her, he said, and he was willing to discuss an equitable settlement. It seemed plausible to Sofie when Justin said they should avoid lawyers because they would simply 'rip them off' and take money out of the mouths of their children. In the meantime, he would put money into a joint account for her and the children – that is, of course, until she found a job.

Sofie was ashamed to tell me of the relief she felt when Justin finally got in touch, even if it was just to address practicalities. She was in an impossible position, however: she had no idea how much money their business was earning so how could she know what was fair? But she desperately needed money to survive and felt she had no choice but to accept Justin's financial arrangements. She also didn't want to 'rock the boat' because she still hoped that he would come back to her once he realised what he was losing.

Justin phoned Sofie the next day to continue the discussion. He seemed upbeat and happy and Sofie couldn't understand it. Didn't he know that he had broken her heart and stomped on any semblance of self-esteem she possessed by moving on with another woman so quickly? How could he be so cruel, then ring to discuss logistics as if it was just an everyday task he needed to cross off his list?

In the end it was agreed that care arrangements would be almost week on week off. Justin would pick the children up from their home on a Friday night as he didn't finish until late and didn't want the children to languish in after-school care (which would also mean extra expense). He would then drop them back to Sofie the following Thursday night. Sofie agreed. She wanted to avoid the anguish of seeing his new home, and it seemed to be a reasonable way for the children to go between the two homes with minimal disruption. How wrong she was.

The first time Justin was to pick up the children, to Sofie's amazement, he came to the door, opened it with his key and proceeded to walk in, sit on the lounge and talk to the children about their day. Sofie felt violated, but powerless to stop this, and she didn't want to cause a scene in front of the children. When he was ready, he simply stood up, cheerily said goodbye to Sofie and left with the most important parts of her world.

For the first time in her life, Sofie would be without her children for nearly a week. She didn't think she could feel any worse – it felt like a punishment when she'd done nothing. Gathering all her strength she stoically walked outside to wave goodbye to her children, only to find the 'other woman' sitting in the front seat of the car, waving at the children as they approached. It turned out she could indeed feel worse.

How could Justin do this? Didn't he know much this would humiliate her? And *her*: the woman who had stolen Sofie's husband and claimed her family for her own: how could one woman do this to another? Sofie held it together just long enough to see the car drive away. She then went inside and, in her words, 'officially lost the plot'. She screamed and sobbed, and all the anger that was just below the surface finally emerged in an emotionally charged text to Justin. She told him what she thought of him. How could he be so thoughtless and selfish? Think of the damage he was doing to their children by introducing another woman so early, how confusing it would be. Just two weeks earlier they'd seen their mother and father together and now they would see him in bed with another woman. She hit send on that text and almost immediately regretted it, for in return his reply was emotionless and to the point.

This is why I left you. You are crazy and are clearly off your medication. Rachel is a wonderful woman and will be a good role model in their lives. You should be thankful for that. Stop harassing me and go get yourself some help. You need it! Goodnight.

This was Sofie's life for the next three months. Justin put just enough money into the account to allow her to get by, and she stretched it as far as she could. She started to apply for jobs that would fit into the children's school hours, but without qualifications she couldn't seem to make the shortlist for even the simplest jobs. Her confidence was shattered and she became more depressed, taking solace in food and binge-watching Netflix.

Each week, three nights before Justin was due to pick up the children, she wouldn't be able to sleep, anxious in anticipation of seeing him again. Each time, he walked into the house as if he still lived there, even pointing out things that needed fixing or cleaning. After he left, it took her three more nights to calm down again. She was in a constant state of either anticipating or recovering from his presence in their home. Her rational brain screamed at her to change the locks but she just couldn't bring herself to do it. Part of her feared the punishment from Justin should she dare to deny him access to 'his' home. Denying Justin access to his property that HE had paid for was inconceivable to Sofie, who had been conditioned to ask for permission to speak much of the time, let alone change the locks on a house that he owned. The other part of her clung to the 'normality' of having him in the family home again, as even after everything he had put her through, she still craved for her family to be back together again. Changing the locks just might destroy her chances of getting her family back, forever.

At each pick-up and drop-off Justin made sure Rachel was in the car. The last time she walked the children out, he incited an argument out of nowhere, accusing her of badmouthing Rachel and him to the children, and saying the children had told him of this. He even told her the children were reluctant to come home; they wanted to live with him.

Sofie could not believe Justin was saying this – the children had told her the opposite. He was accusing her of doing exactly what he was doing himself! In tears Sofie yelled at him to leave, and the distraught looks on the children's faces made her ashamed of having taken the bait yet again. She could see a look of disgust on Rachel's face as she attempted to console the children in the back of the car. Sofie never walked the children out again.

When you have something that no longer serves a purpose for you what do you do with it? You throw it away or perhaps trade it in. What's the sense in keeping something around that is broken and just takes up space? It is with this logic and as much compassion the narcissist disposes of their victim when they no longer see any usefulness in them.

Everyone has a use-by date as far as the narcissist is concerned. People are viewed as replaceable. They are objectified and are only as good as their ability to meet the narcissist's needs. While excruciatingly painful for the victim, it is actually logical if you look at it from the supply and demand perspective of the narcissist. You are empty, and they need a full tank. You are no longer able to boost their ego, so they need to move on to another source. A source brimming with ego–boosting ability because they have not yet been abused.

You were never valued for your unique qualities or the little idiosyncrasies that define you as a person. In simple terms, the narcissist does not love, they attach like a parasite attaches to its host, and drop off to find another host when needed. They won't treat the new target any better – they will go through exactly the same cycle as they did with you.

Lacking empathy, compassion and loyalty, the narcissist is incapable of loving another human being and this is why they move on so readily. They do not look back with fond memories of the special times you spent together. There is no point in trying to remind them of any special moments you shared together such as the birth of your baby, or the day you planted that 'sold' sign on your first home. Your history together will mean nothing to the narcissist. There will be no emotional connection to those memories, and they will view you with nothing but disdain for your pitiful attempts to try and suck *them* back. When they can't see you, you cease to exist for them in any historical or meaningful capacity. They do not look back with regret at losing you. The only thing they feel for anyone else is envy and anger. You are objectified and used for whatever purpose you can serve and discarded when it costs them more energy to keep you than to replace you.

The discard is inevitable, whether the narcissist remains in an official relationship with you or not. If the narcissist does remain in any capacity, it will be because it serves their needs in some way that's nothing to do with love. The narcissist may physically stay with their victim for many years even when they have abandoned them emotionally long ago. If this happens it simply means that you will go through the love bomb, devalue, discard phase over and over, with the love bombing phase reduced to days when they're not abusing you.

The narcissist knows they must dispose of you, but they also know they cannot be alone. To be alone is to be alone with that true self, which must not happen. To avoid this, they must line up and hook another target before walking away from their current source.

Do you have memories of the narcissist's behaviour changing before the discard? Did they start liking different food and music or wearing clothing styles they never had before? Did their routine change – did they start going to a new café, and/or drinking their coffee a different way? Did they start becoming very secretive about their phone and social media accounts? These changes were because they were grooming someone else. They were mirroring their new target just as they mirrored you. You were seeing the likes and dislikes of the new 'soulmate'.

You may remember that the abuse and crazy-making behaviour escalated right before the end, and how you (understandably) reacted to it in a frantic effort to understand why. This was because the narcissist had nothing but contempt for the tired old source that was past its use-by date. They knew the end was near and were just biding their time before moving on with their new soulmate. They did not have to try with you anymore, and they were able to drop the mask for good. In their eyes, you were pathetic because they could treat you so badly, yet you stayed around for more. You were blamed for them leaving.

Another reason the abuse will escalate just before the discard is to pave the way for the narcissist to transition into the new relationship in an acceptable fashion. The idea is to make you look mentally unwell or crazy to the outside world so people will feel sorry for them and accept their new love interest who is making them so happy.

The narcissist will endeavour to make the discard as memorable/horrific as possible for you so that your frazzled emotions serve as a reason for them leaving. Your defences will be non-existent after the psychological abuse you have endured and you will react accordingly to their cruel actions, seeking answers to your questions about your disposal. You will not get any closure because the narcissist wants you to pine for them and beg them to come back. They want you to be miserable to punish you for not worshipping them anymore, for not being perfect, and because you saw behind the mask. They will pick a time that will hurt you the most, such as Christmas, your birthday or when you're sick. They will leave you in a world of hurt and you will be blamed for it. They want you to really hurt so you will remember them, and so they will remain inside your head forever.

Hoovered (the second time)

Sofie was trying hard to pick up the pieces of her shattered life and plan for the future. She still cried intermittently but she had reconciled herself to being a single parent, and about three months after Justin left her, she finally began to think of ways to move forward and heal.

Then she received a phone call from Justin, who wanted to come over to 'discuss' a few things. Reluctantly she agreed. She still couldn't say no to this man, so Justin came to the house while the children were at school.

Sofie could not have prepared herself for the conversation that took place. Justin was having second thoughts and he missed his family terribly. Rachel was not the woman he thought she was, he said, and she had deceived and controlled him, something he said he could not abide. He told Sofie he wanted to give it another go, and when he put his arms around her and cried, Sofie let him. Before she knew it, they were being intimate. In those moments, Sofie had a reprieve from the pain of the last few months, and she agreed to try again. She was overwhelmed with relief. It was over. She would have her family back. Justin agreed that he would break it off with Rachel, and they would try to start over and bring the romance back by 'dating' each other while living in their separate homes. He thought it best they keep this secret from the children for now.

Sofie was beyond happy; she was elated, and she counted the hours down to the sporadic times she got to spend with him while the children were at school. Because she assumed that he would soon move back in, she had no hesitation in signing any documents Justin put in front of her, including signing the house and their business over to him. These, he said, were needed for the best tax outcome when he moved back in. Sofie just wanted her family back together again.

For Sofie, it was worth the wait for their unpredictable interludes, and these times remained intense and exciting. That is, until they weren't. Gradually, the meetings became less frequent and certainly less intense. It seemed that Justin had lost interest, and the visits to her were becoming almost burdensome. Once again, she felt totally confused. The next time he came over she tried to talk to him about her thoughts but Justin as usual dismissed them: 'You're imagining things'.

Sofie thought about the end goal of getting back together, and dismissed her thoughts as irrational – she was too impatient. She continued to ignore her instincts until one day her youngest child, in tears, told her they didn't want to live with Daddy and Rachel anymore.

Rachel? Once again, Sofie's world collapsed as she realised what had been going on for the last couple of months. He was still with

Rachel. Sofie had prided herself in not asking the children questions about life at their father's but this time she couldn't help it. Her son told her that Rachel moved out for a couple of weeks, but she had returned and had been there every time they were there for the last month. Sofie said she felt the first true bolt of fury at that stage. She felt so stupid and worthless for letting him back!

Once again, broken hearted, Sofie had no choice but to try and pick up the pieces and carry on for the children's sake. The children were due to go to their father's place on the Friday as usual. Once again, he let himself into the house to wait for them. This time, however, Sofie remained in her bedroom as she did not want to have to face him. After they all left, Sofie walked into the lounge room and saw that a painting was gone. She also noticed a television missing from another room. She immediately sent him an angry text demanding them back. He made her wait four hours before replying: 'It's my property too. I can take what I want.'

Every time he came to get the children after that, Sofie was forced to see him in order to 'guard' him. It was a set-up and she had to endure the smirk he would give her that said, 'I just played you. There's nothing you can do about it, and I'm enjoying every moment of it.'

When they were with their father, Sofie made a point of calling the children each night around the same time to say goodnight and hear their voices. The night after Justin took the items from the house, she called the children as usual. She called each child's phone and when there was no answer she reluctantly called Justin's. He told her he was concerned about her mental health, and that the children became upset when she called so he was giving them 'a break' from her. He'd 'allow' her to speak to them in a few days.

Sofie was powerless again. She called Justin every day for the next three days until he finally let them answer their phones and speak to her. Sofie was beyond angry with Justin. She knew he wouldn't answer her calls so she texted him that she was going to take him to court and to expect a letter from her solicitor. Maybe that would make him treat her better!

At this point, Sofie was still under the illusion that she could have a meaningful discussion with Justin and that he would come to see how unreasonable he was being.

Justin responded immediately, urging her to go ahead and contact a lawyer, but that she would not only spend money she didn't have, she would also lose the house she was living in which would need to be sold to finance the litigation. The idea of being homeless terrified Sofie and she gave that little surge of power she'd felt right back to Justin. At the moment, she felt, it was better the devil she knew than the one she might face in court.

Sofie once again slumped into a world of hurt, and the couch and TV remote became her best friends. One day, she decided to contact her old best friend whom she had become distanced from during her marriage to Justin. Her friend suggested she try to get out of the house and meet new people. She couldn't believe Sofie didn't even have a social media account as Justin thought it was a waste of time and energy.

When I discussed this with Sofie, she once again took ownership of this issue, because she'd been 'the one who decided to leave social media'. After all, Justin didn't force her to shut it down; in fact he told her to do what she wanted, so how was it his fault? Sofie was still assuming that she bore responsibility for the way she was treated, rather than looking at the puppeteer who was pulling the puppet's strings and telling the puppet they did it on their own. This is the nature of coercive control.

Continuing financial control

Sofie enjoyed her renewed social media access on Facebook and even started up her own Instagram account as well. It felt good to have this access to the outside world and she didn't feel so alone. She reconnected with old friends from school and made new friends with whom she chatted regularly online.

One day Sofie and her best friend Carol decided to have a girls' day and get their hair and nails done. Sofie had been budgeting carefully with the allowance from Justin and had some money left over to afford it. Carol convinced her she deserved a little pampering, and Sofie looked forward to the day, but still felt a sense of foreboding that she was doing something wrong. She tried to brush that feeling off and enjoyed herself. The next week, however, she found the bank account was short $200. When she called Justin, he told her he had noticed on the bank statement that she had been spending money on herself, but that the money he put in was to support the children, and not for her.

'If you want to pretend you're the world's next top model then go and get a job!' he told her, hanging up then blocking her again.

Sofie was forced to adjust her already tight budget so that she could get by until the next allowance day.

What was wrong with him? Every time she thought she was moving forward and getting on with her life, which is what he told her he wanted for her, something would happen, and she would have to answer to him. The kids told her they went for weekend trips away with their father and Rachel, and for regular nights out to dinner, and that Justin and Rachel had just purchased a new car. Why was it so selfish for her to, for the first time in ages, get her hair and nails done? Every time she had seen Rachel at her house, she looked immaculate. Clearly it was okay for her to pamper herself.

Why did he treat her so much better than he treated Sofie? What was so good about her that she got all the good and loving side of Justin and Sofie got all the bad? What made her a better person than Sofie? This consumed Sofie's thoughts day in and day out. She started looking at Rachel's Instagram account and saw photos of her with Justin and her children. They looked so in love and happy! It became like a daily compulsion: her anxiety would build and build until she looked. Of course, she only found pictures and comments that reflected a soulmate connection between the two. But the pain of looking was less than the pain of not knowing.

The day came when Sofie needed to buy groceries and the account was empty. Sofie called Justin and politely stated her case, saying that some unexpected bills had come up and that she needed more money. Justin said that he would 'think about it'. Sofie felt the frustration build again and yelled at Justin around the unfairness. Justin said that he was being more than fair given that she was still lazing around enjoying being a lady of leisure, and that he was not going to argue with her. He was sick of her always causing conflict and he was not going to engage. He would discuss a possible increase when she calmed down.

Sofie knew that every time she begged him to be reasonable, he seemed to enjoy it and it never got her anywhere. She decided to wait a few days, then Justin called her in a seemingly wonderful mood telling her she could have more than she asked for, and that she deserved to go and do something special for herself.

What? She had suffered his wrath last time she engaged in any self-indulgence, as he saw it, and now he was pushing her to do more? But she took the money regardless, and continued to maintain her 'good girl' status to keep this momentum going. Nothing had changed. She was still at the mercy of his moods, and she knew it.

Effect on the children

Adding to Sofie's mounting distress was the impact the separation was having on the behaviour of her three children and her relationship with them. Her eldest, daughter Taylor, was 14, Katie was 12 and Jack was 10. Every time they came home from their father's they would be argumentative and sometimes just plain rude and disrespectful. They would talk back to her. If she asked them to do a chore, they would ignore her until she ended up yelling at them in frustration. Sofie remembers one time 10-year-old Jack started recording her on his phone when she was disciplining him, saying that his dad had asked him to do this. He'd told Jack that his mum had mental health problems and they needed to prove this so she would go and get some help. Sofie took the phone from her child and deleted the video, trying to explain to him at a level he would understand that this was inappropriate.

She didn't know why anything shocked her anymore, but she still couldn't believe the unconscionable actions of her ex. This was parental alienation and it was cruel, not just to her, but to the children. After her talk with Jack, he proceeded to ask her why she hated Daddy so much. Sofie was shocked: she'd made a point of never talking badly about their father to the children but Jack told her that Daddy said Mummy hated him and Rachel, and Mummy was always trying to start trouble. Mummy should like Rachel, Jack said, because she was nice and always gave him lots of cuddles.

The pain Sofie felt hearing this was excruciating. It was as if her son was telling her that she was gradually being replaced as their mother. It took all her strength not to break down completely in front of her son. She hated Justin for what he was doing. Every time she turned around, there was another hoop to jump through and it didn't matter how much she tried to be a 'good girl', there would always be another one. Of course Rachel was supportive; her world wasn't being ripped away from beneath her. The injustice of it all was overwhelming.

With the younger two children, the poor behaviour would settle down after a couple of days, but with the eldest it was a different story. Taylor had always been Justin's favourite, and since the separation she had become extremely belligerent towards Sofie. Sofie knew this could be normal for teenage girls, but this was something different. She would ring her father every time Sofie reprimanded her and would tell him what was going on in the home. Sofie heard her saying that her mother was 'going off' again. Justin would also call Taylor numerous times a day when she was with Sofie, and Sofie felt that he was constantly inside her daughter's head and dictating her behaviour.

One time, Sofie asked Taylor to unpack the dishwasher, and it ended in another argument. Half an hour later, Justin arrived at the doorstep to take just Taylor back to his home – not before berating Sofie about her inability to parent the children and her favouritism for Katie and Jack.

With Justin phoning Taylor constantly, and Taylor reporting back to him everything that went on in their home, Sofie almost felt like she had a spy in her home. It was an impossible situation. If she spoke to Justin about it he would deny all, and deflect all the blame back to her, telling her yet again that she was a bad mother. Sofie was forced to turn a blind eye to much of Taylor's negative behaviour and became very mindful of what she could and couldn't say when Taylor was around.

Child support – dealing with the system

About a month or so after the time Justin had curbed her allowance for her 'selfish expenditure', Sofie went to withdraw funds and found that once again, they were significantly less than they should have been. She was very angry, but this time, instead of ringing Justin to beg him for money, she did the scariest thing she felt she had ever done. She called the child support agency. Why was she afraid of the repercussions for doing something behind Justin's back? She didn't understand it, but she did it anyway. Then she waited.

A week or so later, she received the call she'd dreaded. She didn't answer it but listened to the voicemail Justin left. He was yelling uncontrollably. She could almost picture the veins popping out of his neck as he verbally attacked her for going outside their 'agreement'. He told her that she would get nothing: he'd signed his business over to his partner, and technically he was now taking a small salary from the partner. Sofie had shot herself in the foot in ringing Child Support as she could no longer rely on him to 'have her back'. He'd been extremely generous with her before, he told her, but now not only would he not give her anything beyond what she was entitled to, he would no longer encourage the children to love and support their mother despite her clear shortcomings. The abuse continued via text.

Sofie was terrified. She had tried so desperately not to rock the boat, but now it seemed she had awakened a monster.

Sofie's fears were real for her. Perception is reality. It was terrifying for her to think of doing something that might anger Justin, especially if it had anything to do with his control over money. Sofie began the process of having the children's child support collected by the agency, and she really wasn't sure what was worse: the verbal arrangement she had with her abuser who would dictate what she 'deserved' or the arrangement with a system that seemed to allow the abuser to use every loophole imaginable to avoid his responsibilities. She wished she hadn't called Child Support now, when she had no money and didn't know where her next cent was coming from.

She was forced to borrow money from her mother. Sofie didn't have a good relationship with her, and she knew her mother would enjoy the fact that Sofie needed her help. Someday this good deed would reveal ugly strings attached to it. As with Justin, there was never a gift from her mother that didn't come with a price tag.

The months went by with no money from their father to support her children, and the bill owed to her mother kept going up. In repayment, her mother was demanding a lot of Sofie's time. These interactions were always to badmouth some other family member or ignite Sofie's sense of obligation to her through guilt. Sofie always came away feeling mentally battered and bruised.

Sofie spent nearly every day of the next couple of months on the phone to Child Support. She couldn't understand the hold up. It seemed she spoke to a different person every time but they all told her that Justin had the right to defend himself, and that he had a certain time frame in which to do this.

Sofie knew him well: he would not be told what to do by anyone. With his arrogance and sense of superiority, he would ignore all correspondence from Child Support and wait until the last moment to reply. The Child Support agency could only follow the processes that were available to them in a system that was flawed. The whole process was infuriating, especially when she saw Justin and Rachel pull up in her driveway in their new car. It was the ultimate affront to Sofie.

Sofie knew these issues were born of Justin's desire to punish her. To him, the children were just collateral damage. He knew that she would never see them go without so he could hold out until he was done torturing her or until Child Support finally forced his hand. Sofie knew that Justin would be in control of the situation.

This was to go on for nearly a year as Child Support continued to seek Justin's cooperation, stating they had to go through the correct 'processes' and give him a 'fair' chance to respond. She knew Justin was playing the system. To a narcissist, knowing they are causing you so much anguish is a wonderful feeling, and it continues to be until playing the system affects them.

At the very last moment, when all his chances had been exhausted, Justin finally provided the agency what they asked for, declaring earnings that would leave Sofie a child support figure of roughly $100 dollars a week for three children.

It was less than half of what Justin had previously given her. Maybe Justin was right: maybe he had been generous before. In tears she called Justin, not knowing what else to do. Surprisingly he picked up straightaway. He told her that Child Support had arrived at that amount, not him. He laughed, told her to 'stop being so lazy', to get off her 'arse', and to 'go and get a job'. And Sofie did, managing to get a job cleaning houses for a local company.

It felt good to be earning her own money. Then, just a few days after starting the job, she received a letter from the child support agency asking for income details of her minimum-wage job. Sofie had fully intended to tell them, but Justin had got in first, in her very first week of employment. How he knew, she did not know. It seemed no matter what she did, he was still in control.

He continued to play the system for the next year with constant requests for assessment reviews and employing other kinds of tactics that would require further investigation by the agency. It was mentally draining – and that's what the narcissist wanted. He wanted to wear her out. He wanted her to give up trying.

It seemed that at least once a week there was some new drama created by Justin that Sofie had to deal with, and his bullying behaviour escalated. He had once again taken items from the house while she wasn't there and he sent her texts questioning her parenting ability and mental health.

One text was particularly disturbing in that it contained a photo of her own anti-anxiety medication that she had recently purchased on script, clearly taken when he entered the house without her knowledge. The accompanying message said: 'You might actually know what our children's needs were if you weren't spaced out on your happy pills all the time!'

She tried to make sense of it all, but it was like trying to nail jelly to a wall: one minute he was telling her to get medicated, the next he was abusing her for doing so.

He also managed to turn the teachers against her at her children's school, appearing at parent-teacher nights with Rachel and badmouthing her behind her back. She also had to endure him and Rachel playing happy families at the children's sports events and socialising with the other parents, her former friends, who now seemed to avoid her. Sofie felt like an outsider at all her old familiar and favourite haunts. She knew that the information that had changed their perception of her came from Justin.

Sofie's depression increased with the strain of making ends meet and trying to put a good face on things for the children, but things came to a crisis point when Justin manipulated the younger children into wanting to stay with him longer term. She had to get help, he said, and they'd come back when she was 'better'.

Sofie felt there was nothing else he could do to destroy her. He had taken everything from her. She knew he would show everyone the messages she sent him and he would use them to prove she was crazy. But she just couldn't help it. She was now angry at herself for reacting and giving him exactly what he wanted.

IN SUMMARY

- The narcissist is incapable of love because they lack empathy and compassion.
- When their narcissistic supply dries up they seek a new source with a 'full tank'.
- The discard doesn't mean an end to ongoing abuse. It means the beginning of post separation abuse. (See also Chapter 8, Divorcing a narcissist.)

CHAPTER SIX

Smear campaigns, flying monkeys and the hoover manoeuvre

You've been discarded. The relationship ended in the most horrific way, and you've been told it was all your fault. They tell you and everyone else they're so glad to be out of the relationship because you're crazy, you're abusive, and you've done everything in your power to make their life a misery with your toxic ways. They're distraught, they are trying to heal and recover, but they've managed to find a kind and genuine soul, someone the total opposite of you, who loves them unconditionally. Someone who came along at a time when they were at their lowest point and is helping them to pick up the shattered pieces of their life. It's amazing timing:

it must be fate and they feel truly blessed. They must get on social media straightaway and introduce this god or goddess to the world.

They fill their social media with happy snaps of themselves with this new, perfect person who has saved them, and they thank everyone for their thoughts and best wishes for the new relationship. They are beginning their new life with their soulmate, and they have never been happier.

You'd assume this newfound bliss would mean they'd be quite happy to sail off into the sunset and live happily ever after like Shrek and Fiona in their castle (or swamp), and forget about your existence. This would be the logical conclusion, given they are so relieved to be free of you. Unfortunately, nothing the narcissist does is ever born out of logic, and everything is born out of a self-serving desire to manipulate and top up their ego. When the narcissist discards you, it's often just the beginning of their real plans for torture, which are to destroy what's left of your tattered self and make sure you never forget them.

The smear campaign

Whether they discard you, or you manage to escape, the narcissist will want to punish you for not worshipping them anymore. The narcissist also fears exposure. Once they know you 'know', they are in constant fear that you will tell the world of their secret by revealing your inside knowledge of their true self lurking behind the mask. You may have been discarded (even if they are still with you at this point), but you know the truth about them and they set about annihilating anything that's left of your reputation so that people won't believe you when you begin to tell your side of the story. In narcissistic abuse recovery we call this the 'smear campaign'.

The smear campaign is about implementing damage control. The narcissist knows what you are going to say about them, so they begin creating an alternative reality which they disperse like a crop duster to anyone who'll listen. A reality that paints you as the villain and them as the victim.

The depth of rage the narcissist feels at being 'abandoned' (you are not begging them to return), or simply not wanted anymore, is in direct proportion to the smear campaign they will instigate, with the ultimate goal being to destroy their victim in every way imaginable. Complete annihilation is usually the goal.

Unbeknown to you, the narcissist began smearing you in subtle ways very early on in the relationship. It might have begun with things like their reaction in front of others when you called them. The narcissist might have said: 'Oh, here he is calling me again. This is the tenth time today. I don't know why he's so insecure and needs to check up on me all the time. I try everything I can to make him feel secure, but he just doesn't trust me.'

The narcissist planted the idea in the listeners' heads that not only are you insecure, possibly unstable and stalking them, but that they are a compassionate partner who is trying to help you with your issues. They created an idea that you're unstable which they can expand on at a later time (when probably what you asked them was to get milk on their way home).

They may very 'compassionately' tell others they are worried about you because your anxiety levels have been very high lately and you've had frequent emotional outbursts. Narcissists are particularly fond of this type of smear as it's implemented under the guise of caring. The narcissist broadcasts what they really want everyone to believe, which is you're 'nuts', and they simultaneously come off as Mother Theresa. It's a win–win for the narcissist.

The narcissist is always preparing for you to expose them. They've spent their life creating a facade of an incredible human being and they will protect that facade at all costs. The false self, or the 'mask' they wear, is normally formed very early on in life. This new personality masks that weak and wounded being that was so vulnerable to attack. The false self, which is devoid of a conscience, is worn like a shield of armour to prevent them ever being vulnerable again. You saw their true self. You know that they are fake. You know their love is fake. You have the power, therefore, to destroy everything they have spent their lifetime building. You are a threat and you must be disarmed and neutralised. Consequently, the smear campaign began long before you were aware of it, and when you finally do understand what's happening, the damage to your reputation has been devastating.

Did you ever go somewhere with the narcissist where everyone seemed to be looking at you strangely? As if you had something stuck in your teeth, or you had committed some heinous offence? You were extremely confused, I'm sure, at the sudden change in people's attitudes towards you, and it would have caused you much anxiety as you tried to work out what you'd done. If people you know have suddenly done an about-face in the way they treat you and react to you, it's more than likely the result of the narcissist smearing you.

Sofie was confused by the way people were looking at her so strangely when she attended her children's sports games. She couldn't understand why these people she thought were her friends now wanted nothing to do with her. Their behaviour was governed by Justin's smear campaign.

He could no longer control Sofie's perceptions the way he wanted to, so he was going to control the perceptions of everyone around her.

His other goal was to punish her through isolation. The narcissist wants to cut you off from all support. They want you to feel completely alone; that everyone is against you. But most of all, they want you to suffer.

You have already suffered the heartache of having the person you loved, and who you thought loved you, turn completely against you. Now many other people in your life are turning against you and you have no idea what you've done. It is excruciating for victims when they don't know who they can trust anymore, and people they once thought of as friends seem to drop away. The narcissist plans this very carefully, ensuring it will happen by engaging with everyone and anyone who might be important to you to manipulate their perceptions.

CONFIRMATION BIAS

Most victims are dumbfounded and feel betrayed at the way these seemingly intelligent good friends and family members believe the lies of the narcissist. Why are they so quick to believe your ex before they have heard your side of the story? The answer to this question lies in a concept called 'confirmation bias'.

Confirmation bias is the tendency to process all new information so that it confirms and aligns with our existing beliefs. When a person engages in this process, they tend to ignore other information that is not consistent with what they already know or believe to be true.

The narcissist is very cunning, and to make their version of events more believable in a smear campaign, they will begin by providing their listeners with very small seeds of truth, which they will recognise. The listener will confirm that what the narcissist is initially saying is correct, and then assume that everything else they are saying is also fact. For example, you may have been out with friends one night and the narcissist provoked you into arguing with them. They made sure that you had a few drinks, so you were more likely to erupt, and your friends saw you shouting at the narcissist and crying hysterically. To plant the little seed in everyone's mind the narcissist might say something like: 'Oh my goodness. Remember the night you saw Sofie screaming at me while she was so drunk? Well, that's happening all the time now. Her drinking is completely out of control and her outbursts are just destroying me.'

The narcissist very cleverly or manipulatively provided information they knew everyone would recognise, and they then proceeded to embellish it with untruths. Everyone had seen Sofie engage in this behaviour, so it was a natural progression for them to believe the rest of the story was true.

THE DOG WHISTLE

To set up a solid foundation for the smear campaign, the narcissist will consistently set up such situations while you are still together to pocket those seeds of truth for later use. One tried and true strategy they use is a concept very aptly named 'the dog whistle'. Most of you will have at some stage seen on television or read about a whistle that is used in dog training which dogs can detect but is inaudible to human beings. Dog whistling is a form of gaslighting the narcissist uses to make you appear unstable and lack credibility. Here's an example.

You are having a lovely family get-together to celebrate Christmas at a relative's home. You are all sitting at the dinner table, enjoying the champagne, when someone says to the cook: 'This roast turkey is delicious. You are such an amazing cook!'

The narcissist then pipes up: 'Indeed. My wife is also an amazing cook, aren't you darling? You should have seen the roast she cooked us the other night. It was incredible!' Now to everyone else at the gathering, here was the narcissist singing your praises and appearing to be a loving partner who is grateful for their wife's exemplary culinary skills. However, the truth of the matter is that the narcissist is baiting you because they profess to hate your cooking with a passion. It's a topic for never ending arguments because no matter what you cooked, the narcissist would say it was terrible. No-one at the table knows about this, however, so they can't understand why you glare at the narcissist.

Another example of the narcissist's dog whistle that I regularly hear of may occur when you're about to enjoy a night out. You're in the taxi perhaps. You've spent hours trying to look your most glamorous but the narcissist tells you that you look fat in that dress and that people at the party don't like you. This all happens right before you step out of the cab. You are heartbroken and cannot stop thinking about it all night. Your mood interferes with all interactions, and you act coldly and indifferently towards the narcissist.

The narcissist has the time of their life at the party, and they attend to you solicitously: they get you drinks and a seat and attempt to dance with you. No-one witnesses the narcissist deliberately provoking you in the hope you'll make a scene. They only see the narcissist being gentlemanly and charming. You, however, are viewed as the ungrateful bore who fails to recognise how lucky you are with a partner who cares about you so much. Seed planted. People remember you as unstable, and the narcissist as the compassionate partner who could never please you, no matter how hard they tried.

RAMPING UP THE SMEAR

As I mentioned in Chapter 5, the narcissist will begin to ramp up their abuse when they know the discard is imminent or they know you are about to leave. It is at this time that the smear campaign will escalate to a point where the victim becomes aware that people are treating them differently, or that they are not talking to them at all.

It's at this time too that the narcissist's mask comes right off and stays off in the vicinity of the victim as the narcissist sees any effort with you as a total waste of energy. They have other fish to fry. They have a new source that is full to the brim of life-giving narcissistic supply. However, your reputation, or lack thereof, can serve as a very effective way to make that new target feel sorry for the narcissist. The narcissist escalates their abuse towards you as they drop the mask for good, and you react in a distraught, frantic and volatile manner just as they anticipated. Their plans have come to fruition. You're acting crazy, they had no choice but to leave you, and the new target feels compelled to take care of them. The new target will also despise you, enabling the narcissist to triangulate the pair of you whenever they are up for a good dose of drama.

IF YOU'RE THE ONE TO LEAVE

If it was you who left the narcissist or managed to escape, the smear campaign may be even more horrific, if that's possible. You have wounded their ego. You humiliated them, made them look like a fool to the outside world so they need to smear you as a form of reputation management. In this situation, the narcissist may employ a smearing strategy designed to target your mental health and set themselves up as your hero in the eyes of others.

The narcissist may approach your friends and family members, with whom they have been forging strong bonds just to isolate you from them at a later date. They might say something like: 'Sofie's left me. I'm so worried about her mental health. She's been saying and doing some crazy things lately, and I don't know where she is. I'm so worried about her!'

You then find your loved ones contacting you to see if you're okay and telling you how worried the narcissist is about you. Perhaps they might tell you to contact the narcissist and try again. After all, it takes two to tango, right? The narcissist's smear campaign takes on new meaning when you 'prove the narcissist right' by yelling at your loved ones and telling them to mind their own business. Your loved ones think the narcissist was right – you *are* volatile!

Another example of smearing that I often hear of is when the narcissist contacts police as well as your loved ones to say they believe you are suicidal. They are worried you might kill yourself and they want an immediate welfare check. How embarrassing, frustrating, enraging it is to open your door and have to assure the authorities that you have no intention of killing yourself.

In both these examples, the narcissist has managed to portray you as having mental health issues, and themselves as a caring individual concerned about their ex. They have also set you up in the system as someone who needs monitoring, and this kind of mudslinging sticks. At the very least, imagine the rumours that will abound from your neighbours, who will make up their own minds about why the police and paramedics are knocking loudly on your door.

If you've been pulling away from, or have gone no-contact with, a narcissistic family member, the smear campaign will be just as vicious. The narcissist simply cannot have you ruining their reputation, and it does not look good when you stop talking to them. They need to maintain their image of the perfect family to the outside world and if you fail to support this grandiose illusion, you will be painted as an ungrateful traitor. For example, the narcissistic mother may cry to other family members about how much you have hurt them and let them down. They may sprinkle seeds of ideas in the minds of outsiders and other family members that you stopped talking to them because they wouldn't give you any more money or let you use them anymore. The smear campaign that is dispersed to your family by other family members can sometimes be the most painful and isolating of all, because these people have always been part of your life and you thought you could trust them implicitly.

Smear campaigns are devastating for victims of narcissistic abuse. You have been completely traumatised by the ongoing abuse. You feel so alone and isolated from the real world, and now you are faced with hearing lies that paint you as a terrible person. What makes this even more devastating is that people you once trusted are believing the lies.

HOW TO DEAL WITH A SMEAR CAMPAIGN

When you hear such malicious fabrications about yourself, it's natural to want to defend yourself and tell people what really happened. You want to set the record straight, thinking that once people know the truth, they will see the narcissist for what he is, and they will come back to support you.

Unfortunately for you, the narcissist in their manipulative way has anticipated exactly what you are going to tell everyone when defending yourself and attempting to expose them, and they are prepared. Defending yourself against a narcissist is never a good idea because it's what the narcissist wants you to do, and they have set it up so it will backfire. They have given everyone a very plausible explanation about why you will be saying what you say, and when you do? Bingo. That confirmation bias kicks in, and the narcissist is 'proved' right.

It might sound counterintuitive, but the best way to combat a narcissist's smear campaign is to hold your head high, move on with your happy and successful life and ignore what's being said. If you defend yourself, the narcissist will up the ante. They want to be inside your head; they want you to defend yourself so they can say 'I told you so' to their supporters. They will go to extraordinary lengths to get you to do so, trying tactics like unblocking you and your friends on social media or virtually hand-delivering the smearing information to you.

But when you ignore what is being said about you, hopefully the people who matter in your life will see you moving on, seemingly without giving the narcissist a second thought. Your behaviour will prove the smear campaign wrong: you'll be at peace, doing none of the things the narcissist has said about you.

The narcissist, on the other hand, is still repeating what a horrible person you are. By continuing to badmouth you they end up looking like a liar and a fool.

The smear campaign will destroy you if you engage as the narcissist wants you to, but it can only hurt you if you hear about it, so:

+ Don't ask people what the narcissist is saying about you.
+ Don't stalk the narcissist on social media to see what they're saying.

+ If people want to tell you about the latest rumours, tell them you're not interested. (Get them to document it if they think it might be useful for court.)

+ Get someone else to be your ears and determine anything that needs actioning while you get on with your healing.

Flying monkeys

It takes planning for the narcissist to set up a workable smear campaign. They need to be very careful that when they are dishing the dirt on you they do not come off looking sneaky or cruel. So, like any ruthless businessperson trying to obliterate a rival organisation, the narcissist gathers their workers and followers together, trains them to do their bidding, and points them in the direction of the enemy. We refer to these followers as 'flying monkeys', a name inspired by the monkey henchmen of the Wicked Witch of the West in *The Wizard of Oz*. Flying monkeys are an important resource to the narcissist, as they allow the narcissist's hands to remain clean while someone else does their dirty work. So if you have a narcissist in your life, you also have their flying monkeys, and it's important to be aware of the narcissist's ability to use them to abuse you by proxy.

The narcissist engages flying monkeys so they can maintain their fake charismatic persona to the rest of the world. The narcissist will dispatch flying monkeys when seeking to punish their victim for any perceived slight that wounds their ego.

Leaving the narcissist and rendering them insignificant is the ultimate 'sin' of a victim, as is appearing to be getting on with life without the narcissist, and healing. Flying monkeys engage in rumour-mongering and toxic manipulation to punish the victim by either bringing the victim back under the narcissist's control or destroying their reputation. They may pretend to be the victim's friend, the goal being to act as the narcissist's eyes and ears, so the narcissist continues to have updated surveillance of their victim.

Flying monkeys are not 'friends' of the narcissist. They are followers who get their own distorted fulfillment, or self-worth, from the narcissist's approval. Their blind loyalty knows no limits as they are often completely dependent upon their leader for their livelihood and lifestyle. They are also 100 per cent disposable and replaceable, and would suffer a similar fate to that of any other victim should they fail in their duties to 'hear no evil and see no evil'.

Some individuals may be unaware they are being used as flying monkeys. For example, a couples counsellor may unwittingly become one. A narcissist will engage in DARVO (deny, attack, and reverse victim and offender) during the counselling session and the counsellor then believes the victim is actually the abuser. In Sofie's story in Chapter 3, Justin manipulated their counsellor to re-victimise Sofie.

Other people and organisations narcissists may use as unaware flying monkeys include the police and child protection authorities, as well as your friends and loved ones.

Many of the narcissist's entourage are aware their job is to hurt you and they can be just as toxic as the narcissist. They may be intensely loyal to the narcissist for a myriad of reasons, but the main reason they are chosen is they are easy to manipulate. The loyalty, however, does not go both ways, and the narcissist has no qualms in discarding a flying monkey if they displease them.

The narcissist loves to use so-called mutual friends to act as their flying monkeys. But you will soon realise that any friend of the narcissist is against you and never was your friend. Perhaps you are in hiding from the narcissist and are trying to implement no contact when all of a sudden who should appear on your doorstep but the narcissist's wingman, the chief flying monkey otherwise known as their best friend.

The friend may say they know about what is going on between you both, but they don't want to get involved and they still want to be friends with you. My advice: don't fall for it. This is probably the ugliest flying monkey of the narcissist's troop, and they will have anything but goodwill for you. They will be there to gather information, take photos if they can, and report back to the narcissist. The narcissist does not have friends. Friendship requires trust, good faith, genuineness and unconditional love and support. The narcissist has followers and butt-kissers. That's it.

The more powerful and influential the narcissist is, the more power they have to delegate to their troop of flying monkeys, who will not question the actions they are asked to engage in, despite the obvious ruination of an innocent victim. These types of narcissists often succeed in climbing the respective social and career ladders quickly, and may become celebrities such as high-profile sports stars, CEOs of large organisations or politicians. They can also be found in the church and leading charitable organisations, where trips to children's hospitals are mistaken by the community for kindness and generosity, rather than an effort to gain attention and admiration through photos and videos on social media.

The actions of a loyal flying monkey who is dependent on their leader knows no limits. I have heard numerous stories from my clients about vicious smear campaigns where videos they had filmed of their abuser are doctored to produce a fictitious scenario to support the narcissist's agenda. The irony is that my clients were often recording the videos after months or years of gaslighting to prove to themselves they were not crazy. Many were also recording to provide evidence to the narcissist of their abuse — abuse which they would conveniently forget about or deny, especially after a particularly terrifying rage when they were intoxicated or high.

The motivation of the victim becomes twisted by the flying monkeys, who relentlessly go into full damage-control to protect their master, and victims can have their lives ruined by online misinformation which changes a little with each retelling, like a game of telephones. The victim may endure a relentless 'trial by TikTok' and other social media platforms. Their lives may be destroyed by the very footage they recorded themselves.

Like any ruthless leader, the narcissist will also lie about how many troops they have and who their troops are. A classic example of this is when the narcissist says something absolute along the lines of 'Every one of my friends hates you!' After hearing this, your perception of these people changes, you stop engaging with them, and then they really do begin to dislike you because you have seemingly shunned them. Even perceived flying monkeys are extremely useful when it comes to hurting you and making you feel all alone. The narcissist also takes a great deal of joy in turning your own friends and family into flying monkeys and will engage someone they know who is special to you. With the smear campaign, not only does the narcissist turn your loved ones against you, but they ensure your loved ones are now their allies. They know it will be doubly painful for you to have a loved one turn on you and side with your abuser.

FRIEND OR FLYING MONKEY?

There will be individuals in your life who will tell you they won't be choosing sides: they want to have both you and the narcissist in their lives. It's not their fault the pair of you 'broke up', and they make it clear they will still be engaging with your ex.

In their broken state, many victims give credence to their friends' justifications, and they resign themselves to possibly having to see their abuser at some social gatherings. If this situation sounds familiar to you, consider this. You have suffered psychological, emotional and perhaps physical abuse at the hands of the narcissist, and you have spoken to your friends about the abuse on numerous occasions. You have sought support from them consistently throughout the 'troubled' relationship, and they have comforted you and expressed their understanding and sympathy. After you've escaped the toxic relationship, you're invited to a birthday celebration at your friend's house, and you find out your abuser has also been invited and is going to attend. What do you do? You don't want your abuser to come between you and your friends, and you don't want them to dictate your social life. You also don't want your friends to feel like they must choose between you because that wouldn't be fair, right? So, you go. You go, and you have a miserable time because the narcissist has brought their new partner with them, and is playing the room so much that you wish the ground would swallow you whole.

HOW TO DEFINE A 'FRIEND'

A friend is loyal and trustworthy and will defend you against those who hurt or speak ill of you, even when you're not around. A friend will not befriend your enemy. How could someone who has seen you suffer so terribly, has listened to you describe in detail how much this person has hurt you, remain buddies with the perpetrator of your abuse? A friend shouldn't throw their hands up in the air and say, 'I'm Switzerland' and 'I will no longer be able to hear you over the sound of my neutrality'. If you're being asked to accept new contractual conditions in this friendship, which means they will be providing the same friendship benefits to your abuser as they do to you, then I believe you are now in the company of a flying monkey. Re-evaluate the relationship as any information you provide to them may be taken back to your abuser. It is not just that you now can only engage in superficials with these people as any expression of emotion would be like handing the enemy a loaded weapon; you can no longer trust them.

It's true that some of these people may not be completely aware of the extent of the abuse and will fall into the category of 'innocent' flying monkey. However, the result is the same. There is so much loss after narcissistic abuse, and your inability to completely trust these individuals as you once did is part of that loss. If they are friends with the narcissist, the reality is they're being manipulated and you either go no-contact with them, or you adjust your communication with them. No contact with the narcissist means no contact or limited contact with their flying monkeys. It is once again lose–lose for you, but at this time you need to think in the context of healing.

Don't wonder whether you didn't make the extent of your abuse clear enough and think maybe that's why they remain friends with your abuser. Don't think you are being unreasonable or selfish or that you really should just 'suck it up' if you decline invitations to gatherings your abuser will be attending. Resign yourself to the fact that these people, whether they know it or not, will be used as flying monkeys to spy on you and report back to the narcissist.

If you plan on telling them something, you may as well pick up the phone and call the narcissist yourself.

It is always my advice to erase contact with anyone who is a connection to your abuser and who will keep you in the toxic environment you are trying to heal from. Hopefully these individuals will one day see how they're being manipulated by the narcissist, but for now you need to say to yourself, 'Not my circus, not my monkeys', and leave the chaos behind.

The hoover manoeuvre

I would love to say that once you feel confident enough to run the gauntlet of the smear campaign unscathed while sidestepping all flying primates, you'll be in the clear, but I can't. While you are running and sidestepping, you may also have to manage a very confusing 'hoover manoeuvre' by the narcissist to bring you back under their control.

As mentioned earlier, 'hoovering' refers to the narcissist's actions to bring you back, or suck you back into the vortex of the abuse. In Sofie's story in Chapter 5, when Justin had discarded Sofie but continued to abuse her, he then returned to her when she was trying to heal and reactivated her hopes for a reunion. Why didn't he just leave her alone if he despised her so much? The reason the narcissist comes back to 'hoover' you is quite simple. The narcissist comes back to see if you'll accept another round of abuse, to make sure you don't heal and to regain control of you. For the narcissist, it's a huge ego boost to know they have the power to suck you back after they've treated you so badly for so long.

The narcissist likes to save all their exes for a rainy day – when they feel bored or when they need someone with whom to triangulate their new primary source (to remind that source they are replaceable). A bit like having a harem, they like to keep as many exes as possible waiting in the wings because it's an extremely tedious and dangerous exercise to have to find a reliable source on short notice if the current one has broken down.

The narcissist may have discarded you, their old primary source, but that doesn't mean you're allowed to move on with your life. The narcissist put a lot of work into love bombing you and getting you hooked. It was thoroughly exhausting and the upshot of this is that you now owe them for life. When they come back to hoover you, they are staking a claim for something they worked very hard to get, as well as tapping into a reliable source of narcissistic supply. That supply seems potent to the narcissist now you're moving on with your life: you've fuelled up; you're re-energised. You're starting to look all shiny and new again. The narcissist is delighted with all the work you've been doing on yourself because it will be such fun to tear you down again. The most valuable thing for the narcissist, however, is that they don't have to go through the extremely arduous task of love bombing you again because that work, my friends, has already been done. A few mere breadcrumbs of 'niceness' or kindness will suffice this time, and they know you'll be putty in their hands.

Just as the narcissist knows exactly when they can relax and drop the mask after they have love bombed you, so too do they know that the most opportune time to begin a successful hoover manoeuvre is usually when it looks like you are starting to heal, to move on and possibly forget about them. You're out grocery shopping one day and who should you happen to run into but your ex, or that family member you're trying to go no-contact from. The narcissist catches your eye and seems taken aback with surprise that they ran into you, even though they live four suburbs away away and always said they disliked that particular grocery store. Your plan was to leave the ice cream in Aisle 3 and make a run for it before they saw you. Too late. The narcissist bails you up and it's like butter wouldn't melt in their mouth.

The narcissist might say something like 'How have you been? You're looking beautiful today. I was just thinking about you yesterday because I went to that amazing restaurant we used to go to. Oh, by the way, my child misses you. They talk about you all the time. I'm so glad I ran into you – I'd really love to remain friends for my child's sake, and I think we're big enough to leave all that awful stuff in the past and let bygones be bygones. By the way I'm also going to counselling like you suggested which has really helped me a lot!'

They're going to counselling? Let me just reiterate that a narcissist will only ever go to counselling to manipulate the counsellor, because the narcissist thinks they are perfect. Why would they need counselling? So telling you they've taken your advice by attending counselling is nothing but a big old hoover manoeuvre – and most probably a big old lie. To expand on this notion, narcissistic personality disorder is possibly the only disorder in which the person with the disorder is not negatively impacted by it. It's everyone else around the narcissist who finds themselves in therapy, to cope with the trauma resulting from the one person who should be in therapy!

Your head is spinning. The ice cream is melting in the trolley, and before you know it, your mouth, which is not aligned with your brain at that moment, says, 'I don't know, maybe'.

As soon as you possibly can, you hightail it out of there so you can process what just happened. You go home and you perhaps think to yourself, 'No, I am *not* letting you back into my life', and you feel empowered by having the upper hand for once. 'You're doing so well!', you congratulate yourself.

Two days later, however, it's a different story. The toxins have entered your bloodstream again and your dopamine receptors are craving another hit. Consequently, you haven't been able to stop thinking about the narcissist since you saw them at the store and now you just can't resist the urge to unblock them and see if they've called. And they have. Five lovely voice messages stating how much they've missed you that you listen to over and over again. You unblock them on social media and notice that they've already unblocked you. Game, set and match to the narcissist. They know you will be checking out their profile, and they post accordingly to make you miss them. Another successful hoover. They are back in the game. They are back inside your head.

The old 'I just wanna be friends' line is a trusty old chestnut the narcissist uses to keep you under their thumb, to make sure you don't get away from them and betray them by healing from the abuse. You cannot be friends with someone who abuses you, and if you are even considering calling this person a friend then ask yourself why. My guess is that you haven't fully come to terms with the reality that the 'nice' person who love bombed you does not exist, and you accept the breadcrumb of just being 'friends' to keep the 'drug' (the narcissist) in your life.

If the narcissist says to you they want to remain friends, what they are really saying to you is that they want your narcissistic supply with absolutely no strings attached to it. Now that you are just 'friends', they will call on you to talk about their current conquests and ask for your opinion. They know you still have an emotional connection to them (a trauma bond) and they can rely on your pain at hearing about their relationship with the other person. It's win–win for the narcissist as they can keep an eye on you, hurt you by making you listen to the stories about their new life, and call on you for sexual and monetary benefits when they feel like it. They know you'll be hoping that if you stick around and provide that empathetic ear to listen to all their relationship problems with the new source, they might come back to you. Keeping you as a friend provides a never-ending source of negative and positive energy for the narcissist, and you have even less power in this relationship than you did before because you are not officially 'together'. They simply want all the benefits of a primary source, without the commitment.

Just 'happening' to run into you at a place they know you frequent is a common strategy the narcissist uses to hoover you and start you thinking about them again. Remember, they have already done all the hard work by planting those invisible buttons inside your head (conditioning you), and now they just need the right moment and proximity to you so they can push on those buttons and reactivate the addiction. The narcissist may appear a changed person and talk about all the work they have done on themselves, which starts you thinking they really have changed. You start to entertain thoughts such as: 'Maybe they didn't realise what they had until I was gone, and now they realise how much they miss me.'

It's been a while since you were abused by this person. The memory of just how terrible those times were has started to fade, and their voice, and possibly their tears, pull at your heartstrings. You are taken straight back to those love bombing days when you felt so special and loved by this person, and it's only a matter of time before you call them. They are so glad you returned their call;

they invite you out and before you know it, you are spending every second together again. Things go so well for a while, and you are so happy to be back in the arms of your soulmate. Life with your 'soulmate' is wonderful, until it isn't anymore and you find yourself not just back at square one in this abusive relationship, but two squares before that. The abuse becomes worse than ever.

There are numerous other ways the narcissist will try to hoover you back into engaging with them so they can regain their sense of power over you. They have gone on with the business of being a narcissist and they now have a new faithful source of supply, but that source has now lost its shiny newness and they are annoyed that you are not begging them to come back to you.

If you haven't blocked them, you may find yourself getting a call out of the blue acting like nothing has happened because they remembered it was your birthday coming up. This will be very confusing for you. The last time they spoke to you they told you to lose their number and never contact them again, and here they are happily chatting.

Maybe the narcissist will contact you at a time when they know you will be particularly vulnerable, to give you some hope — then smash your dreams to smithereens. This makes for great narcissistic supply as they can relive the satisfaction they received in the initial discard. Justin engaged in this hoovering strategy with Sofie at a time when she was still strongly trauma bonded with him and susceptible to his fake love. He had left her to marinate in her pain for just the right amount of time for a highly successful hoover. He used her, then topped up on the energy of her distress when he once again abandoned her and returned to his new primary source.

Maybe the narcissist will call you because they have all of a sudden developed a conscience and want to return some clothes and other items you left at their house. Or maybe they will remember the favourite pink toothbrush they left at yours – maybe they can pop round Friday night with a bottle of wine and pick it up?

The 'You're the only one who would understand' line is always a handy hoover manoeuvre. They might call you telling you their child or their parent is gravely ill. They pull at those empathy strings of yours, knowing you'd feel terrible if you didn't offer compassion and assistance.

If you have been successful in blocking them, they may even engage one of their flying monkeys to contact you (see Flying monkeys earlier in this chapter). Whether you respond or not, the narcissist can feign complete ignorance of their friend contacting you. The narcissist is hedging their bets with this manoeuvre: if it works and you do respond, they can either say, 'I didn't know they were going to do that but it's great to hear from you', or 'I never asked them to contact you. I had nothing to do with it. You must think I'm desperate if you think I want to see you again!' Either way, they've managed to suck you back so they can control and feed off your emotions.

If one strategy doesn't work, they will try another. Be prepared for the narcissist to go to extreme lengths to regain control of you. One of my clients thought she had the narcissist in her life completely blocked at every level, when they found her on Facebook Marketplace via an item she was selling.

Hoovering is not used only to suck you back into an intimate or friendship relationship with the narcissist. It can just as often be used to re-engage you in arguing with them, so they are able to garner that negative supply from you. Justin would repeatedly hoover Sofie by calling her about trivial issues to do with the children. Things would get relatively quiet for Sofie, and then out of the blue she would get a phone call or message from Justin that would have them arguing back and forth, and Sofie continuing to try and defend and explain herself to the likes of a brick wall. Another particularly damaging hoovering strategy that Justin engaged in with Sofie was to present his new lover, Rachel, to her after the discard, and getting Rachel to pick his children up from Sofie's home. Things were getting a little dull for Justin, and this was a great way to provoke Sofie into a reaction.

JADE-ING

Another acronym we use in narcissistic abuse recovery is JADE: justify, argue, defend and explain. Jading is something that you should never do with a narcissist but it's very easy to walk right into their trap and reward them for baiting you. Never again are they going to be able to hoover you back by saying something or throwing accusations at you that will have you justifying yourself, arguing with them, defending yourself or explaining yourself.

You don't have to explain yourself if you co-parent with a narcissistic ex, you don't have to defend your decisions, and you are never again going to argue with someone who will engage in word salad and deflect from any topic that does not suit their agenda. Resist the bait to JADE with them. You will have less frustration in trying to explain yourself to a brick wall.

WHAT TO DO IF YOU'RE BEING HOOVERED

If the narcissist tries to hoover you, remember why they are trying to get through to you and be proactive rather than reactive. Make it impossible for them to do so by blocking them everywhere. Make sure all of their belongings are gone from your home so they have no excuse to visit or drop in. Retrieve all of your belongings from their home if you can do so safely, or forget about them. If they will not return items that are important to you, do not JADE with the narcissist for their return. Employ a third party to help you such as the police, or perhaps a lawyer. Don't wait for the hoover to happen because when that happens, the narcissist slides back into your life and you must jumpstart your healing process again. Ignore their attempts to pull you back. Deprive them of their narcissistic supply and watch them choke and splutter, just like a broken down old vacuum cleaner that is so clogged up it can't suck anymore.

IF YOU HAVEN'T BEEN HOOVERED

Some clients worry because the narcissist hasn't hoovered them. They've read so much about narcissistic hoovering and they wonder why that is not happening to them. If you are not being hoovered, it's because the narcissist sees that it is too much effort – in other words, you are too confident or strong. They don't think you'll be easily manipulated again because you saw the person behind the mask, and you made it very clear you would not make yourself a target for the narcissist ever again.

If you are concerned that you haven't been hoovered ('is there something wrong with me?'), then ask yourself: do I subconsciously want the narcissist to contact me again? If the answer to this question is yes, then re-evaluate where you're at on your healing journey. If you are not being hoovered, the narcissist has plentiful narcissistic supply elsewhere, and/or you have been deemed too much work to target again with all the healing work you've done. Either way, not being hoovered is a positive thing and one that you should savour.

When the narcissist hoovers you or tries to suck you back into some kind of engagement with them, it is only ever to inflict more emotional damage and to reclaim you as a reliable form of narcissistic supply. The narcissist is incapable of loving because they do not have the traits needed to love another human being, such as empathy, compassion and loyalty. They attach to you like a flea to a dog, and they drop off and move on to a new host when they are full.

The narcissist does not miss you no matter how much they say they do when they attempt to hoover you. They have not changed no matter how much they sound or look as if they have. Any changes are short-term to manipulate you back into the cycle of abuse. You cannot miss something you never loved in the first place. The only thing a narcissist misses about you if they ever think about you at all is what they can get out of you, such as attention, money, sex or maybe your house that they once lived in.

IN SUMMARY

- Whether you leave or are discarded you may face a vicious smear campaign as the narcissist seeks to protect their false self by discrediting you and thus anything you say about them.
- They may enlist their followers or 'flying monkeys' to smear you by proxy.
- Hoovering is a tactic often employed post-discard when the narcissist may attempt to reel you back into the cycle of abuse to top up their narcissistic supply.

CHAPTER SEVEN

Am I the narcissist?

Sofie told me of a time when she screamed uncontrollably at Justin and threw three glass kitchen plates on the ground. She remembers just begging to be understood, but Justin twisted everything she said and told her she was crazy. She remembered her actions during this argument but she couldn't remember how the argument started. It always seemed to be some trivial thing that she didn't think was a big deal, but greatly offended Justin.

Another time, she remembered being shown a video Justin recorded of her during a heated argument. In the footage, she truly looked and sounded out of control, yelling and crying to the point of hyperventilation while Justin remained calm.

In a third example, Sofie related spending two hours banging and screaming at the front door like a lunatic (in her words) to be let in because Justin had locked her out. They'd been out to dinner and had a few drinks. She'd thought they were having a lovely time when suddenly Justin said the night was over and they had to go home. He didn't talk to her all the way, and when they arrived, he proceeded to lock her outside because apparently, she had drunk too much and had offended him. She said she went 'crazy' because she just wanted to get inside the house that belonged to her as well.

Was she a narcissist? she wanted to know, because she couldn't see Justin's point of view in these arguments no matter how much she tried. Was she a narcissist for 'flying off the handle' and not being able to control her temper? For being so selfish and never happy with what he gave her? It was so confusing. She needed to know that she *wasn't* that person who needs the world to revolve around her, but Justin's words rang in her head: 'I'm not the narcissist, you are!'

Of all the men and women I have spoken to who have been abused by a narcissist, I don't think there is a single person who didn't struggle with the notion of whether they were a narcissist themselves. It is a terrifying thought for these people to think that they might be an abuser, and they might be responsible for the constant chaos in this relationship. They examine and re-examine their behaviour and compare it to behaviour they know constitutes narcissism. They reflect on numerous times when they acted terribly and appeared angry and out of control. They remember occasions when they lied and sneaked around so their partner wouldn't find out they had spoken to a friend their partner didn't like, or they accused their partner of cheating without any clear-cut evidence. They desperately didn't want to be that person as they continued to reflect, but all they could see was behaviour that caused them immense shame.

Reactive abuse

Reactive abuse occurs when the victim reacts to the manipulative tactics of the narcissist by retaliating, often in frantic and explosive ways that are out of character. The victim might scream and yell just as Sofie did, they may hurl insults or they may even engage in behaviour to hurt their abuser such as messaging their family and friends to inflict harm on the narcissist's 'impeccable' reputation. Some victims even lash out physically when confronted with ongoing devaluing techniques such as gaslighting and projection in an attempt to gain some control in the situation and make the abuse stop.

When abuse is ongoing, and the victim is pushed to the point that they can no longer take it, their survival instincts kick in and their fight-or-flight response activates. They automatically act to protect themselves, which results in a normal reaction (given the circumstances) to abnormal abuse.

MOTIVATION IS KEY

Abuse is *never* okay, but to understand why a victim might react in such volatile ways, we need to look at the intentions behind the behaviour of both abuser and victim. It may be confusing for some who do not understand the dynamics of narcissistic abuse to comprehend how there is any difference between the abusive actions of the narcissist and the 'abusive' reactions of the victim when the outcome is the same.

Imagine an elderly woman is walking down the aisle of a store carrying a basket of groceries. Suddenly she slips and drops the basket, and fruit and vegies spill out onto the floor. Most people would race to help: making sure she was okay, picking up the items she'd dropped and helping her carry them to the checkout. Most people would do this out of empathy for the woman – their motivation would be altruistic. However, if it was the narcissist who saw what happened, instead of feeling empathy and desire to help someone in need, the narcissist would view the situation as an opportunity for admiration and attention. The narcissist would check first to see if they had an audience for their good deed before helping and later might brag to others about what a good person they were. The results are the same: the woman was helped. However, the *motivation* behind the actions of the narcissist differed. Theirs was selfish and ego-driven, the other a desire to help another human being in need.

When Sofie was locked out of her own home she reacted to Justin's antagonistic and manipulative behaviour in an explosive outburst out of frustration, and in an attempt to regain some control. Justin, the true abuser, was then able to ascribe the role of abuser to Sofie. Once again, Justin had engaged the strategy of DARVO (deny, attack, reverse victim and offender). The roles of victim and offender had been neatly reversed and Sofie felt immense shame in having engaged in the very behaviour she deplored.

SETTING UP A RESPONSE

Sofie's volatile reactions to the abuse were a provoked response to intentional abuse. In these situations the abuser will poke and prod, mostly in ways that are covert and not obvious to others. The abuser's goal is to get the victim to act in exactly the way they do: crazy! Frustrated! Frantic! They want the victim to scream, yell, throw things – and if they're really good at their game, they'll get the victim to hit them, because they know the victim will reflect on their behaviour afterwards and experience shame and confusion. The abuser wants to prevent the true victim exposing them by setting them up to react so they will have 'proof' that the victim is the abuser and the 'crazy' one.

As mentioned, victims experience great shame and regret when they recall some of the behaviour they engaged in while seemingly unable to control their emotions. As they look back, they are humiliated by their out-of-character actions.

When she told me of the incident in which she was locked out of the house, Sofie's version of events was that she was acting irrationally. Justin told her that she was a disgrace and that he would not let her in while she was behaving like that, but she just kept getting angrier while he remained calm and coherent. When she thought about her behaviour the next day (she was finally let in two hours later), she was disgusted with herself. She even defended Justin's actions – she simply couldn't calm down. She knew she had anxiety issues and the difference between Justin's and her behaviour that night was proof to her that her anxiety was causing major problems in the relationship. The next day she begged him to forgive her for her unfathomable outburst. He would not talk to her for a week after this incident, and when he finally did, the relief she felt was palpable.

I listened to the story Sofie related very carefully, and through the lenses of FOG (fear, obligation and guilt) and the blinders of gaslighting, blame-shifting and projection, I was able to see a more realistic version of the events that ensued that night.

Sofie and Justin went out for a night of fun at the local tavern that included dancing and a few glasses of champagne. Sofie was having fun, innocently laughing and chatting with Justin and other patrons on the dance floor when she got up to groove to her favourite song. Sofie could see Justin glaring at her as she danced so she came back to the table to see what was wrong. Justin was standoffish at first, then he grabbed her arm roughly and told her they were leaving. He gave her the silent treatment the whole way home and Sofie started to cry and yell at him to tell her what she'd done. He calmly told her she was a drunk, she'd embarrassed him by flirting with other men and she was out of control. Her behaviour right then and there, in yelling and crying hysterically, was proof. He then played judge, jury and executioner by locking her out of her own house to punish her. Sofie was powerless and distraught, and of course her frantic behaviour escalated because she could not get into the 'safe' environment of her home.

Justin had successfully manipulated the situation so that he was able to punish Sofie for having fun. His pathological envy ignited watching Sofie having a wonderful time enjoying the company of others. He could not feel this genuine happiness and her ability to feel this brought out the eternal shame he harboured inside, as well as rage that he was not the centre of her attention. He proceeded to not only destroy her happiness but provoke her to a point where she would be guaranteed to react in a strongly emotional way. Then he would blame her for it. His calm demeanour compared with her seemingly crazy behaviour not only provided proof that she was the one who ruined the night out but also gave him ammunition to use against her in the future.

Now let's look at the time that Justin recorded Sofie on video while once again she was crying uncontrollably and screaming for him to leave her alone. Prior to Justin recording her, they had been out to dinner. Back at home, as Sofie continued to listen to the music she loved while enjoying a glass of wine, Justin told her that the waitress had been looking at him all night and he talked incessantly about how attractive she was. Sofie finally reacted and yelled at him because the way he was talking was so disrespectful to her. Justin then called her insecure, paranoid and jealous, and the argument escalated as Sofie became increasingly upset. It was at the point when Sofie was at her most volatile that Justin got out his phone and started to record her. On the video, Sofie was hysterical while Justin could be heard talking calmly and quietly, supposedly trying to calm her down. He played the video back the next day for Sofie and she was mortified at her behaviour and once again proceeded to ask for his forgiveness just to stop the silent treatment he was giving her. Once again, she owned the behaviour, and absorbed all responsibility for how her actions were impacting the relationship.

A NARCISSIST WILL NEVER TAKE RESPONSIBILITY

As you know, the narcissist will never take ownership of their toxic behaviour. To take responsibility for their actions is to admit they are flawed and destroy the grandiose image they have of themselves. It would mean they are less than perfect. They will never admit they are wrong — unless of course they need to in order to manipulate, deceive and have their needs met. They wear their fake mask to hide the true self they loathe, which is weak and vulnerable. To admit they have imperfections is to bring that internal shame to the surface, and they call on numerous strategies to ensure that doesn't happen.

Two of their most potent weapons are deflection and blame-shifting. They use these strategies when intentionally setting up a situation to elicit a negative response from their victim. Having no empathy, the narcissist can engage in unconscionable behaviour to purge themselves of this shame, such as deflecting their despicable behaviour onto someone else, and blaming them for the outcome.

This is exactly what the narcissist is doing when they manufacture a situation designed to make you react in such a negative way. With great skill, they monitor their own behaviour to appear as the calm and rational one, while passively attacking their victim, who is unaware they've been set up and responds accordingly. The abuser continues to monitor their own behaviour while ensuring the behaviour of the victim escalates to the desired level at which point the narcissist will paint the victim as the abuser. Game, set, match. Your behaviour is proof that you are the toxic one.

You are *not* the narcissist

When Sofie finally had a label for her ongoing confusion and suffering in her relationship, she wanted to shout it from the mountaintops. At the very least she wanted to tell Justin that she knew what was wrong because now they had a diagnosis. Maybe this could be fixed! So Sofie did what all victims do when they don't know any better, and she told Justin he was a narcissist. Of course, then, Justin did what all narcissists do: he projected all the narcissistic traits she had researched straight back onto her.

According to Justin, *Sofie* was the one with no remorse or empathy. She was the one who was selfish and thought she was better than everyone else, and so on. Sofie had unknowingly shown Justin all her cards, and he took full advantage of the heads-up. He researched the topic of narcissism himself and he made sure that in every possible situation Sofie could think of, *she* was the one who looked like the narcissist. And it worked. Justin had worn out Sofie's ability to trust herself and she was putty in Justin's hands. Justin knew exactly which buttons to press to make Sofie feel shame and guilt because it was he who had set up those hypothetical buttons.

The best reassurance I can give you to alleviate those painful and confusing thoughts is the very fact that you are worried about it. The thought of it fills you with dread: if you are a narcissist, you want to get help to stop the behaviours that are hurting other people. You experience shame, regret and remorse around your behaviour and will endeavour to regain the trust of those you have hurt. This means you have the capacity for introspection. You can reflect on your behaviour and acknowledge your flaws. You have the capacity for empathy and remorse and to lay your vulnerabilities on the line at the risk of being hurt. You can take responsibility, be accountable for your actions and admit you're not perfect.

A narcissist will never engage in self-reflection because that would damage their perfect image of themselves. Narcissists see everyone in very black and white terms, as either 'all good' or 'all bad'. The capacity for introspection would reveal imperfections, so they will never go down that route. They feel no shame and remorse for their actions and will always justify everything on the grounds that the victim deserved what was coming to them. It was their fault!

Do you remember how heartless the narcissist was when you were sick, or when you were sobbing uncontrollably on the floor because of their cruelty, and how they could literally flop themselves down in front of the television and ask you to pass them the TV remote? The narcissist thinks the victim is pitiful for crying. In their eyes, crying is only appropriate when you are trying to manipulate someone, and that is when fake or crocodile tears will be produced. Consequently, you are either extremely weak or you are trying to manipulate them, or both. Either scenario will result in contempt that reflects the narcissist's disregard for the feelings of others.

Your capacity for compassion and kindness is at odds with all that constitutes narcissism. A narcissist will never reflect on what they have done and ask themselves: 'Am I a narcissist?' They will never experience remorse for their actions (unless it is for themselves because they got caught). They will never seek help to address their problems, because that would require self-reflection and acknowledging that they had a problem. Their self-image will remain untarnished as they project and deflect all that is negative onto you.

Just as Sofie did, you will experience (or have already experienced) your own lightbulb moment when you realise that you were the victim of abuse by a toxic narcissist, and that your abuser tried with all their might to project the role of abuser on to you by engaging in DARVO (deny, attack, reverse victim and offender). It will be so tempting to tell them you know who, or more appropriately, *what* they are. Don't. When you have that epiphany it is so important to hold those cards close to your chest. You are just too vulnerable and 'human', and the narcissist too cold and reptilian. They will be entirely convincing as they portray themselves as the victim, and while they gaslight and lie pathologically, their pulse will not change.

Imagine that someone you love very dearly has been the victim of ongoing, insidious psychological and emotional abuse, and perhaps physical and sexual abuse as well. Will a victim act like the charming, charismatic, magnetic individual the narcissist portrays themselves to be, or will they be more likely to appear withdrawn, on edge, hypervigilant, anxious, full of self-doubt, frantic, frustrated, unravelled and mistrusting?

A true victim is unlikely to appear cool, calm, rational and coherent as they talk about the abuse. They are more likely to be emotional; they will stumble over their words and struggle to articulate the nature of the abuse.

The true abuser will be exactly the opposite as they provide an articulate analysis – and personal diagnosis – of their alleged abuser.

The true victim will also focus on the abuse and their struggles to cope. In trying to convince others that they are the victim, the abuser is more likely to talk about the victim and what a terrible person they are.

SURVIVAL MODE

There is a poignant analogy used in narcissistic abuse recovery to describe the behaviour of victims when they are concerned they are starting to behave in the same way as their abuser: 'When you lie down with dogs, you get up with fleas.' We use the term 'narcissistic fleas' to describe these undesirable behaviours. The longer you remain in the relationship with your abuser, the longer you are having those behaviours role-modelled to you, and you will tend to 'take on' some of these behaviours as being 'normal' in the context of this relationship. You may start yelling and swearing in order to be heard, or you may attempt to get back at your abuser by disposing of something they value. These behaviours are out of character and will usually create feelings of immense shame and anxiety for the victim, who will reflect on and experience remorse for their actions.

Victims develop numerous coping mechanisms to be able to survive their trauma and being able to 'fight fire with fire' is one of them. You need to survive, so, just as someone in an old Western movie wouldn't take a peashooter to a gun fight, the victim develops survival strategies that ensure they are not handicapped when placed in a fighting arena with their opponent. By picking up 'fleas', you are arming yourself to ensure the most level playing field possible in a trauma zone designed to destroy you. This does not make you a narcissist. It makes you a victim who is in survival mode.

The narcissist is always reversing the roles of victim and abuser, and it is an enjoyable experience for them when they can manipulate you to retaliate. I have had numerous victims report to me that their abuser would antagonise them and provoke them intentionally to the point where they knew they would 'explode', and then encourage them to hit them. The narcissist might point to their chin for instance and say something like 'Hit me. Come on, you know you want to!'

They might even grab the victim's hand and place it on themselves to entice a physical reaction. The victim may actually lash out physically in response to this manufactured situation, and the abuser will dramatically fall over, or heavily land against a wall, which is completely at odds to the minor physical retaliation. What better proof that the victim is in fact the abuser than bruises and marks on the narcissist's body? The true victim then has 'evidence' they are abusive, and they further absorb the notion that they are in fact the narcissist.

It's even more enjoyable for the narcissist if they can make you retaliate in front of an audience who will then support the narcissist's claim that you are abusive, which further cements your feelings of responsibility. Unlike the narcissist, the victim, deeply ashamed, acknowledges their 'abusive' actions. These sincere emotions are vastly different from the narcissist's 'Look what you made me do' attitude, should the true victim be the one carrying the injuries.

* * *

If you are considering the notion that you are a narcissist, I want you to consider every one of the scenarios I've described. The narcissist in your life wanted you to believe this so they could further manipulate and control you. Like a chess player, they set you up to fall and to take on the blame for the toxic mess that you believe you created.

A narcissist would never let you blame *them* for the abuse. It always must be someone else's fault. They never feel sorry for what they have done to you and will always find – or create – a way to ensure you feel the guilt and shame that should be theirs. They will never reflect on their behaviour as you do and ask themselves: 'Am I a narcissist?'

The fact you have asked yourself this question, and your consideration of all your behaviour that brings you such shame, means the answer to your question is a resounding 'No!'

IN SUMMARY

- Reactive abuse occurs when the victim is manipulated into uncharacteristic retaliation.
- A narcissist will never take responsibility for their behaviour; instead they will deflect and blame-shift.
- If you can ask yourself 'Am I a narcissist?', you are *not* a narcissist.

CHAPTER EIGHT

Divorcing a narcissist

Sofie needed to get help. With Justin's smear campaign ramped up, she was angry: She needed to get help. He was not going to take her children from her.

After Sofie told me this, my next words to her were: 'You are going to get yourself a lawyer, Sofie. A kick-arse lawyer who will have your back and fight for you. This is when you take your power back!'

I wish Sofie had taken my advice immediately. However, her conditioned fear responses were still strong, and she wasn't yet ready to go down that path, because in her mind that truly would mean the end. When Sofie left my office, she didn't call a lawyer. She called a mediator: she thought this would make Justin less angry than a lawyer.

Suffice it to say, it did not go as Sofie would have liked.

After a number of individual appointments with the mediator, the day finally came for Sofie and Justin to have a joint meeting.

In the car park, Justin gave her a smirk that sent her anxiety levels spiralling and ensured she was unnerved before the mediation even started.

During the mediation, Sofie sat opposite Justin with the mediator at the head of the table. Sofie was nervous and felt intimidated by Justin's presence. The mediator talked to them about their wishes regarding arrangements for the children, and Justin was his usual charming self. Sofie knew him too well: he was flirting with the mediator. And as the mediator laughed at his corny one-liners, Sofie realised she was not immune to his charms.

When it was time for Sofie to speak, the emotions she had tried so hard to hide overwhelmed her. With the help of her notes, however, she was eventually able to speak about her wishes and answer the mediator's questions. But it was a pointless exercise, as Justin wanted it all his own way including choice of schools and extra days with the children, claiming he was being generous. When there was no agreement from Sofie, he changed his mind: he wanted fulltime custody, citing Sofie's mental health issues as his main concern. With nothing resolved, the mediation ended and the mediator asked that Sofie and Justin use email to communicate with each other about the children only.

After the appointment, a very emotional Sofie hopped in her car, drove around the corner and turned the engine off. She did not turn that engine back on until, after a lot of research, she'd made her first appointment with a lawyer. She now realised that she couldn't fight this thing on her own, and she prayed the lawyer would have more of an idea about personality disorders than the mediator did. She also called a locksmith to come and change the locks on her home that very afternoon. She had finally had enough. She sighed and thought to herself, 'Let the games begin'.

Why mediation doesn't work

Mediation is a great way for a narcissist to engage you with promises of some closure, just to pull that carpet out from beneath you at the last second.

If you're attending mediation with the narcissist, take your lawyer with you to protect you and provide you with legal and moral support. It's rare that these processes go so smoothly that an agreement is reached straightaway. Mediation is just another way your abuser can string the divorce process out. Narcissists love to prolong your agony and make the court process go on for as long as possible. This is aptly referred to as 'litigation abuse'. They will litigate you to the ends of the earth if they can, to keep themselves inside your head, to punish you, to make you spend all of your money on lawyer's fees, and to wear you out. They want you to give up and let them have what they want so they make sure the process is as costly and stressful for you as possible.

When you've made the decision to divorce

Once you decide to divorce, here are 11 steps to bear in mind.

1. IF YOU HAVE TIME (AND YOU FEEL SAFE), DEVELOP A SAFETY PLAN BEFORE YOU LEAVE

If you are thinking about leaving the narcissist, develop a safety plan before you go.

+ Make a list of what you need to do such as get a lawyer, call a counsellor, call Centrelink, call Child Support, take inventory of your furniture, etc.

- Go to a bank and open an account of your own. Pay in small amounts that your abuser will not miss.
- Locate important documents such as passports and birth certificates. If you cannot take them without the narcissist noticing, then photocopy them.
- Gradually, start gathering anything that has sentimental value to you such as gifts from loved ones, photo albums and special memorabilia.
- Every day, take something over to a loved one's house to store it there.
- If you can access the narcissist's records, take screenshots of everything, including bank accounts, emails and social media.
- Tell the narcissist nothing. Keep your cards very close to your chest. Do not give them the heads-up – they may move money around and put property into another name. If they've already done this, then document it.

This is going to go against your integrity and every moral fibre in your body, but you're protecting yourself against someone who is wired completely differently to you. Someone without empathy or a conscience. As soon as the narcissist realises they have lost you, their goal is to make your life unbearable, and take the things you value the most just to destroy them.

2. GET A LAWYER IMMEDIATELY (YESTERDAY) AND REACH OUT FOR SUPPORT WHEREVER POSSIBLE

Sofie told me that walking into that lawyer's office for her first appointment was terrifying. She was experiencing so many emotions she feared she'd burst into tears the second she opened her mouth to speak. She was angry, she was sad, and she was fearful of all the unknowns. The most terrifying thing for Sofie, however, was that she would make Justin angrier and he would do something to hurt her that was even worse than what he'd done already. However, Sofie reminded herself that she was strong. She had to be to survive trauma that was designed to destroy her. If she could survive that, she could do anything.

I was very happy when Sofie told me she had finally worked up the courage to secure legal advice. But I knew that going up against a narcissist in a system that doesn't understand the nuances of narcissistic abuse would be one of the toughest battles she would face.

It took a long time for Sofie to seek emotional support from me and then secure legal advice to protect her future. And no wonder: the ongoing trauma she had experienced and the clear symptoms of complex post-traumatic stress disorder (CPTSD), depression and anxiety made it impossible for her to think about anything other than surviving day to day.

Justin knew that he'd done a great job in wearing her down, and he wanted to keep her there as long as possible to retain his control over her. He would do everything possible to keep her from finding the strength to access support from those who might loosen the invisible chains his victim was secured with.

Divorcing a narcissist is probably going to be the hardest thing you do in your lifetime (other than living with one). You need to prepare in every way possible because you're going up against an enemy who knows every intimate detail about you and is hell-bent on destroying you. It is so important to get legal advice about what you can do and what you're entitled to.

Even if you're still with the narcissist and thinking about leaving but it all just seems too much to contemplate, find and talk to a lawyer. If you have limited funds because the narcissist has all the resources in their name, there are still steps you can take to secure a lawyer:

+ Ring Legal Aid.
+ Call local shelters and community services for advice about accessing legal services.
+ If your money and assets are inaccessible, research lawyers who will work pro bono.
+ Reach out to your loved ones.

Remember: the narcissist lied when they told you that you'd get nothing if you left them. That's what they wanted you to believe so you would remain in their control and not take 'their' property.

Ideally, within the boundaries of being safe, talk to a lawyer before you leave the home. A lawyer may be able to get an order to have your abuser removed from the home so that you and the children can remain there. Again within the boundaries of being safe, they may advise you to stay there for a time as once you leave, your abuser may be able to change the locks and you won't be able to access your belongings without a great deal of trouble and stress.

3. MAKE SURE YOU SECURE A LAWYER WHO IS EXPERIENCED IN DEALING WITH NARCISSISTS

Sofie found a lawyer she felt extremely comfortable with, who was empathetic and experienced in dealing with narcissists, sociopaths and psychopaths. Sofie was confident in her knowledge of narcissistic abuse, and her capabilities to support, protect, and fight for her.

After lengthy discussions about providing relevant documentation to begin child custody arrangements, they discussed subpoenaing Justin's records and beginning the process of property settlement so that Sofie had fair and sufficient resources to support her children.

Sofie was dubious about getting any information whatsoever from her ex, and as she'd predicted, every time her lawyer requested documents from Justin, she was either ignored or given the run-around, receiving partial or wrong information. At one time Justin decided to get rid of his own lawyer and represent himself, and then months down the track he hired another lawyer. They had to subpoena documents numerous times. He would not be told what to do by anyone. His narcissistic sense of superiority and entitlement meant that he didn't respect anyone in a position of authority.

Numerous clients tell me about terrible experiences with lawyers they felt were not listening to them, and even strongly advising them to co-parent with their abuser.

It is absolutely vital to find a lawyer who understands personality disorders and has empathy for the trauma you've experienced and will continue to experience. Hire a lawyer who is experienced in dealing with narcissists, sociopaths and psychopaths and who can help you to take back your power in all areas, including the mediation process.

4. DOCUMENT ALL INTERACTIONS WITH THE NARCISSIST NO MATTER HOW SMALL

To defend yourself against the narcissist's lies in court you must start documenting all interactions with them as early as possible:

+ Diarise everything, no matter how small or insignificant you think it may be.

- Communicate with the narcissist only via email or parenting app so you have written proof of what they have said. Keep communication minimal and with no emotion. Do not give them any reaction, and do not engage when they try to provoke you. Do not discuss anything to do with the court process and refer all questions to your lawyer.
- Prior to meeting with your lawyer, start writing. Think back over the abuse so you can paint an accurate picture for your lawyer.
- Gather evidence that supports your side of the story: any phone records that prove the narcissist was accessing escort services, for example; screenshots of messages between them and their lover while you were still together; any conversations with the narcissist you recorded; bank statements (if you have any) that may prove their indiscretions. Pull out those malicious voicemails the narcissist left you and the vicious text messages that totally negate that charming exterior they are showing the court.

5. LET YOUR LAWYER DO THE TALKING

One of the most frustrating and upsetting things for Sofie was that Justin kept contacting her outside of the lawyers to try and negotiate with her directly and avoid legal costs. She still did not have the strength to hang up on him and she listened as he tried to wheel and deal an agreement that benefited him. Sofie occasionally came close to agreeing because she just wanted it all to be over. Thankfully, she told her lawyer, who sent out a swift and concise letter telling him to cease contact with her client. She also seconded my advice to Sofie to block Justin on her phone. All contact from then on was to be via email and that email was to be only on her computer, and only pertaining to urgent matters concerning the children.

Never discuss or negotiate terms with the narcissist. That's what your lawyer is for. You need time out from your abuser to heal. You need to be able to get through your day without hearing the voice that triggers your anxiety. You need to be free from their capacity to manipulate you.

6. PREPARING FOR COURT

Sofie knew that Justin was a liar, but even in knowing her own truth, it was very painful to read the lies in his affidavit. He was so charming: would the court believe his lies? In his affidavit he went for the chinks in her armour; every vulnerability she possessed. He attacked the things she valued most because he knew she would fight the hardest to protect them – he attacked her identity as a mother. He wanted a reaction from her! He wanted her to feel his wrath that was cleverly wrapped in the cloak of the law. She was depicted as a violent drunk with mental health issues that would prevent her from parenting their children. Her mental illness meant she didn't take adequate care of herself and he was worried about the safety of his children. He depicted several incidents in which he believed she had failed to care for the children appropriately. The upshot of all his 'evidence' was that the children were at risk of harm in her care.

For court, Justin put on his best suit as well as his best mask to 'perform' in court. The mask he wore reflected a charismatic person who only wanted what was fair, equitable and appropriate given the hardship that his business had endured. Sofie felt the tears welling as she watched and listened to the man she had once loved with all her heart try to annihilate her. All under the guise of wanting what was 'fair' for himself, for Sofie, and for the children, and all implemented with such stealth and conviction. What she wouldn't give for that mask to come off and for everyone to see him for the person he really was.

Know what to expect and be prepared. There is a saying in narcissistic abuse recovery: 'The only thing a narcissist changes is masks and victims, never themselves.'

The family court experience can be daunting for anyone, let alone victims of abuse who may have to face their abuser in court. Victims are a shell of themselves and also worry that their mental health issues, resulting from the abuse they endured, will stand in the way of fair proceedings. This is exactly what every abuser wants. They know they have the capacity to intimidate their victim simply by being in the same room, and if they can catch their victim's gaze? That scores them bonus points. It's all a game for the narcissist, and the family court is just another platform on which to extend the domestic violence.

Before the court date, Sofie was concerned she wasn't going to be able to understand the court proceedings on the day and would look like a fool. I reassured her that her lawyer would protect her, but urged her to share her concerns with her lawyer so she could make sure that legal jargon was minimised. Sofie was also worried about her anxiety: she didn't want to break down on the day.

What I advised Sofie is what I advise all my clients. Breathing exercises, meditation and no caffeine on the day (a stimulant, it can exacerbate anxiety) can all be helpful, but most important of all is preparing mentally. As mentioned, the narcissist uses the family court as another way to further abuse their victim. They know how their victim will be feeling. They know they can cut their victim down with just a glance and a raised eyebrow, and they know what to do to get a reaction from them.

Do not give the narcissist the opportunity to intimidate you outside or inside the court. Prior to mediation, Justin began his intimidation tactics with Sofie in the car park. The smirk he gave her sent her anxiety levels sky-high, which made it difficult for her to concentrate during the mediation. Wear dark sunglasses to and from the court. *Do not look at the narcissist, ever.* If our eyes are the windows to our soul, the narcissist will want to look squarely into yours to activate those conditioned fear responses they enjoy so much.

To deprive the narcissist of an initial 'high' before entering the court, take a support person with you who can help you monitor the narcissist's presence and be another source of strength for you. There is safety and strength in numbers and if you can take your whole family there for support, then do so.

The narcissist puts a great deal of work into getting their victim to act 'crazy' or unpredictably on demand, and they will use their day in court to prove this to others. The narcissist is an actor and a chameleon who will put on the performance of their life before an audience of lawyers, barristers, social workers and more. This is what you must expect. They are going to do what narcissists do best: lie. You must prepare to hear falsehoods about yourself and about the pool of property.

The narcissist will do and say whatever it takes to get what they want. They have no respect for the judicial system, and they think you deserve whatever they dish out to you. Their sense of entitlement and superiority makes them feel righteous about their lies: if telling the truth goes against them, they reason, they are entitled to lie because a system that would deny them what they want is 'useless' and beneath them.

However, it's one thing to make claims and accusations that support your case, but you have to be able to prove them. The narcissist can say you're a serial killer if they want to. They can show pictures of syringes or empty bottles of alcohol you supposedly imbibed. They can say whatever they want to, but *they must support their claims with evidence*. They will have no evidence, and if they do, it will be manufactured and/or irrelevant.

Sofie was worried that she would have to defend herself against Justin's claims about the state of her mental health, as he had told her many times that he'd make sure the court knew all about her 'problems'. She worried that if she broke down, she would prove him right and it would be game over. Narcissists brainwash their victims with great skill to fear them in court with threats such as this. Victims fear a type of self-fulfilling prophecy, whereby their abusers' accusations of instability become a reality. This is why preparation is so important. The narcissist is not a doctor. They are not a psychologist or a psychiatrist and they cannot make a diagnosis. Even if they did possess these qualifications, they STILL would not be permitted to diagnose you because of the conflict of interest. Their lawyer will hopefully have informed them of this, but the narcissist knows they have laid the groundwork to make you fear having your mental health issues exposed and used against you.

Victims fear punishment for the residual effects of the abuse. They sometimes fear attending counselling and support groups or taking any medication to make them feel better in case these records are subpoenaed, and it somehow 'proves' the narcissist's claims. In essence, they fear the paradoxical notion that the results of their abuse such as depression, anxiety, CPTSD and panic disorder will be the very things their abuser uses to win against them.

Again, *prepare, prepare, prepare*. Prepare to hear hideous lies about yourself. Imagine what the abuser might say and give an internal chuckle at the absurdity of their arrogance. Write down the lies you expect to hear so you are not blindsided and shocked when you hear them, and go through them with your lawyer who can then prepare their responses. Practise breathing exercises, and when you hear the lies in court give no reaction whatsoever. It's your reaction the narcissist wants, and you're going to deprive them of their intended supply.

Every victim of narcissistic abuse worries their abuser will fool the court into believing they're the trustworthy, reliable and compassionate soul they pretend to be. And why wouldn't every victim think that? That's been their experience for the entire relationship with the abuse taking place behind closed doors and the rest of the world seeing only the narcissist's charming mask

The victim knows too well the sadistic person behind the mask and knows how easily the narcissist can fool people. But remember: in court there will be boundaries, rules and processes. The narcissist will need to rely heavily on their covert strategies to get you to prove by your reactions that they are right. Wearing their mask, they will exude confidence in their words, mannerisms and posture. They will portray you as the liar, the crazy person and a terrible parent. All these statements will be pure projection – descriptions of the narcissist's own behaviour.

It will be hard not to react when you hear lies about yourself, but remember what the narcissist is trying to do. Remember what they always did when you were together, when they would blame-shift and gaslight you, then punish you for your reactions to the abuse. What happened if you failed to act as you were supposed to, ignored them and didn't take the bait? Ego wounded, they would get agitated and do something even worse to get your attention – even fly into a fit of narcissistic rage – and their true self would be revealed.

In court your lawyer will be asking for evidence of their claims or telling them they have not answered the question properly. The narcissist will be held accountable. There will be firm boundaries around their behaviour and they won't have your narcissistic supply to feed off. With no fuel to sustain them, they will get angry, hopefully giving the court a small taste of the real person you endured for so long.

I've heard of narcissists yelling in court at their ex's lawyer, their own lawyer and even the judge when things weren't going the way they wished. This will only work in your favour and expose the narcissist as a tantrum-throwing toddler who stomps their feet till they get what they want.

7. DO NOT USE NARCISSISTIC TERMINOLOGY IN COURT

One of the hardest and most frustrating things for victims to remember in court is to not call their abuser a narcissist. You know what they are, and you want to make sure everyone else is aware of this too. However, just as the narcissist cannot diagnose you, you cannot appear to be making a diagnosis of them either. The court will not look favourably at individuals who take it upon themselves to diagnose without appropriate qualifications. To circumvent describing your partner directly as a narcissist, I suggest that instead, you describe their behaviours. Here are some examples:

+ To describe them you might say: 'I would get very confused because they never seemed to have any empathy for me when I was sick, or any remorse when they made me cry. They just seemed to feel entitled to whatever they wanted, and they believed that everyone was envious of them.'

+ Instead of 'projection', you might say: 'They would accuse me of doing something, and then I would find out they were doing the very thing they were accusing me of.'

+ Instead of ' gaslighting', you might say: 'They would provoke me then tell me I was oversensitive when I reacted. They would tell me they didn't say something when I know for a fact they did.'

8. NEVER ALLOW YOURSELF TO BE ALONE WITH THE NARCISSIST WHERE THEY CAN MANIPULATE YOU

Never allow yourself to be alone with the narcissist where they can provoke you, or manufacture a situation they can video and use against you.

If you can, install cameras at your home. Even when there has been no physical violence in the past, many narcissists become more aggressive when they start to lose control of you. Victims have had their property damaged in the wake of a divorce from their abusive partner, or they see the same car regularly driving by and slowing down outside their home. Cameras will either act as a deterrent or they will record the offences. Change the locks on your home as soon as possible, to stop your abuser gaining access to your safe place. Don't wait like Sofie did.

Never underestimate the narcissist's desire to punish you for leaving them or being able to live without them.

9. IF YOU ARE BEING THREATENED OR INTIMIDATED BY THE NARCISSIST, SEEK HELP IMMEDIATELY

If you have any fear whatsoever, go to the police, and demand action until the police ensure you are protected by a restraining order at the very least.

Most police do a wonderful job in protecting us and put their lives on the line every day to do so. For that I am so grateful; however, lack of resources and education around domestic violence means often a victim's concerns are minimised, and not enough is done to protect them.

This means victims may not even contact the authorities because they think their concerns will fall on deaf ears, and it will just make their abuser angrier.

Once again, if you fear for your safety, be the squeaky wheel that gets the grease. Insist the police take action on your complaint. Tell the police that *you* want to write the statement – that way, you can express all the emotions the abuse provoked in you rather than have a police officer writing from a template, which may make the abuse seem trivial. If you have your children with you at the police station, ask that someone help you with them so that you have the time to adequately document your abuse. (Many victims who flee their abuser are going to have their children with them. I wish this was something that you could take for granted.)

As a victim you need to 'speak, even if your voice shakes'. Remember that police have a sky-high pile of domestic violence applications on their desk and many of them are not trained in dealing with domestic violence victims. Let the police know that you are in fear for your life and don't let anyone talk you out of your application. You are leaving an abuser. Don't allow yourself to become another statistic because there was no physical abuse in the relationship and you don't think it will come to that. Past physical violence is not the only pathway to murder. Worldwide, thousands of victims are murdered every year by their intimate partner despite no evidence of previous physical abuse, but rather ongoing coercive control, stalking and verbal/emotional abuse.

10. PREDICT THE NARCISSIST'S BEHAVIOUR AND WORK OUT STRATEGIES TO AVOID THEM, OR RISK-MANAGE IT

Once you actually leave the narcissist, making your life unbearable becomes their next mission. Predict their routine, and avoid them. It may help you to view this stage as 'anti stalking', where you work out where they're likely to be so you can steer clear of those places. Find a new grocery store, join a new gym. They may not be as convenient, but your capacity to relax while you are there will be worth it. Pick ups and drop offs with the children are another example of a situation you can avoid by allowing third parties to do the handovers, or engaging the services of supervision clinics.

11. PREPARE MENTALLY AND PHYSICALLY FOR BATTLE

Your self-care at this time is everything. You need to be mentally and physically strong to get through this process so make sure that you are looking after yourself in every way you can. Regular exercise, even if it's just a daily brisk walk, a healthy diet and attention to your spirit with perhaps meditation or yoga will all help you to feel stronger and better equipped to face the challenges ahead. Find a counsellor who specialises in narcissistic abuse recovery and process what is happening to you in a safe environment.

Shield the children as much as you can from the court process. This may be hard at times, for example when family reports need to be carried out so that courts can decide where children should live.

Don't engage with your abuser, no matter how reasonable they may sound at the time. They will always be manipulating you. Keep all communication concise, unemotional and to a bare minimum.

Above all, never underestimate the narcissist's desire and ability to stoop to unthinkable levels to punish or damage you. Divorcing a narcissist is like going into battle. They will take precise aim at your credibility, your emotions and your capacity to ever be independent of them and happy. But now that you know who and what they are, you can level the playing field and prepare. As the old saying goes: 'Know thy enemy and know yourself; in a hundred battles, you will never be defeated.'

IN SUMMARY

- Develop a safety plan before you leave the narcissist.
- Document everything.
- Prepare thoroughly for court: mentally and physically as well as with your paperwork.
- Mediation (often a compulsory prelude to court proceedings) will not work.

CHAPTER NINE

Co-parenting with a narcissist

Co-parenting with a narcissist is impossible. Sofie gradually realised this once she found herself in the unfamiliar territory of being a single parent of three children, all of whom had their own needs and deserved to feel the love of both their mother and father. Sofie wanted this so badly for her children that she regularly subjected herself to Justin's passive and overt aggression just to ensure some kind of stability in their lives. She reasoned that her needs should come last, and the ongoing anxiety she felt every time she had contact with Justin was the price she paid for choosing this man to be the father of her children. She needed to make it work for their sake. What she didn't know at the time was that she was embarking on an impossible mission in which her efforts would be thwarted by a parent whose only goal was to use her attempts at co-parenting to extend the abuse. The children were just collateral damage. Sofie would soon learn that she needed to develop other strategies to parent her children, knowing that she could never rely on Justin to place their needs first.

As Sofie discovered, you *cannot* co-parent with a narcissist. This is one of the most common things I get asked by loving parents who have children with a toxic ex-partner. There is nothing you can do to change the fact that this person is your child's parent so you need to put in place a system that allows the two of you to effectively communicate to ensure your children's needs continue to be met.

Why do your knees shake though, at the thought of having to discuss the care arrangements, medical needs, clothes, haircuts, schools and all the other hundreds of foreseeable and unforeseeable needs of your children with your abuser for years to come? They shake because this person is your abuser: the thought of having to co-parent with your abuser creates fear grounded in the reality of historical abuse. You *know* that teamwork with the narcissist is impossible. You *know* that the narcissist sees you as enemy number one and regards the children as an unlimited source of ammunition to maim you with. You *know* that this person's only interest in their children is self-serving and that they will make your life hell while they control what you love most in the world.

Co-parenting requires the ability to cooperate, coordinate and collaborate under the umbrella of a united front – in other words, teamwork. It entails two people coming together and having reasonable discussions to ensure the children's needs are prioritised and the transition from one household to two causes minimal disruption to their lives.

When you were with the narcissist, do you remember ever having healthy conversations resulting in best outcomes in which you felt heard and understood? Of course not. If you do, you now know you were being manipulated. Now that you've escaped (or you've been discarded) communication isn't going to magically improve. You've committed the sin of being able to survive without the narcissist, and meaningful chats with them over coffee are just not on the cards.

Co-parenting can be difficult and requires work when there are two non-disordered parents trying to establish a new life for themselves and their children. But when one of those parents is a narcissist, all bets are off.

The narcissistic parent will use any attempt to co-parent with them as an opportunity to secure narcissistic supply from you by gaslighting you, sabotaging your plans, making you beg to get what you need for the children or just not responding to you when you try to communicate. They will in essence counter-parent everything you try to do for them. They will see any attempt to discuss the children's needs as being something that will benefit *you*. They will delight in the fact that you want something from them and will do everything in their power to make sure that you're disappointed. If you're trying to plan a holiday, they will say that it doesn't suit their schedule. If you're trying to enrol the children in school, they will say that your choice is not good enough, too expensive or not close enough to their work. If you have a special event that requires the children's presence on a night they are with the other parent, they will deny you access because it interferes with their allocated time, even if the children will just be sitting at their place playing their video games.

'That is *my* day with them!' they will insist, telling you to change the children's weekly softball game to fortnightly (as if that would be possible). The narcissist views their children as their property and you are a thief trying to steal what belongs to them.

To explain just how futile and counterproductive it is to try and co-parent with the narcissist, here's an example that may sound familiar.

Little Johnny needs braces. Taking a deep breath, you call the narcissist and explain what the dentist has said to you: Johnny's teeth are crooked and braces will ensure they straighten, improving his confidence as he gets older.

Do you think the narcissist will be grateful that you are attending to the child's needs and say: 'Of course! Thank you for bringing this to my attention. Which account would you like me to put the money into?' Or is it more likely the narcissist will say something like: 'I've looked at his teeth and I think his teeth are fine. If you want him to get braces, then *you* pay for it. I'm not paying for something he doesn't need. Don't bother me again with your idiotic requests.'

Even if you did get them to agree, they would make it so difficult to make consistent payments that you end up paying the bill yourself. Whether it's braces or something else, when you ask the narcissist to join forces with you to help the children, all they hear is that you want a favour from them. When you tell them what you want, it doesn't matter how nicely you ask, they're either not going to do it, or they're going to do the complete opposite. They want your life to be a shambles. They want to put as many roadblocks in your way as possible, and they want you to continue to beg for what you need. In other words, asking for what you want gives them a weapon to use against you because you have told them what's important to you.

Finding solutions

Now we've established that it's impossible to co-parent with your narcissistic ex, you may be thinking: 'Well, what the hell do I do?'

PARALLEL PARENTING

The concept of parallel parenting provides a more realistic way of parenting together when one parent is a narcissist.

In a nutshell, implementing parallel parenting means that you do what you do on your time with the children, and the narcissistic parent does what they do when they have the children.

Parallel parenting enables the non-abusive parent and the children to live with minimal stress in their lives by implementing firm boundaries. These boundaries limit the narcissist's ability to disrupt the other parent's routine with the children, providing a happier, healthier environment for the children to thrive in. Sofie was lucky enough to find a lawyer who was experienced in dealing with narcissists and encouraged her to parallel parent right from the start.

Parallel parenting can be difficult for loving parents to come to terms with initially. It means not knowing what goes on in the other home, the other home where your children reside with your abuser. You are certain they will be gaslighted, the rules will clash with the rules in your own home, and there will be no thought for the children's emotional welfare as they are introduced to new partners immediately. Not knowing is going to destroy you if you let it, because short of overt child abuse (God forbid) that can be reported to the police and/or child protection, you are never going to be able to control what goes on in that home. This is where I urge you to put all that energy you are putting into something you cannot control, into what you *can* control. Put that energy into making your home a happy and emotionally safe environment that provides a stark contrast to the chaotic environment of the narcissistic parent. The children do not want a perfect parent; rather, they crave a happy parent. You cannot be that happy parent if you are constantly anxious and stressed about what is happening in the other home. You need to work with what you've got.

Parallel parenting doesn't mean that everything is always going to go smoothly. It's not foolproof, but it will provide you with space from your abuser so that the children have at least one home where they do not have to walk on eggshells all the time.

Parallel parenting also means recognising the narcissist's attempts to step over those very firm boundaries any chance they get. They will try anything. Sofie told me about numerous times the children came home from Justin's completely overtired. The children would tell Sofie that Dad had taken them out the night before they were due to come home. The children would be tired, cranky and argumentative with Sofie because of their lack of sleep. At Justin's house, the children's bedtime was 10 pm, an hour and a half later than the 8.30 pm bedtime at Sofie's house. Sofie was aware that Justin did not even enforce his own rule, and the children played on their phones and video games until they fell asleep. This lack of appropriate rules and boundaries at Justin's house was exasperating for Sofie, but she knew that talking to Justin about the issue would get her nowhere. She could only control what happened in her own home and that's what she needed to focus on.

Not being able to do what they want when they want with their 'property' is going to outrage the narcissistic parent. While you will eventually come to terms with the fact you cannot control what goes on in their home, they never will. If they can't openly control what goes on in your home, they will do their absolute best to have as much negative impact on your home life and relationship with your children as possible.

With no concern for the emotional welfare of their children, the narcissist wants to destroy any happiness and stability in your home. Remember the pathological envy they feel at your ability to be naturally happy, and their need to ruin that happiness so they feel better about themselves. They will not allow you to be 'better' than them by having a loving, healthy relationship with your children. In their quest to destroy your happiness, the narcissist will use their own children as pawns. It matters not that the children are miserable, only that your home is unhappy, and you do not have meaningful time with your children.

PARENTING ORDERS AND PARENTING PLANS

To make parallel parenting as practicable and low-stress as possible, any arrangements should be set in place with detailed parenting orders – a set of orders made by a court about parenting arrangements for the children.

Alternatively, a parenting plan is a written agreement worked out and decided jointly that sets out the arrangements for the children without going to court. (However, always seek legal advice before agreeing to a parenting plan.) This plan is not legally binding, unlike a parenting order.

When you apply for a parenting order make sure you cover every contingency: you will save yourself a lot of heartache, not to mention the expense of having to go back to court to have orders adjusted.

Do not assume that just because the narcissist is being 'nice' at the time of having orders or a parenting plan written up, any suggestions they have will be in the children's, or your, best interests. You are dealing with a pathological liar and someone who wants to punish you because you have control over their 'property'. *You* are your children's only appropriate parent and you need consistency, stability and predictability to provide them with a nurturing environment in the years to come. So consider every decision that may be needed until your children are adults, no matter how tiny, and account for it.

MINIMISE CONTACT WITH THE ABUSER: GOING 'GREY ROCK'

In order to punish you, it is simply not enough to destroy your relationship with the children and the peace in your home. The narcissist must also go after your sanity, that which you have managed to resurrect in the time of establishing boundaries with your abuser.

To limit your contact with the narcissist, I suggest implementing a concept called 'grey rock'. Just like a rock that sits there doing nothing at all, you are going to appear so boring to the narcissist through your lack of engagement that they will need to seek their narcissistic supply elsewhere. Emotion equates to energy or fuel to the narcissist. By going grey rock, you deprive them of that energy, and they will soon learn they can no longer rely on you to have their needs met.

A tried and trusted measure by the narcissist to extend your mental anguish is the 'imperative' 24/7 capacity to contact you about the children. If you were dealing with a non-disordered ex, this would be taken for granted to ensure transparency and a free flow of information between the parents. However, a toxic parent wants that continued access to you not for the children's sake, but so they can ruin your day at the drop of a hat. Think about that last time your ex called you at work to abuse you for not packing enough underwear for the children when they went for their scheduled week. How did you feel? Were you able to function to the best of your ability for the rest of your day at work, or did your efficiency flounder, or maybe you even had to leave work and go home?

Consequently, my advice is always to block the narcissist on your phone and all other devices except for an appropriate parenting app or email address.

Contrary to what the narcissist and naive people might tell you, you don't have to allow your abuser 24/7 access to you simply because you have children with them. This person harmed you. You are trying to heal from the devastating effects of psychological and emotional abuse inflicted on you by this person.

Your phone should be your safe place that connects you to the world and to people you love. It should not be a device that you associate with your trauma. It is so freeing for victims when they take that little bit of power back to choose when they take on the manipulative contact of the narcissist.

Parenting apps such as Our Family Wizard, 2Houses, or WeParent, or email, allows you to communicate with the toxic parent while all conversations are documented. The narcissist is less likely to abuse you as they know the messages can potentially be read in court and used against them. By using these methods, you don't have to hear your abuser's voice, and you can get through your day in peace knowing they have no way to disrupt you and cause you anxiety.

Create a new email address or download a parenting app and install them on your computer only. Make a time once each day when you check for messages, but not before bedtime, so messages don't interfere with your sleep.

To enable parallel parenting to be effective as possible, you are going to have to work around the narcissist's attempts to get you to react even when their contact is reduced to email.

Only respond to the narcissist's emails when it is absolutely necessary. Treat all correspondence as if you are writing an affidavit which is factual and devoid of emotion. If you can find a valid question regarding the children somewhere within a five-page written assault on your character, respond *only* to that question. If you can get away with one word such as 'Yes' or 'No', then that is all you give them.

Your minimal responses are going to drive them crazy and hopefully they will give you some wonderful evidence to reflect their character. That is a bonus, but not the goal. The goal is to get them to leave you alone; to let you to live your life in as much peace as possible.

If the narcissist counters the phone ban with 'What if there's an emergency?', simply provide a phone number for a loved one who's agreed to be the emergency contact and who will in turn contact you in such an event.

Problem solved. You can get through your day, your week and your life without that nagging thought in the back of your mind that your abuser might ruin it for you, and you have a reliable way to communicate with the narcissist and monitor that communication. If it's only the children the narcissist wants to talk about, why should it bother them?

You've just learned how to take away the narcissist's daily top-up of their energy sources by removing their ability to contact you via phone. This limits your abuser's capacity to get inside your head and trigger painful conditioned responses. However, what good is removing phone contact for this purpose when you have to see the narcissist regularly at pick-ups and drop-offs? The narcissist loves these occasions because it provides an opportunity to intimidate you face to face. Justin thrived on the times when he could provoke Sofie into a reaction by pressing on those imaginary buttons he'd planted inside her head, and it worked every time. Whether he was being horrible or being nice as pie, Sofie had to look into the eyes of her abuser, and the physical and emotional response she had to this was debilitating.

Just as Justin did with Sofie, the narcissist who never misses an opportunity to make you squirm will use these times to extract maximum supply from you. They may insist on coming to your door, even though the children are old enough to walk out to the car themselves. They may incite an argument with you in earshot of the children, but will do this insidiously, without raising their voice, so when you react you appear hostile and unprovoked. A favourite tactic of the narcissist is to bring their new partner with them to inflict maximum pain and feelings of anger and jealousy in you. They may even send the new partner by themselves to pick up the children, hoping a dramatic scene will ensue, or at the very least, a perfect chance to triangulate. The narcissist knows that it will be agonising for you to see your children in the arms of the new target. They want you to hurt.

Even if you've chosen a neutral place to meet for the exchange, the narcissist won't let you get away untarnished. You may sit in your car with the windows up to avoid confrontation and the narcissist will walk up and lean on your car, motioning that they'd like to talk to you. They may appear the opposite of aggressive, merely wanting to exchange pleasantries. You know, however, that their desire to interact with you is all about intimidation. It's all about invading your space, and making you writhe under their predatory gaze.

Some suggestions to avoid seeing your abuser at these times include using a third party such as your mother or best friend as a go-between for the changeovers. Ask the narcissist to pick the children up from (or drop them off to) a person you trust, someone the narcissist is least likely to attempt to intimidate. Schools and day-care centres are also great places to utilise, so you don't have to have contact with the narcissist and the children are not subjected to a horrific atmosphere when the narcissist provokes you. If it's the school holidays, you may also want to take advantage of supervision clinics where the children can wait to meet their other parent. You can search for these clinics on the internet, but talk to your lawyer or perhaps your local community centre who will be able to recommend some reputable places to you.

These arrangements aren't ideal, but if you're apprehensive about setting up such arrangements, think about this: if your abuser had broken every bone in your body, if they regularly gave you black eyes and a busted, bloody nose, would you contemplate talking to them on the phone, or seeing them at handovers? No. You have been emotionally and psychologically abused by this person, and it makes perfect sense to remove any opportunity for them to hurt you again.

MAINTAIN SEPARATE HOUSEHOLDS

Once you've established a system in which you have as little contact as possible with the narcissist, you also need to be mindful to keep your households very separate. I have spoken to clients who shared clothes, toys, sporting shoes and accessories – even pets! The non-disordered parent always has the best intentions for their children in that they want to make the transition from household to household as easy as possible with their children's emotional stability in mind.

This is a wonderful concept, and in a normal parenting relationship should be encouraged. However, the narcissist views arrangements like this as a means to control you, not as a way of making their children happy.

The narcissist will attempt to get a reaction from you by keeping clothing you have bought, especially the expensive items. Every time you get your children back, they will be missing something, and one day you will find you have practically no clothes left for them at all. The children may leave their tennis rackets behind or their favourite toys, and you will be forced to beg the narcissist for their return. By sharing items with the narcissist, you are putting yourself in harm's way because it is only a matter of time before the narcissist 'forgets' or refuses to return these items. These items provide a connection to you and the narcissist will use this connection to create drama and conflict.

Whenever possible, keep *everything* separate. It will mean doubling up on expensive items occasionally, but the protection of your sanity will be worth it. Strategies include having older sets of clothes the children can wear to and from the other parent's house which are not going to break the bank to replace. The children may not be happy about this arrangement to begin with but they'll get used to it. Remember, you have to parent these children, and disengaging from the narcissist in every way possible is going to benefit them in the long run.

MANAGING THE NARCISSIST'S PHONE CONTACT WITH CHILDREN

As mentioned earlier, when you cut off phone contact from the narcissist you will be giving yourself space to breathe and heal without continued pressure from the narcissist to remain in a trauma zone they control. The narcissist will see this as war because you are also cutting them off from 24/7 access to their property, the children. They may call to speak to the children at the most inopportune times. They will call when they know you're out for dinner or at a special event because the children have told them excitedly about your plans. They will call around dinnertime, homework time or bath time. They will call regularly when you're away on holidays. Any time that will provide the most disruption to your life is the time they will call.

Phone access to the children is a way of infiltrating your home so you can never enjoy the quality time you and your children are entitled to. The narcissist wants the children to be thinking about them. The disruption they seek is not always just as simple as calling numerous times a day to annoy you. Much of the time it's about covertly shifting the children's mindset so that you are left with an unhappy or angry child who was quite content prior to the phone call. The narcissist loves to make the child sad by producing crocodile tears during the phone call, voicing their sadness at missing them, and saying things like 'I wish you didn't have to go there and leave me'. The child inevitably feels guilty and becomes sad themselves. You are left to comfort a distressed and perhaps resentful child, and your quality time is ruined.

Phone contact between the narcissist and your children is something you are going to have to think about and risk-manage, especially if you are still in the process of family court proceedings. You deserve to have quality time with your children that is not negatively impacted by the narcissist's attempts to implement chaos.

My suggestion to ensure the narcissist has regular contact with young children is to get yourself a landline. Provide the narcissistic parent with a time they can call that suits you and will not interfere with your household's routine. Perhaps you might decide that 7.30 pm each night might be a good time, when the children have completed their chores and have been bathed and fed. Or perhaps a morning time before school is more appropriate, enabling them to 'recover' from any manipulations the narcissist engages in. Whatever time you decide, it must suit you. This is *your* time with the children, and you are trying to provide them with consistency, stability and predictability in their lives. You do not contact the narcissist and intentionally try to destroy their time with the children, and you are only making sure the courtesy is reciprocated.

By having a landline, you know the only time that phone rings it is going to be a scheduled call from the narcissist, and you can plan your life accordingly. If you choose to, you can also monitor the phone call on loudspeaker for very young children (but bear in mind this may be very triggering for you, and you may want to get someone else to supervise the phone call if you can).

In this day and age, many parents want to ensure their older children's safety by providing them with a mobile phone. The narcissist will ensure even very young children have this device as a way of circumventing their inability to get at you directly. A phone will be handed to each child under the guise of caring. In reality, the narcissist has simply handed their children a tracking device, through which they will monitor their movements at your home, and call whenever they feel like it.

Have you noticed the look on your older child's face when the narcissistic parent calls, and how they need to go to their room out of earshot from you? This might be quite normal behaviour for teenagers especially, but in this situation, the child has been conditioned to keep secrets from you. Even if there is no great secret to maintain, the narcissist wants you to worry about the conversation taking place.

Putting boundaries around phone contact with older children who have their own phone is going to be challenging, and the narcissist will play this card for all that it's worth. If you try to restrict your child's phone usage, the narcissist will denigrate you to the child, saying that you are trying to alienate them from speaking with their other parent. There is no clear-cut answer here, other than to provide as little reaction as possible, so the narcissist is deprived of hearing how their phone calls caused major disruption in your home, and in your relationship with your child.

Talk to children who have their own phones at an age-appropriate level so they can understand your boundaries, and how they come from a place of love, not punishment. Above all, remember that putting these boundaries in place is about self-care, and minimising the narcissist's ability to harm you, which in turn harms the children.

MANAGING THE NARCISSIST'S MANIPULATION OF YOUR CHILDREN

When it comes to punishing you, the narcissist will use any means at their disposal, and this includes using their own child as a spy. The narcissist will instruct their child to listen and gather information they are seeking. They will be asked to provide the narcissistic parent with updates about purchases the other parent has made, whose home they've visited, and potential new partners. They will even instruct their child to take photos or videos inside the home to be used as evidence against the non-disordered parent, or ask them to steal something and bring it back to the narcissist. Of course, the child will be brainwashed by the narcissist into believing the acts they are engaging in are justified, as the narcissistic parent has convinced them of how unfairly they've been treated.

The act of using one's children to get to the other parent is clearly despicable but to the narcissist it's the equivalent of asking an employee to make them coffee. It matters not that they are modelling to their children that it is okay to steal and lie if it gets you what you want. Or that they are modelling ego-driven behaviour that reflects a massive sense of entitlement. Or even that they are modelling a system where you just take whatever you want and use other people to do your dirty work when necessary. It only matters that the narcissist wants something, and their child is a means to an end.

It is a terrible thing to feel you can't relax in your own home, and that innocent actions and conversations may be relayed to the other parent by your child. If this is happening in your home, your first thought might be to talk to your child about respecting your privacy and not telling the other parent about what goes on in your home. The problem here is that it places a lot of burden on the children's shoulders, who may innocently blurt out what they have been doing at your place. It is also exactly what the narcissist will be doing. The narcissistic parent will confuse the child by saying they are not allowed to keep secrets from them, yet tell them they will be punished if they dare discuss what goes on in the narcissist's home. Unless of course the narcissist wants certain information to get back to the non-disordered parent – which confuses the children even more.

Sofie remembered her youngest child telling her that Dad had forbidden him to talk about what they did with Rachel. Then one day he came home and said that Dad had told him it was okay to tell Mum that Rachel had left. This was right before Justin manipulated Sofie back into a short-lived relationship with him. How convenient.

Assume that anything you do in front of your children will get back to the narcissist, so be mindful of your behaviour while they're with you and give them nothing of importance to take back. Watch what you say, what you leave lying around and who you talk to in front of them. If you're not prepared to see your life on the front page of the *Daily Mail*, then don't do it in front of the children. It's not your fault and it's not their fault. It's a situation out of your control, designed by the narcissist to keep an eye on you. Put your energy into what you can control and give the narcissist nothing to feed off.

The child most likely to be asked to infiltrate the privacy of your home will be the golden child. The narcissist has assigned the role of golden child to the child who will shine the most positive light on the narcissist's persona. Much of the time, this will be the child who is most similar to them, an extension of themselves – or it may be the most talented child, who'll be the source of ongoing admiration and accolades to the narcissist from outsiders.

The scapegoat child, on the other hand, can never please the narcissist.

The golden child will be groomed and conditioned to need the praise they receive from the narcissistic parent, and they will likely do whatever is asked of them by that parent to avoid a fall from grace. They will have been conditioned to believe that the victim has somehow wronged the narcissistic parent, and they will be used as the narcissist's missile to obliterate harmony in your home as the narcissist pits the children against each other – and you.

As we saw in Chapter 3, in Sofie's family, the eldest child, Taylor, was Justin's favourite and she could do no wrong in his eyes. With younger daughter Katie it was the opposite: she could never please her father. The roles Justin had assigned to them, with Katie being the 'scapegoat' child, set up a turbulent, competitive relationship between her and her 'golden child' sister.

The narcissist knows what this rivalry will do to the harmony of your home. They don't want you to play happy families, they want you always on high alert and 'putting out fires'. Through the dynamic of triangulation, they have set up the equivalent of a UFC grudge match. You will need to develop your own rules and strategies to referee the ongoing bouts while the narcissist cheers on the clashes remotely.

For more about golden child versus scapegoat child rivalry, see Chapter 10: The children of narcissists.

* * *

As noted earlier, parallel parenting is not perfect, but it is better than having to negotiate with the narcissist. You will have to risk-manage many different situations and develop your own strategies to look after your family and home. It will take time, but when you come to a sense of peace in knowing that you cannot control the children's other home in any way, and that their homes need to be as separate as possible, you can work on making your own home as happy, nurturing and high functioning as possible. You will never be able to co-parent with this person. You are coming from two completely different frames of reference. You want what's best for the kids; the narcissist wants what's best for the narcissist. You will never be able to attend such things as parent–teacher interviews together as the narcissist will just use these occasions to intimidate you and create conflict. If you must see them at certain functions for the children, take a support person with you, and do not feel compelled to stand next to your abuser for appearance's sake.

Make an investment in counselling for the children as early as possible. Remember to have this put into orders at the start as the narcissist will hate the children airing their 'dirty laundry' to a non-follower, who may expose the narcissist for who they are.

No matter what the narcissist does, never talk to the children in a derogatory way about their other parent, and of course, never argue with that parent in front of them. Children don't stop loving their abusive parent when they are subjected to this conflict, they stop loving themselves. Children have an innate ability to make everything their fault, and if they had just been better, less naughty, if they didn't regularly spill their cornflakes on the table, then Mummy and Daddy wouldn't be fighting.

Invest in your self-care. You are captain of this ship and if you are emotionally and physically sick, the rest of the crew will suffer.

Above all, you need to provide a stark contrast between your own home and the narcissist's home in every way. No matter what they tell you, children thrive on rules and boundaries that are enforced with consequences for inappropriate behaviour, and they get lost when there is no order in their lives. You are the only parent they have who will provide them with unconditional love and support. Model the behaviour and attitudes you wish to see in them, such as kindness, empathy, and respect for others. Provide them with the opposite of what they have in the narcissist's house, and ensure they never have to walk on eggshells wondering what is expected of them or what sort of mood you'll be in. Provide them with a safe place when they return from the narcissist, where love and respect are taken for granted, and abuse and love do not go hand in hand.

What if my ex won't parent?

Not all narcissists want to have their children. For narcissists trying to love bomb a new target, the children may be a nuisance they don't want to be bothered with. Loving parents often tell me they put a great deal of energy into trying to make the narcissist have contact with the children and bending over backwards to accommodate the narcissist's demands. This is not your job. It is not in the children's best interests to force contact with a parent who cannot be bothered putting in any effort to see them, and will only do so if you drive 100 kilometres, place the children on their doorstep, then drive back two days later to retrieve them. Just because a parent is with the children, it doesn't follow that the children are benefitting emotionally. Making the contact happen for a parent who doesn't care may be doing the children more harm than good.

When you stop bringing the children to the narcissist's doorstep, or stop allowing the narcissist into your home to see their children (please, never allow them into your home – this is your safe space) expect them to react. When you stop doing everything for them, that's when they will stake a claim on their property. Let them get a lawyer. Again, make sure all care arrangements are documented in orders or a parenting plan. It's amazing how many narcissistic parents lose interest when they have to get a lawyer.

If you're trying to force contact between the children and the narcissist, think about your motivation. When I ask my clients to dig deep and reflect on why they are doing this, the answer is usually because in doing this they get to see the narcissist. They are still connected to their abuser by that very powerful trauma bond, and the children provide an excuse to see the narcissist and maybe remind them of what they are missing.

IN SUMMARY

- 'Parallel parenting' is the preferred option when your ex partner is a narcissist.
- Get everything in writing as a parenting order or plan.
- Go 'grey rock' (no contact).

CHAPTER TEN

The children of narcissists

It's one thing to meet your abuser later in life and be sucked slowly but surely into a relationship that will destroy your self-worth. But imagine if you had never known any different. Imagine if your abuser had been there your entire life and had shaped your perceptions of how you should be treated and the value of your feelings. Imagine if your abuser had taught you what to expect from, and search for, in every other relationship in your life. Imagine if your abuser was your mother or father.

The narcissist is *always* a narcissist. This is who they are, and their needs do not change just because you are connected to them as their child. Narcissists view their children in the same way they view everyone else: as a source of narcissistic supply.

As a child of a narcissist, you are born with the job of feeding narcissistic supply back to your parent that they are special and to be revered. The job description includes spending the rest of your life repaying the debt to your parent for being born, but it doesn't include any scope for being an individual, being independent or having needs of your own. No-one else will understand your problem with the job description because to every one else it will look as if you have a great boss. The job will require you to be at the boss's beck and call and available at a second's notice. In the position you will be micromanaged and subjected to ongoing criticism 'for your own good'. If you ever try to leave this position your employer will call on others to make you feel bad for failing in your duty to care for the one who was responsible for bringing you into this world.

This job takes priority over everything else in your life and penalties will apply should you dare to be selfish enough to have needs of your own. This job will consume you, and no matter how hard you try you will never please your employer. This job will destroy you, but you will keep hanging in there because it is your duty. You can never quit no matter what the conditions. This job is your life.

Why narcissists have children

The narcissist's desire to have children is never born out of love; it's the result of self-absorbed intentions, and the child of the narcissist will be shaped and influenced for impression-management to the outside world. The narcissist's world revolves around their image so the child will be used to create the impression of a great family person. A narcissist receives never-ending narcissistic supply not just from the child but from the community as well. The role of parent provides the narcissist with another platform for attention as they interact with the community under the guise of a caring and generous parent. It also serves to 'trap' the other parent into a lifetime of abuse thanks to a permanent connection that will constantly be used to extract supply.

Growing up as the child of a narcissist

The process of ensuring the child victim never abandons their narcissistic parent will start the minute they are born and continue forever, unless the adult child can escape the cycle of abuse. Whether the narcissist responds to the adulation or not, they love it when their children are young and 'besotted' with their mummy or daddy, as most young children are. To the young child, their parent is the most important person in the world.

As the child becomes older and enters their teenage years it is a natural progression for the parent to be knocked off their pedestal and unceremoniously replaced by the child's peers. In adolescence the child wants to find out who they are, start to spread their wings and express their individuality. Their family takes a back seat to other pressing issues in their life such as boyfriends and girlfriends, and they are keen to have as much independence as possible.

For the child of a narcissist, however, becoming a teenager is probably the most traumatic time in their lives because they are discouraged from and even punished for wanting the things that other teenagers take for granted. The child's peers are a threat to the narcissist as they distract the child from their obligation of attending to their parent's insatiable need for attention. They also provide an avenue of support for the child and the child appears to be happy in their company.

The narcissist experiences feelings of envy, abandonment and subsequent anger towards their child for enjoying the company of others. To the narcissistic parent, it's an act of betrayal for their child to enjoy anything that isn't the direct result of the narcissist's actions. A narcissistic injury has been created which can only be healed by restoring 'order' – when the narcissist regains their position of power as the most important person in their child's life. The child is allowed to be happy, but only if the narcissist can take ownership of the cause of their happiness. There must always be some benefit in it for the narcissist, and if the child is deriving happiness elsewhere it will be sabotaged if possible.

The narcissist cannot come off looking like the bad guy, however, so the sabotage of their children's friendships must look as if it's of the child's own doing. Coercive control at its finest.

Knowing that overt measures may risk the narcissistic parent's impeccable image, the narcissist uses their powerful influence to plant seeds in their child's mind about why some particular friends are not good friends at all, and they deserve so much better. The narcissistic parent may interpose themselves into their child's friendships to gather information and set up situations for triangulation. The parent may bring to their child's attention that their friend is spending so much more time with someone else, or that they heard 'a little rumour' that their child's friends were speaking ill of them. Childish games of rumour-mongering are never beneath the narcissist parent. Any action will be justified in their mind if their child prioritises someone else in their life. The punishment will be swift, and the child will be conditioned to take responsibility for what has happened.

With the narcissistic parent approving of very few people in the child's life, the child becomes more and more isolated from the outside world, and their dependency on their narcissistic parent increases. The narcissistic parent is delighted that their 'wayward' child has realised the error of their ways and is once again taking up their dutiful position of being the narcissist's emotional punching bag.

Golden child versus scapegoat child

The narcissist considers their child to be an extension of themselves, therefore the child will have to perform in a way that enhances the narcissist's reputation. Accordingly, the narcissist will take ownership of all their child's good qualities and achievements, and will brag about them to the world, but will relegate responsibility for any other children's 'failings' to someone else, such as the other parent or a teacher, who will be shamed if they don't meet the narcissist's standards.

The narcissistic parent knows their children aren't going anywhere, especially when they are little, so they set about creating an environment that will provide them with maximum supply. To this end, they will use their children's natural desire for love and approval to set up an arena of competition in which their children will compete for parental love, something that should be taken for granted. The narcissist's goal is to triangulate, or pit, family members against each other in a quest to win the 'love' of the narcissistic parent. This puts the narcissist at the top of the triangle where they can watch their offspring battle it out to please them.

As described in earlier chapters, triangulation starts with the narcissist assigning the roles of scapegoat child and golden child to one or more of their children. The golden child will usually be more like the toxic parent, with the same interests and talents. The scapegoat child is typically the one who is more intuitive and sensitive and who will voice their displeasure at the narcissist's actions. In comparison to the narcissist's great interest and involvement in all the golden child's talents, they will make it clear they have little interest in what talents the scapegoat child has, and that child will get no encouragement to excel in what they're good at. The narcissist punishes that child for daring to be different, and the scapegoat child will become the vessel for the narcissist's projected internal shame.

The golden child is the favourite child of the narcissist and is raised with the expectation that they will reflect positively on that parent. They will often feel immense pressure to perform, as anything less than perfect will result in withdrawal of the praise they have become dependent upon. The need to please the narcissistic parent becomes part of their make-up and they become indoctrinated into a way of life where success is everything, and failure unacceptable.

In comparison to the other children in the family, they will be praised and rewarded for their achievements, setting up a dynamic for sibling rivalry. Children with narcissistic parents rarely grow up with a close bond because the difference in the way they are treated leads to animosity and resentment. The golden child does not want to lose their position of favourite, so will often sabotage the scapegoat child's attempts to please. The scapegoat child continues to try, but it seems the goalposts always shift and they never quite get there.

The roles of scapegoat and golden child may stay the same for life, or they may change at any time, depending on how the children please or displease the parent. For example, the golden child may make the 'selfish' decision of choosing a university course the narcissistic parent doesn't approve of. They are swiftly demoted to the role of scapegoat, and the parent promotes the old scapegoat to the role of golden child. The parent lavishes the new golden child with the attention that child has been craving all their life and the ex-golden child feels shunned, so changes their university course. The narcissistic parent revels in the fact that their children are trying to outdo each other to try and please them. Their lack of morality and empathy means they don't care if they are preventing natural bonds from forming between siblings. Divide and conquer. The last thing a narcissist wants is united siblings joining forces to expose them. No, they need for each child to have a totally different perception of their reality so that future exposure of the narcissist's true self will be disputed by the golden child, and the narcissist will be protected.

Sofie was assigned the role of scapegoat child by her narcissistic mother at an early age. Of course, she didn't know this at the time, and she always thought there must be something wrong with her because her narcissistic mother found fault in everything she did. She was chastised for being 'sulky' and 'oversensitive' if ever she wanted what all children crave such as a genuine cuddle after hurting herself. A quiet, creative child, she loved to paint. Her older sister, however, was a sporty academic who excelled in maths and science. She was the golden child whose achievements were plastered on her mother's social media page while Sofie's beautiful artwork did not get a mention. Sofie loved her sister but, as with her mother, she could never please her, and she always seemed to look down on Sofie. As they got older, the relationship between Sofie and her mother and sister became even more fractured, with Sofie feeling 'ganged up on' by her parent and sibling.

Sofie's father was away most of the time, but even when he was there, he would never intervene in the family dynamic set up by her mother. Although not outwardly abusive himself, he'd always support his wife when she called on him to join forces with her to demean Sofie.

The narcissistic mother

Sofie hoped that as she got older the relationship with her parents would improve, especially with her mother. It didn't; it got worse. Her mother seemed to resent everything she did, from getting her hair coloured to the type of clothes she wore. It was as if she was in competition with her own daughter. She always made Sofie feel bad with comments like 'You would look so pretty if you only lost a few pounds' or (in front of Sofie's boyfriend at the time) 'Sofie, have you been taking your anxiety medication? You don't want to ruin this relationship too.' Every time adult Sofie saw her mother the exasperating comments would flow. Yet Sofie went back for more, hoping the next time would be the time her mother approved.

Sofie's perception that the relationship with her mother was competitive was correct. To the narcissistic mother, a daughter is a threat to their grandiose idea of themselves. Their same-sex child represents everything they may have lost, such as their youth and their looks. They will feel threatened by anything their daughter does or has that makes them feel 'less than'. The narcissistic mother will try and outdo her daughter in ridiculous ways such as buying a house when they do, buying the same clothes only better quality and/or more expensive, or getting a new hairdo when the daughter has just decided to.

These mothers may have such deep-seated envy of their daughters they will even resort to flirting with their boyfriends – sometimes the teenage daughter doesn't know whether their crush is coming over to see them or their mother. The competitive nature of the narcissistic mother knows no limits and they will sabotage their daughter's relationships whenever possible because their daughter's happiness reflects back to them their own misery.

The narcissistic father

Children of narcissistic fathers can never measure up to their father's expectations. They spend their lives trying to be better than they were yesterday, not because they have a healthy sense of motivation, but because their father has told them that yesterday's efforts were not good enough.

Just like the toxic mother, the narcissistic father loves to triangulate his children, in particular enjoying pitting two sons against each other. The golden son may become the narcissistic father's 'right-hand man' and will be prepped to join him in a self-owned business. The scapegoat son sees his father favouring the golden son, with the usual rivalry resulting. In reality, the adult golden son has no choice but to engage in the father's wishes, because to have dreams of his own is to lose the breadcrumbs of the father's approval that he is dependent on. Like the narcissist mother, such fathers may flirt with their son's girlfriend or wife to exert their dominance over the son and create conflict in their son's relationship.

A teenage girlfriend of the son sees in the narcissist a 'confident' older man, and their immaturity sees them drawn to this person. The son naturally becomes jealous and the father plays dumb, feigning a complete lack of awareness of the attraction. Once again, the son feels he can never be as 'good' as his father, and that anything that makes him happy will be short-lived if his father finds out about it.

The narcissistic parent wants their child to do everything in their power to try and please them, but the golden rule is that the child can never be better than them. The narcissist wants to reap the rewards of their child's achievements, but those must always fall just short of their own.

Children of the narcissist are in a constant state of confusion about what will make their parent happy. Even if they do achieve highly, the narcissistic parent will distort their perceptions and downplay their achievements so they can never be proud of themselves. It will never be good enough. For this reason, it is very common for children of narcissistic parents to have a complete lack of confidence in themselves and to have anxiety disorders which they carry with them into adulthood.

Anxiety

Anxiety is something we experience when we lack control in our lives. If you had a narcissistic parent, think back to your earliest memories. Did you ever have predictability in your life? Did you ever know for sure that when you cried you would be comforted or that the narcissist would be happy you went from a C to a B on your report card? Did you spend your childhood trying to work out what would make the narcissist happy but never seeming to be able to achieve it?

The abused child cannot predict the consequences of their behaviour, good or bad. Therefore, there is no scope to control their own lives, no matter how much they try to be a 'good' boy or girl. Consequently, their developing brain works on overdrive to do its job of keeping them 'safe' in the ongoing trauma by regularly causing the amygdala (part of the limbic, or emotional control, system) to send signals to the hypothalamus (concerned with visceral responses), and the resulting fight or flight response becomes the norm rather than the exception.

Abused children are in a continual state of hypervigilance to danger (walking on eggshells), and anxiety disorders do not disappear just because the child grows up. Anxiety often becomes debilitating for adult children of narcissists, impacting every aspect of their lives. Many victims grow up self-medicating their anxiety, which leads to addictions to alcohol and other drugs, and their compounding effects. Victims require much understanding and support to manage their anxiety and comprehend the trauma behind it.

Parent of the year

As the child of a narcissist, your job is also to make sure that everything looks 'rosy' to the outside world. Image is everything, and anything that doesn't reflect favourably on the family must remain behind closed doors and be denied if spoken about. To all and sundry, the narcissistic mother or father will appear to be an amazing parent who cherishes the ground their children walk on. They will take advantage of any situation that will portray them as parent of the year.

I'm always amazed to hear of a narcissistic parent taking their child to therapy to address the behavioural issues resulting directly from the abuse by that parent. The narcissist receives positive attention from anyone they brag to for being such a good parent and addressing their child's mental health. The child goes to therapy to be 'fixed', but they know better than to talk negatively about the toxic person waiting outside, playing the role of the dutiful parent. The child cannot and will not talk about their abuse, either for fear of punishment because they must go home with that parent, or because they have no idea that what they're going through is abuse. It's then reinforced that the problem is with them: they are a problem child. And they grow up believing they're a problem adult.

'Parentified' children

Many child victims of narcissistic abuse become 'parentified' – taking on the role of a 'friend' and 'emotional leaning post' to their parent and perhaps caregiver to their siblings. The lines between parent and child can become blurred at a very young age because of the narcissistic parent's selfish needs. The narcissistic parent may rely on their child for support in dealing with adult issues that a child should never be burdened with, let alone aware of. It places a huge weight on the shoulders of a child to ask them to provide commentary on matters such as financial issues or relationships.

Instead of thinking about what they're going to wear to the school dance, the child is filled with anxiety about whether they're going to have a house to live in because they've been told the other parent did not pay their child support. It becomes normal for Mum or Dad to ask them for advice in their relationships, and to be taught to hate that person one week and then love them the next week because their parent has got back together with them.

One of the devastating effects of parentification for the child victim is that it strengthens the trauma bond. One day the child is pushed away and made to feel irrelevant because they're not pleasing the narcissist parent, the next they become Mum or Dad's best buddy and confidante – and Mum or Dad want to talk to them and cry on their shoulder. For a short time the child feels important to the parent and these breadcrumbs of 'niceness' will outweigh any abuse. It also makes the child feel very grown-up to be having these kinds of conversations with their parent. They feel very 'special' to be included in the dynamics of such adult issues. However, the result is they spend their time worrying about their parents' problems instead of being allowed to grow and develop emotionally as a child should.

Making them crave those breadcrumbs of special treatment is just another way the narcissistic parent ensures their child never 'abandons' them. Yes, children also become trauma bonded. A powerful emotional bond is formed with their abusive parent as a result of the lifetime cycle of abuse with intermittent positive reinforcement. The child suffers every time they cannot please that parent, and the parent becomes the only one who can bring an end to that suffering by being 'nice'. The child experiences such relief that the silent treatment or other punishment has come to an end, that the times the parent is nice to them seem like heaven. It is for this reason that it is especially rewarding for the child victim when the narcissist parent engages them to take on the adult role of their caregiver and/or best friend.

The narcissist's need to control any type of happiness in their child's life relates not just to their relationships, but to any decision that child makes or any behaviour they engage in that they enjoy. It is especially frowned upon if the other parent is deemed responsible for that happiness. There will be callous disregard for the child's feelings as the narcissistic parent puts roadblocks in the way to punish the other parent and to punish their child for being happy with someone else. The narcissist's child feels either rejected or suffocated. There is no in–between.

Becoming an adult

The university course or job you choose must be approved as one that will align with the narcissist's image. You may only leave home with their blessing no matter how old you are, and while you are living at home you must never have any needs.

When you do engage in the aspects of your adult life that are approved by the narcissist, the same rules will apply. You will get the validation you have become dependent upon only if you continue to allow the narcissist's needs to be paramount.

As children of narcissists become adults, they start to realise that something is very wrong in their relationship with their aging parent. Where their friends have positive and appropriate relationships with their aging parents, the adult child of the narcissist has a relationship with their parent that is permeated by feelings of obligation and guilt. They feel like they can never have any boundaries with their parent, and their adult lives and relationships continue to be manipulated by the narcissist. In narcissistic abuse recovery we refer to them as ACONs, 'adult children of narcissists'.

The feelings of helplessness and never being good enough for the narcissistic parent do not improve as both parties age. They get worse. There is no recognition on the part of the narcissistic parent that their child is now an adult with dreams and goals of their own. The debt for being born will never be paid in full.

There are several reasons these feelings of helplessness become worse. Firstly, the narcissistic parent is aging. They have spent their lifetime destroying people and creating enemies. They can't walk down their street without running into someone they have burnt. Secondly, they are starting to lose their ability to secure narcissistic supply because their looks are starting to fade and they just don't have the energy anymore. Aging has meant they may no longer be working or engaging in other activities that provided a platform from which to extract narcissistic supply. So who do they fall back on when sources start to dry up? Their trusty children of course.

Now they are old, they're going to call in that 'debt' you owe them – with interest. The narcissist's dependency on you increases, and your dependency on them for validation and your obligatory role to meet their needs have never ended. You continue to base your self-worth on their opinions as you have your entire life, and they have ramped up the attention-seeking behaviour because you are one of the few sources of narcissistic supply that remains. Another perfect storm.

As an ACON, you will also have extra supply to provide to the aging parent, in that you will very often have a family of your own. Your family will provide an absolute smorgasbord of narcissistic supply to the aging narcissist as they gaslight and triangulate family members, and watch you struggle to maintain order in your own home. The narcissistic parent will love to interfere in your marriage and cause rifts with your children. Perhaps they will express their dislike of your spouse out loud and make it extremely uncomfortable for you at family gatherings. Or it may be the reverse: your spouse doesn't like your parent because they can see through the manipulation. You start to resent your spouse because this is *your* parent, and you have a lifetime history of minimising, rationalising and defending their toxic behaviour.

Or perhaps it is you who is trying to distance yourself from the toxic parent, and that parent is 'sucking up' to your spouse, pretending to be a caring parent whose child is just so ungrateful. This becomes a bone of contention in your marriage as your parent triangulates and causes conflict between you and your spouse. The spouse of course thinks they are acting in your best interests, because after all, you only get one parent.

A great source of entertainment for the narcissist lies in manipulating their grandchildren. An ACON will be told that everything they do as a parent is wrong. The narcissist cannot have you outshining them with children who actually love you! You will never cook them the right meals. Their behaviour will be chastised and ascribed to your bad parenting. Your house will never be clean enough, and you will iron their clothes the wrong way.

At the same time, the narcissistic grandparent will be pulling some or all of your children onto their side of the arena. They will be the world's best grandparent to your child so that if you try to go no-contact, it will be incredibly upsetting for the child. Of course, the manipulative grandparent will be gaslighting the child into believing your reasons are purely selfish. You may then feel like your hand has been forced into organising contact between them to keep the child happy. This is extremely frustrating when you know your parent's motivation is more about punishing you than spending time with their grandkids.

Perhaps they will have a 'favourite' child of yours which sets up an arena of competition between siblings. How do you explain why their grandparent 'loves' one of their grandchildren more than another? If you talk to your parent, you'll only be gaslighted and talked out of your reality. They will either deny it and tell you that you're imagining things, or they will agree that they do treat that child better, but only because the other child is such a terrible child – because of your parenting no doubt – and therefore undeserving. Either way, it will make you feel terribly sad for your children and absolutely powerless to completely remove them from that environment.

You are not like your narcissistic parent

It's not just the ongoing abuse from the controlling, narcissistic parent that causes ACONs to have ongoing feelings of low self-worth and a lack of identity beyond 'obedient child'. Many ACONs worry they may have inherited some of their parent's genes and traits. They may look at behaviours they've engaged in with their own children or intimate partners, behaviours they were not proud of that brought about feelings of deep regret and remorse.

If this is something that resonates with you, please remember that narcissists do not have the capacity for introspection. They do not look at their behaviour and experience remorse. Everything they do that causes pain to someone else will be justified. Isolated incidents that bring about remorse and a heartfelt desire to change do not indicate Narcissistic Personality Disorder (NPD). They are more likely to be the feelings of someone who has been traumatised. Someone who has grown up in an abusive environment and watched the most important role models in their life teach them how to react and how to treat people. These behaviours may also be the result of subconsciously having to defend yourself your whole life, because you were always under attack, or of frustration in never being able to articulate your feelings. Not everyone who was raised by a narcissist becomes a narcissist.

Here's a story I tell my clients to help ease their minds.

Twin sisters who were raised by a narcissistic, alcoholic mother went on to have very different lives. Their alcoholic mother psychologically, emotionally and verbally abused them throughout their childhood. They remembered her screaming at their father nearly every night while she was drunk, and then they'd be subjected to her hungover wrath in the morning. The girls didn't received any affection from her unless it was in the presence of others, and they learned to walk on eggshells around her moods.

As the twins got older, the mother started to become even more abusive. She hated the fact they were so pretty while her own looks were fading, and she'd punish them by either yelling at them or giving them the silent treatment.

One of the twins started to drink to seek relief from the acute anxiety she felt as a result of the abuse. Her dependency on alcohol worsened over time until she became a full-blown alcoholic. She in turn went on to abuse her own children in the same way her mother abused her.

The other twin used exercise instead of alcohol to manage her anxiety and ended up going to university to study physiotherapy. She became a nurturing mother and teetotaller who doted on her husband and children. One day, the alcoholic twin was asked what she believed led her to become an alcoholic. She replied, 'I became an alcoholic because I watched my mother'. When the other twin was asked why she'd never drunk alcohol, she replied, 'Because I watched my mother'.

Please remember this story when you experience deep remorse about something you have said or done that may have hurt someone else. You are allowed to be human and make mistakes. It does not mean you are like your narcissist parent in any way.

Is your child likely to develop NPD?

Unfortunately, it is impossible to predict whether your child will develop the narcissistic traits of their abusive parent. Nature, nurture and lifetime events that are beyond your control will impact on their personalities as they develop.

However, children learn through role modelling, so when you, their only appropriate parent, model and reinforce the behaviours you wish to see in your developing child and counter the selfish and destructive behaviours of the narcissistic parent, you minimise that risk.

When you were still with the narcissist you were deep in the FOG (fear, obligation and guilt), focused on survival, and with limited power to mitigate the damaging parenting tactics of the narcissist. As a single parent you now have the power to parent the children with strategies that encourage them to have healthy self-esteem and self-worth. The parenting you provide needs to be in stark contrast to that of the narcissist, meaning your child is taught the importance of empathy and compassion for others, respect is earned, not taken for granted, and love is not a conditional commodity based on control and getting your own needs met.

Adult relationships

It's nearly impossible for any child of a narcissist to articulate that what they're experiencing is abuse. This is their 'normal'. They've grown up this way, conditioned to believe that everything that happens to them is their own fault. Consequently they grow up with low self-esteem and absolutely no self-worth, which often leads them to partners who will support their beliefs. Many child victims of narcissistic abuse grow up to find themselves with partners who mirror their abusive parent. It is a shock for many victims of child abuse when they realise the relationship they are in is so similar to the one they have with the toxic parent. My clients often shout: 'I can't believe it: I married my father!' or 'I married my mother!' Without knowing it, they've found someone who supports and reinforces their subconscious notion of what constitutes a normal relationship.

The scapegoat child especially may find themselves in a relationship in which they are forever trying to please their partner and never expecting any gratitude. They just take it for granted that they should never have any needs of their own. This is familiar and normal for them. Their expectations of how they should be treated are extremely low because this is how they were treated as a child. They were conditioned throughout their life to believe that people who love you take advantage of you. One, or both, of the most important role models in their life showed them either how to abuse someone else or how to tolerate abuse. The scapegoat child will normally fit the mould of the latter.

The dilemma of leaving

If a narcissist has projected an image of your 'perfect family' in the community your whole life, how hard is it for an ACON to walk away from their abusive parent when people are saying to them, 'But they love you so much, they'd do anything for you!'

Perhaps you love the non-narcissistic parent despite their enabling of the abuse that they never protected you from. You reason you should just put up with the toxic behaviour from your abusive parent so you don't have to give up the parent you love. This is the dilemma victims face when considering how to stop being treated this way, and how to stop feeling so bad. It feels like a no-win situation. Either stay and put up with the abuse and nothing changes or go no-contact and feel an overwhelming sense of guilt. (This is my parent! You can't just abandon your own parent! What will people think of me?) These are normal reactions from someone who just wants to be loved by their parent.

The adult child of a narcissist is going to need a lots of support, not just to break away from the toxic relationship with the narcissistic parent, but to realise that the toxic parent is not going to change.

The adult child who is most likely to attempt to break free is the scapegoat. They have been the recipient of all their parent's self-hatred their entire life, and their intuitiveness provides them with a level of understanding of the toxic behaviours of their parent.

The golden child is more likely to stay chained to that parent for good because their sense of self is completely wrapped up in their parent's approval. Their self-worth has always been completely dependent on their parent's validation. This connection is strengthened further if/when the scapegoat manages to escape, because without the scapegoat child to rely on for supply, the narcissistic parent relies more heavily on the golden child. Even if the golden child starts to succumb to the pressure of providing all the supply, the narcissist parent, through fear, obligation and guilt, will make it virtually impossible for that adult to leave and maintain their sanity.

You were abused by a narcissistic parent because of who *they* are. You didn't do anything to deserve it, and you have every right to sever ties with anyone who abuses you, regardless of biological connection. *No one has the right to abuse you.*

Reflect on your self-worth: why is it so low? It's because the narcissistic parent made you believe that everything was your fault and you've carried this into every aspect of your life. Maybe you are highly dependent on others because your parent conditioned you to believe that you could never be independent. Or on the flip side, maybe you are so distrustful that you never allow yourself to depend on anyone, which can be just as debilitating. If you can't trust your own parent then who can you trust? Or maybe you are terrified to make any big decisions for yourself in life because your narcissistic parent decided everything for you and your ideas have always been ridiculed. The list goes on. ACONs often suffer debilitating anxiety and depression from a lifetime of walking on eggshells. They may have anxious and insecure attachment styles and fear abandonment if they are not the 'perfect' (i.e. submissive) partner. Consequently, they develop incredibly high tolerances for abuse. They become people-pleasers at the expense of never having their own needs met. They may not even know what their needs are because they've never been allowed to have any. As mentioned earlier, ACONs will often shy away from healthy unfamiliar relationships, and find themselves in another toxic relationship where they are treated in a way that feels familiar. No one deserves to feel like this!

It's a terrible thing to grow up unloved and then not be allowed to stop trying to love the person who wouldn't love you. You do not owe your parents. There is no debt to be paid in a loving relationship between parent and child. If a relationship exists simply out of a sense of obligation and guilt, it is not a loving relationship. It is simply a connection. A connection you are allowed to either maintain at some level on your terms or sever.

Sometimes the relationship is simply too abusive to maintain at even a superficial level, and no contact is the only answer. If you choose to maintain some kind of connection, keep your boundaries firm and provide consequences when the other person fails to observe your boundaries. Stop explaining yourself – don't JADE with them (justify, argue, defend and explain).

Grieving

Whether you stay in contact or not, you must grieve the parent you never had. There is such a sense of loss in coming to terms with the fact that you will never have that loving bond with your parent. Your toxic parent is who they are, and their behaviour has been consistent over a long period of time. Therefore, it's highly unlikely they will ever change. Grieve the loss of your hopes and dreams that one day, *one day*, you might genuinely please them. Grieve the loss of a parent that never was and never will be, and give yourself closure and permission to move on and be happy. Give any guilt away to the universe, and don't listen to people who have never walked in your shoes.

* * *

As children, we are taught that our parents love us. We are told not to talk to strangers because they might hurt us; that the people we can love and trust are the ones at home: our parents. Unfortunately, the notion that all parents love their children means that children of narcissistic parents grow up believing that love and abuse go hand in hand. Our brains do not stop developing until approximately age 25. If a brain that is still growing continually receives the message that toxic love is normal, then that is what is going to be hardwired into that child's belief system and dictate their behaviour. Consequently, the child of the narcissist grows up believing that love is conditional, and that their needs must always come last.

The truth is, love is unconditional. When you were born, you were a blank slate to be written on, and the messages you received from your toxic parent were not love. Stop believing you ever deserved to be treated this way. Start believing that you deserve better. And the people who fulfil their own selfish needs by walking all over your boundaries and self-worth? They don't deserve a place in your life. No matter who they are.

IN SUMMARY

- For a narcissist, parenting is just another platform for attention and narcissistic supply.
- For the child, it's a role that will last a lifetime unless they break free.
- The narcissist will assign the roles of 'golden child' and 'scapegoat' to their children and pit them against each other.
- Low self-esteem may lead ACONs (adult children of narcissists) to partners who will support their belief that everything is their own fault.

CHAPTER ELEVEN

Boys don't cry: Male victims of narcissistic abuse

During one particular session with me, reflecting on the way Justin had pitted her own children against each other and regularly attempted to turn them against her, Sofie realised that history had repeated itself: this was exactly what had happened during Sofie's childhood. But in that case, her mother had turned Sofie and her older sister against their father.

Sofie's mother discouraged her from having any kind of positive relationship with her father, and constantly put him down to her. Sofie remembered her mother's constant verbal attacks on her father, telling him that she was going to leave him because he didn't earn enough money, that she would take the children, and that he would never see them again. This terrified Sofie, and she recalled yelling at her father to just give their mother whatever she wanted so they didn't have to leave.

She also remembered her mother saying 'don't tell your father' when a male 'friend' of hers regularly visited while their father was away working, telling them their father got jealous and did not want her to have any friends. She felt sorry for her mother, who was so 'lonely', and angry that their father left them all alone so often. She recalled her mother telling him that she only married him because she was pregnant with Sofie's older sister, and that he had 'trapped' her. Her mother even screamed at him in front of them that she 'should have got an abortion!'

It was only now, as an adult, that Sofie realised the long-term damaging effects these words had had on her and her sister's self-worth. During one particularly horrendous attack when her mother yelled at her father for what seemed like hours, she kept poking him in the chest, telling him he wasn't a man because he 'just sat there' and wouldn't 'stand up for himself'. That was the first time Sofie heard her father yell back at her mother. Soon after, the police arrived at their door and told their father to leave the home for a while to 'cool off'. As a child, Sofie could not understand why he was the one who had to leave and not their mother.

Sofie remembered other terrible names her mother had called her father, and the insults to his intelligence and manhood that her mother regularly threw at him. Now, talking to me, it all started to make sense. Just as she had been, and still was, the victim of her narcissistic mother's abuse, so too was her father. He was as powerless in that relationship as Sofie was in hers, and as a male victim of narcissistic abuse, suffered in perhaps even more silence (if that's possible) than a female victim. Sofie's mother was half his size. Sofie could not conceive of her proud father telling anyone, let alone understanding himself, that he was being abused by a tiny woman. Sofie knew that her father had been raised in a society that instils in its men from a very early age that 'boys don't cry'.

Sofie's memories of her father's love for her were tainted by the brainwashing tactics of a vindictive narcissistic parent engaging in parental alienation. Using various methods of coercive control, both male and female narcissists use this strategy to punish the other parent by altering their child's perception of the non-abusive parent, turning their natural love into ambivalence or hatred or preventing that love from developing in the first place. As an adult, it was painful for Sofie to realise that she had been denied her right to develop a loving relationship with her father. She felt natural anger towards her mother as the one responsible for ensuring this loving connection never developed. She admitted that she also felt anger towards her father for not 'trying harder' to protect her. She then felt guilty for being angry at him.

I would work with Sofie to process these feelings at future sessions, but for now, Sofie wanted to understand her father's trauma so that she could better understand her own. She also wanted to have a better relationship with him now as an adult, and for that to happen, she needed answers. How had her mother sucked her father into the same vortex of abuse that Sofie found herself in? Shouldn't a man have more power to just leave? Isn't it normally the man who abuses the woman? Why did her diminutive mother seem to have so much power and control over her burly 1.9-metre father?

Through no fault of her own, Sofie was like many others who fail to see how men can also be victims of narcissistic abuse. She wanted to know more, so we discussed it often.

As I noted in the Introduction, since a diagnosis of pathological narcissism would necessitate an acknowledgement from the perpetrator that they may be a narcissist (and what narcissist is going to concede to this?), very few narcissists have actually been diagnosed as such. Narcissists do not believe there is anything wrong with them. The likelihood of a narcissist walking into a therapist's office and asking for help with their suspected narcissism is almost zero. It is only the people close to the narcissist who find themselves in therapy.

Unfortunately, the lack of research and the subsequent lack of reliable statistics on narcissism and the gender breakdown of perpetrators means that traditional societal ideas that domestic violence is always 'man abusing woman' continue to be reinforced. Consequently, male victims of this type of insidious psychological violence find little empathy in society, and therefore very little support.

To illustrate how difficult it is for a man to seek help, let alone recognise that he has been abused, here are two stories representative of male clients I've counselled in recent years. The first is the story of Michael, who was victimised by his narcissistic wife. The second story concerns James, who was abused by his male partner.

Michael's story

Michael came to see me several years ago in relation to 'issues' he was having in the relationship with his wife. He could never please her no matter how hard he tried, and he described genuine psychological cruelty by her over the years which had turned him into a 'shell' of the strong and confident man he once was. The textbook narcissistic love bomb, devalue, discard and hoover cycle occurred repeatedly in this relationship, and the cyclical wounding and healing resulted in a powerful trauma bond to the woman who was abusing him.

Michael was a member of the military who had fought in the Middle East. He talked about the terrible atrocities he had seen, the loss of mates and the devastation he had felt as a result of these traumatic experiences. He was a courageous soldier who had survived a number of deadly incidents that his mates did not. And yet in the relationship with his toxic wife he felt completely powerless. The rules of engagement in this particular war were unknown to him. But despite his unhappiness he found himself unable to leave.

Like most people who come to see me, Michael had started to google his wife's behaviour. After further research, he was certain his wife was a narcissist. He described ongoing affairs, pathological lying and cruel patterns of narcissistic behaviour that were consistent over time and in which he would be gaslighted and demeaned, and his manhood ridiculed.

He earned good money yet they were always in debt as his wife (who controlled their finances) would exhaust the limit of one credit card after another. Any attempt to address the ongoing issue of debt with her was met with either confusing arguments in which he would end up apologising to her for 'not trusting her', or rages that ended up with lengthy, torturous bouts of the silent treatment. It was easier for him to just keep paying off the credit cards than to subject himself to these 'discussions'. He also described her threats to leave him and take their children to another state. Despite all the toxic behaviour that Michael described, he admitted that he couldn't stop loving her. He told me that she wasn't that person all the time, and he lived for the moments when she'd be 'her old self'. The thought of losing his wife forever was terrifying for Michael. He desperately wanted answers: how could he get that 'old self' back for good; that amazing woman he'd married who'd once put him on a pedestal? And how could he stop her treating him so badly? Despite his extensive research and his confidence in labelling her a narcissist, he still hoped I'd be able to provide him with some magic recipe of communication that would bring back the non-existent person he'd fallen in love with.

Initially, Michael had resigned himself to staying with his wife, a decision supported by the magical thinking that she would change. However, as Michael began to process his trauma, he realised that his decision to stay was based on more than just the deep trauma bond he felt to his abuser. Michael's situation had the added complexity of society's stereotypical notion of men as the aggressors. These societal ideas dictated Michael's entire sense of self, and because he was a man he struggled to believe that what he was experiencing was abuse.

These stereotypical roles in which the woman is viewed as nurturing and much weaker than her stronger, aggressive male counterpart reflect most of the research on domestic violence. That research shows the indisputable fact that women are far more likely to be murdered by an intimate partner than a man is.

The problem for male victims of narcissistic abuse like Michael is that even in the face of current research indicating that one in six men suffer emotional abuse, men are still not having their trauma validated by a society that typically views them as the aggressors, and stereotypes continue to be perpetuated by the research that reflects and supports women as the victims.

The fact that psychological abuse/narcissistic abuse, a non-gendered form of domestic violence, is under-reported, particularly by men, and the lack of credence given to available research on male victims, means that men like Michael are misrepresented and disadvantaged. As there is little or no research on female abusers, there is little support for male victims. Coming forward as a male victim of a woman makes you an anomaly. It is easier for society to fall back on conventional beliefs and stereotypes that men can't be abused by women 'because a man is bigger/tougher' than to provide empathy and support for such an anomaly.

The research relating to male victims of domestic violence is limited not only because of stereotypical beliefs around violence and gender, but because the violence that men endure is typically (though not always) non-physical. It is virtually impossible to measure the prevalence of domestic violence in the form of psychological abuse when the injuries aren't visible and psychological abuse is still ignored or downplayed as a factor. The upshot is that, as stated previously, victims hesitate to report psychological abuse, and even fail to recognise the abuse for what it is. How many times have I heard from my female clients that they would have felt more like a 'victim' – and more supported – if they were obviously bruised and battered. (Think too of these very common statements in the context of a man coming forward to report psychological abuse.)

Statistics are clearly less reliable when victims hesitate to come forward, especially when one gender feels they would be ridiculed if they did. This is one factor that differentiates a male victim's reluctance to report their psychological abuse from that of his female counterpart. A woman fears that she will not be believed. A man fears not only that he will not be believed, but that he will be ridiculed and become the laughing stock of his workplace and community.

Michael articulated to me that he was not willing to risk his career and reputation by talking about the abuse to anyone associated with his job, and he was not willing to risk losing his children by talking to a lawyer. It was easier to stay and manage as best he could. His wife, who appeared the doting mother and loving partner to everyone on the other side of their closed front door, had complete control over the most important parts of his world: his children.

She had also succeeded in manipulating the perceptions of outsiders by covertly smearing him and engaging in DARVO (deny, attack and reverse victim and offender) on a number of occasions when Michael had tried to make her accountable for her behaviour. It stands to reason that if society presumes that the woman is always the victim, then a manipulative, narcissistic woman like Michael's wife is going to use those stereotypical ideas to her advantage. The narcissistic rage she felt in being 'criticised' resulted in her planting seeds in the minds of people that he worked with, and their wives, that he was erratic and unstable. She also planted seeds to suggest that she was scared of him at certain times. Because she was smaller than he was she knew they would believe her. She also knew that these seeds of information would be watered with the plausible notion that a man who had witnessed and experienced violence during war might have problems with aggression. She actually used his service to his country as her own weapon to maim him with. To twist the knife even further, she consistently reminded him that 'everyone' thought he was crazy.

Being a member of the military, Michael had access to free counselling services, yet here he was with me, paying for my services to support him with his trauma. I was sure that I knew what the answer to my question would be, but I proceeded to ask Michael: 'Why would you make that financial sacrifice when you are entitled to and deserve the counselling support of your employer?'

His answer: 'Because I don't want anyone to know that I need help. I don't want them to think that I have mental health issues. No matter what anyone says to you, if someone finds out that a bloke like me has been talking to a counsellor on a regular basis, they are going to look at me differently.'

As he put it, 'Who wants someone who has "mental problems" fighting beside them during war? Who is going to trust you with their life in battle when you're telling them you can't even handle your missus yelling at you?'

He had seen it happen before. For one of his fellow soldiers, talking to a counsellor not only resulted in a change of attitude from other men and his exclusion from normal 'bonding' activities outside work, but also lack of advancement. The unspoken (and unsupported) belief among his fellow soldiers was that the promotion was denied to him, an obvious candidate, because that man had 'mental health issues'. At any rate, Michael believed that seeking counselling was viewed as a 'weakness', and 'frowned upon', and would result in blacklisting.

Formal counselling aside, Michael believed that he would be jeered at by his mates if he spoke about the psychological abuse by his wife, who was loved by all. Not only was he up against the social stigma associated with mental health issues, but for him, talking about emotions was only 'acceptable' to your peers if they were 'manly' emotions like anger. Discussion about your feelings being hurt because someone yelled at you too much? That was what 'girls' did. Michael felt totally isolated from any type of support that was available. 'Man up!' he regularly told himself to survive the trauma of narcissistic abuse that made him feel weak and anything but manly. But Michael felt powerless to do this. As a male victim of narcissistic abuse, it seemed that he must suffer in silence. There was too much to lose, and the punishment for a man seeking support for narcissistic abuse was the desecration of the last little piece of his manhood, which he was not prepared to lose.

TECHNIQUES OF FEMALE NARCISSISTS

A female narcissist will use the same strategies as her male counterpart to entrap her victim quickly. She will love bomb them, giving her victim little time to think about anything other than this relationship and how utterly amazing it feels to be 'idolised'. In the beginning she will listen with 'empathy' as her victim pours his heart out to her about previous relationships, perhaps when he was hurt by other women. She will of course appear to be the complete opposite of those women, and the things she has in common with her victim will be astounding.

There will be slight variations to the manipulation tactics she uses, simply because she is female. One of the weapons that she will commonly use is sex. A female narcissist assumes 'men like sex'. She will typically seduce her victim with sex that many of my male clients describe as incredibly intense and fulfilling. My clients describe to me a feeling of chemistry they've never experienced before, saying they had never been with someone who wanted to please them so much, or so often. However, sex is no more an act of intimacy for a female narcissist than it is for a male, and as soon as she knows her victim is hooked (specifically: hooked on the sex) she will use sex as a weapon to control him, by either denying him or rewarding him as she sees fit. She will also use it to emasculate him when she is particularly keen to destroy his confidence and self-worth, by ridiculing his sexual ability, and, as I hear frequently from my clients, the size of his penis.

Emasculation is a powerful and toxic strategy that women use to abuse men. Narcissistic abuse in all its forms is about power and control, and to exert her dominance over her victim a female narcissist must annihilate his self-esteem and any signs of strength that threaten her power. It is typical for female abusers to attack their partner's job, their qualifications or lack thereof, and their ability to provide. Societal norms promote the idea that strength is a quality to be expected and revered in a man. These norms also support the notion that a man is expected to be the protector and provider to his family. Depriving her victim of the very qualities that enable him to 'fit in', and achieve what society expects from him, may create extreme feelings of shame. He feels like a failure, and in many cases this results in depression, which the narcissist further uses to attack him. Depression can be debilitating and decreases one's capacity to be productive. If this happens, particularly if the victim has self-medicated with alcohol or other drugs, the narcissist is able to reinforce to her victim that she was right: he *is* a failure. And like every other victim of narcissistic abuse, he will start to believe that he is the problem and deserving of the abuse. Feeling unworthy to fulfil his role in society isolates the victim further, and his abuser has free rein to maintain her dominance over him.

Female narcissists will use every method at their disposal to ensnare their victim quickly, and one very common strategy is to intentionally get pregnant. I hear this regularly from my male clients, that during the passionate throes of the love bombing stage, and with her discouraging him from using protection because she was 'taking care of that', she 'inexplicably' found herself pregnant.

'I don't know how this could have happened!' or 'I'm going to sue that doctor who told me I couldn't get pregnant!' are typical phrases men hear as the woman denies any accountability for this 'act of God'. The female narcissist has chosen her victim wisely: she knows her victim won't abandon her. He will take care of his child and, hopefully, the mother of his child. Regardless of whether her victim stays in the relationship, she knows that child will be a permanent connection to him and she will use that child to trap him. Should they divorce, the child will provide years and years of potent narcissistic supply as she uses them as a pawn to punish him with.

Just like male abusers, female abusers attempt to isolate their victim from any type of support system and will have 'problems' with his friends and family. Even if she 'allows' her victim to engage in the company of one of his mates, she will ensure that this enjoyable activity comes at such expense to his sanity that he will either have a miserable time or cancel his plans. She will get sick, start an argument or feign a crisis to coerce his actions. These strategies to isolate and monopolise his time are yet more examples of the coercive control she uses to dominate him and sabotage any source of enjoyment in his life. The attention must be on her! She will enjoy creating drama and building his hopes and his manhood up just so she can tear them down.

Her victim soon learns not to look forward to anything, knowing that disappointment is inevitable and his hopes will always be destroyed. She will use his natural masculine desire to protect his family, to persevere and to 'tough it out' against him, should he even think of leaving. '*You* tell the children that you're the one who is breaking up this family' and, *You* be the one to break their hearts!' are common statements my clients tell me they hear if they try to leave. This is gaslighting, of course, because the abuser is the one responsible for breaking her children's hearts should her victim leave. It is an effective strategy, however, as she knows her victim won't want to be responsible for his children's pain.

The female abuser will produce tears at the drop of a hat to manipulate her victim, to make him feel guilty, to make him do something to please her, or to stop him from doing something that will please him. She has intimate knowledge of the empathy her victim possesses, and she knows that tears will pull at his heartstrings. But in reality these are fake or 'crocodile' tears, mechanical in nature, and are simply another tool with which to manipulate him. Should her victim cry, however, he would be either ridiculed or accused of trying to manipulate her. Whether a male victim shows emotion or not, he is potentially doomed. If he shows 'feminine' emotions like tears to her he will punished. If he holds back his tears, he will be accused of being callous and unfeeling. She will gaslight him to make any of his reactions the wrong reaction.

Michael described to me the numerous affairs his wife had during their marriage, but admitted to feeling somewhat responsible for her finding affection with other men because he was away from home for such long periods of time. His wife continued to reinforce to him that it was his fault, yet at the same time she did not want him to get another job. It was so confusing for him (gaslighting) because she would not give him the solution that would fix this 'problem' in their relationship. She would further confuse him by regularly saying during outbursts that she wanted a 'real man'. The contradiction for a male victim like Michael when they hear this very common put-down is that the female abuser has been systematically stripping away every ounce of masculinity they possess, and then using their victim's lack of self-worth against them. Again, the victim is blamed for the effects of their abuse, and is unable to discern that their inability to be a 'real man', as their abuser puts it, is not the cause of the abuser's actions, but the result of it.

The reality in Michael's situation was that the narcissist did not *want* to find a solution. Like all narcissists, she enjoyed cheating and she felt entitled to cheat. She just needed to find a way to make her cheating *his* fault. Cheating is not an acceptable behaviour in society, so the narcissist needs to cover all bases should she be found out so that she is not viewed by others in a negative light. Carefully thought out covert smear campaigns labelling their partner as abusive, an alcoholic or mentally unstable enable the female narcissist to 'find comfort' in the arms of someone else without too much scrutiny. Narcissists cheat. It's what they do, and female narcissists are no different. However, a 'heartbroken', 'neglected' woman who cries copious tears to anyone who'll pay attention? A woman who tells all that her partner was abusive and she just wanted to feel loved? That woman is going to be able to cheat with impunity, and get the sympathy of others for doing it.

FINANCIAL CONTROL

Women are also able to exert financial control over their victims. This control may differ from that of a male narcissist. Yes, many women will have complete control over all resources and make their victim beg for a handout. But this control can also be implemented by creating financial debt and engaging in reckless spending sprees that are self-serving.

Like Michael, victims often report that they regularly experience financial crisis while their narcissistic wife continues to rack up debt they cannot afford. Their abuser will spend money they don't have on luxury items, and will pay for numerous 'self-enhancement' procedures using money that should be going into paying off the mortgage. And while she consistently puts off paying the children's school fees because there's no money left in the account, she has the most luxurious car of anyone in their street, while he is left driving around in a rusty old pick-up.

The difference between these female abusers and someone who has an addiction to shopping lies in the intent and the motivation behind the behaviour. The toxic narcissist doesn't care that she is placing her family in financial crisis as long as she is getting her needs met. She feels entitled to spend as much as she wants and will exploit her victim at any given opportunity. The narcissist will rage if her victim tries to make her accountable for her actions, and he is forced to continue to 'rob Peter to pay Paul' in a toxic relationship he feels unable to leave.

LEAVING THE FEMALE NARCISSIST

Male victims of narcissistic abuse who have families, like Michael, fear leaving their abuser, believing the family court system will naturally sympathise with the mother and he will lose his children. The female narcissist is very aware of her victim's fears, and she will regularly ignite those fears with words like: 'You and I both know the courts will give the kids to me!' In this day and age, this should not be a natural assumption, but it has been in the past. A 'clever' (manipulative) woman is going to be able to use those past assumptions to prevent her victim from leaving her. Her dismantling of his sense of self, the destruction of his ability to trust his instincts and make decisions, and most especially his distrust of a system that seems to support only female victims of abuse, means that many men choose to stay in the toxic relationship. They feel powerless to leave and choose the devil they know in an environment that is familiar to them, rather than face the devil they don't (the family court system).

REMAINING WITH THE FEMALE NARCISSIST

A man remaining in a relationship with his abusive partner is *never* what's best for the children, despite what the narcissist may tell their victim. It's what's best for the narcissist so they can continue to have power and control over their male victim. Children remain the ultimate weapon for the female narcissist to use to control her victim, and she will not only do everything in her power to stop him from leaving, but she will also prevent him from having a healthy, loving connection with his children if he stays.

Surviving this type of trauma requires energy, and sadly, this often means that male victims feel incredible guilt when they don't have the emotional availability for their children that they would like. Once he has fulfilled his obligations as a man to work and provide for his family, which is never enough for the narcissistic wife, while continuing to risk manage her toxic behaviour as best as he can, there is little energy left to give to the children. In turn, she will use his depleted energy resources against him. The words 'You're a bad father' sting in the ears of every male victim who hears them, and all too often, he starts to believe them himself.

A female narcissist is just as skilled in baiting her victim into reacting to her abuse as a male. She will poke and prod until she finally gets the explosion in frustration she was after. She will then use his reactions against him. The added power she has in doing this when her victim finally does erupt comes from the fact that anger and 'anger management issues' are associated with men. It is relatively easy for the female abuser to twist the narrative and have not only outsiders believe that he is abusive because he yelled at her, but the victim himself, who feels shame and remorse for 'scaring' a woman who is 'half his size'. The provoking behaviour may include intimidating physical behaviours such as poking and slapping where the man feels powerless to respond. She may even attempt to entice him into hitting her, to garner 'evidence' to use against him. She knows her victim is in a lose–lose situation. If he retaliates physically, even to simply push her out of his way, he will be at the mercy of a system that would not believe that he was the victim. In not retaliating, he is at the mercy of her rages – and not retaliating may make her even angrier.

James's story

When James came to see me, he looked like, and described himself as, a 'shattered man'. The tears flowed intermittently as he described the toxic relationship he felt trapped by. Like Michael, he also felt that the pain of leaving would be greater than the pain of staying. Like Michael, he had spent many hours researching the confusing behaviour of his partner with whom he had such intense chemistry in the beginning, a partner who now seemed to yo-yo between loving him and hating him. The latter periods would result in punishments and threats to destroy him. Unlike Michael, however, James initially did not want to label his partner as a narcissist, as he had been the victim of terrible abuse as a child. Like many victims of narcissistic abuse, James's empathy was being used against him.

James was 28. He described to me his own unhappy childhood in which he witnessed ongoing bouts of domestic violence when his father would regularly beat up his mother. His father never beat him, but the poisonous words he directed at James throughout his life created wounds that had never healed, and were far more painful than any physical injury he had ever experienced.

His father detested James's gentle nature, and would regularly refer to him as a 'girl' or a 'sissy', as if these names would somehow 'toughen him up'. Even though James was tall and solid like his father, he did not fit the mould of what his abusive father defined as a 'man'. Nor would he ever. James was a gay man who still suffered from the wrath of his abusive father, and the thought of coming out to his family terrified him.

James's abuser stored away this little piece of information (scored during a particularly good display of empathy in the love bombing stage) and utilised it any time he needed to pull James into line. And outing James's 'secret' became a weapon that the narcissist would covertly threaten him with should he ever think of leaving.

This is a common experience for gay men who are being abused by a narcissist, and further cements the narcissist's power and control over them. Coming out and revealing one's gender or sexuality can be a scary thing for anyone to do in a society where homophobia still very much exists. Throw child abuse into the mix, along with fear of an abusive, homophobic father, and the narcissist had complete control over James's life, which he knew he could destroy with one phone call.

James's story illustrates another difficulty that men face in being recognised as victims of narcissistic abuse, and the subsequent lack of support. Domestic violence in all its forms is viewed by society as a 'heterosexual' issue. James supported this notion when he told me of a time that his partner, Mateo, had slapped him in the face, leaving a red mark under his eye. This was not the first time Mateo had physically assaulted him; it had happened numerous times before. But it was the first time that James worked up enough courage to report it at his local police station. The memory of that incident was etched on his brain, not because of the assault, but because of the reactions of the police. Their whole demeanour told him that they were not taking him seriously, and it was obvious the officers were somewhat amused by James's injury, which they described as 'needing a magnifying glass to see'.

James felt humiliated and totally unseen and unheard when an officer said, 'I'm sure you blokes will sort it out', and promptly left him to attend to someone else. The issue that resonated for me in James's experience was this: men are typically viewed as the aggressor in an intimate relationship, and if you're a man, it's expected that you should be able to defend yourself and 'sort things out'. The old 'boys will be boys' adage rings true, as domestic violence occurring in the context of two men is scoffed at when viewed through the lens of heterosexuality. The premise is that 'man on man' is a fair fight. The abuse is regarded as 'mutual' and it is assumed that two men have an equal ability to defend themselves.

Here I'll reiterate that mutual abuse is a myth in the context of domestic violence and narcissistic abuse. There is always a power imbalance in these toxic relationships, with only one abuser and a victim who reacts to the intentional abuse.

The societal idea that abuse is mutual in gay relationships is clear in the incident when James sought help from the police. Even though James's abuser was a man, he was not supported as a victim of abuse, reinforcing the stereotype that only women can be victims. (This brings into awareness the conflict that exists for a victim in a lesbian relationship seeking support. Even though the victim is a woman, she would most likely not be given the same support that she would had her abuser been male. Once again, society looks at conflict in lesbian relationships as 'mutual abuse' where there's an even playing field.)

Gay men, it seems, have even less chance of being recognised as victims of narcissistic abuse than heterosexual men, isolating them further and pushing them deeper into the controlling clutches of the abusers they are trauma bonded to.

James told me that he regretted going to the police because not only was he not supported, but Mateo punished him for 'betraying' him. Not only did Mateo ghost him for an entire week, not telling him where he was going, but he sent James numerous photos of his nights out partying at clubs with their mutual friends. He even sent photos of himself with his arms all over another man who James did not recognise. James was distraught. The silent treatment was 'killing' him, and here was Mateo out enjoying himself, punishing him when James was the one with the injury.

There were other variables at play here that made the punishment even more devastating for James and compounded the isolation he experienced as a gay male victim of abuse. Because no one outside his community knew that he was gay, he cherished the friendships he'd developed in his community, and it was the only place he could truly be himself. James had sensed a change in his friends' attitude towards him a few months prior, but it was growing increasingly obvious that they were treating him differently. James later found out that Mateo had begun smearing him to his friends much earlier, with lies suggesting his infidelity, something he was pretty sure that Mateo himself was guilty of, and of course the narrative of James's visit to the police station was completely distorted. Mateo's smear campaign implied that James had in fact abused *him*, and that James had betrayed Mateo with his lies to the police. As all narcissists do, Mateo was engaging in classic projection while smearing James and destroying not only his credibility but his friendship circle. James simply couldn't comprehend the intentional cruelty in Mateo's actions. James described the utter hopelessness he felt at the time as being like 'waves of gut-wrenching, painful betrayal, colliding with waves of crippling grief and loss, to form a perfect storm of soul destruction'.

It was not lost on him that Mateo would overtly, or covertly, imply to his friends that James had betrayed them too with his 'lies'. James told me his reluctance in coming forward to report the abuse reflected not only his loyalty to Mateo and his belief that domestic violence was something that only existed for women in heterosexual relationships, but his loyalty to the gay community. He said, 'It's still hard for a gay couple to be accepted as just a regular couple with all the same wants and needs that any other couple has. In trying to be accepted, we've survived so much oppression, discrimination and often downright hatred. Why hand society the tools to smash us down again?'

James was describing the unwritten value system of many people in the gay community, certainly within his own circle of friends, by which you don't talk about issues that reflect badly on the community – you don't 'air your dirty laundry'. And any type of violence in the relationship was one of those issues. He felt so guilty, he had let them down. And for what? No one believed him. Not even his friends. His community, the gay community, the only community where he felt accepted, was now rejecting him. The loneliness he felt was indescribable, and he prayed for his abuser to return, the only person James felt he had left in the world, to heal the wounds that very abuser had created.

In telling me this, James was inadvertently also describing yet another reason why it is so hard for a gay man to seek support as a victim of abuse. The stereotyped idea that a gay man could not possibly be monogamous suggests that it should be easy for them to just get up and leave their relationship – as if being gay somehow makes someone immune to the powerful trauma bond that occurs when an abuser engages in manipulative strategies to hook their victim and keep them hooked. Even though there is general lack of understanding of trauma bonding in the context of abusive relationships, first responders are very aware – and often assume – that victims will return again and again to their abusers, and the abuse will continue. Female victims, that is.

Consequently, there will be little empathy or understanding for a man who can't seem to leave or stay away from his alleged abuser when that man is assumed by society to be non-monogamous, and in a relationship that society deems lacking in any type of genuineness, structure, stability or substance.

James also told me that being a lot larger than Mateo, who was also less 'masculine' (masculinity as it is perceived by society, at least) in appearance and personality, meant that much like a man being abused by a narcissist in a heterosexual relationship, he felt powerless to defend himself. Mateo had verbally and physically assaulted him in public on a number of occasions and people had simply watched, doing nothing to help him. This included security guards at a nightclub, and even the police, when during one horrific display of alcohol fuelled narcissistic rage, they witnessed 'tiny' Mateo verbally and physically attack James. The police did nothing to protect James. They simply used their presence to stop the 'argument', asking the men to 'break it up', even though the abuse wasn't mutual and James was clearly the one under attack:

Mateo had backhanded him, screamed obscenities at him and loudly threatened to destroy him.

This behaviour adds yet another layer of complexity that makes it difficult for a gay man to be recognised as a victim, because it supports the notion that the bigger/stronger, 'more masculine' person is more powerful, and therefore cannot be a victim of their 'weaker' partner. Abusers who exhibit consistent patterns of narcissistic behaviours over space and time, are not always more physically powerful than their victim. James's abuser presented as a classic example of that. He was able to lash out physically and verbally at James in full view of the public, knowing that he would suffer less scrutiny than perhaps even a woman who was seen hitting a man.

It saddened me to hear James regularly allude to the fact that he might have 'deserved' the abuse. He had been told his whole life by his father that there was something wrong with him and that he was not good enough. As he was growing up, he heard regular verbal attacks by his father directed at the community that James belonged to, the cherished community that was now his family. Imagine growing up and being continually pummelled with 'information' from the most important male role model in your life that it was bad to be someone like you. Imagine the confusion in the mind of a boy who was scared to grow into the person they knew they were.

Sadly, this type of 'induction' into claiming their identity is all too common among my clients. Stigma, stereotypes, discrimination, child abuse and numerous other factors that men like James experience often lead to feelings of internalised homophobia for the victim. Many victims like James experience, and absorb, a lifetime of negative associations with being gay, and internalise the social prejudice that surrounds them. The subconscious shame that results from being so 'different' from everyone else leads to core wounds that restrict any capacity for these men to be happy in who they are, and they are extremely vulnerable to being abused by a narcissist.

Narcissistic abuse is not gender-specific. This creates a dilemma for a society that requires all domestic violence victims to fit neatly in one box and, more importantly, it creates a risk of harm for gay men who are being abused that is completely unacceptable.

The issues that James told me about are just some of reasons that gay men are at risk of abuse by narcissists. Not only do these issues create an unacceptable risk of harm for gay men, but gay men are far less likely to be able to access support to leave the abuser.

In a society that still does not understand that psychological and emotional abuse constitute violence, and looks for 'visible bruises' or broken bones as evidence that you were abused, male victims of narcissistic abuse suffer perhaps in even more silence than women.

* * *

This chapter relates specifically to male victims of narcissistic abuse. Please know, however, that no matter what your gender or sexual orientation, or what pronouns you choose to use, the abusive and ongoing narcissistic patterns of behaviour and the traits of the ego-driven narcissist remain the same. As all forms of domestic violence are, narcissistic abuse is about power and control, so I'm confident that you will relate as a victim of narcissistic abuse to these victims' stories. Many of my clients, who come from various cultural backgrounds and are involved in a wide range of relationships (which don't always fit the traditional male–female model), say: 'It's like they all went to the same school for narcissists!'

As they read and hear each other's stories online and compare their research, they realise they are not alone, and that anyone, particularly the individual with existing core wounds, can become the victim of a toxic narcissist. Their experiences reflect the fact that not only is narcissistic abuse becoming an epidemic in today's society, but the principles of narcissistic abuse are universal. The support you receive as a victim, however, depends on the rules of the society you are governed by, and whether that society (and you as the victim) believes you deserved the abuse.

CHAPTER TWELVE

The healing journey begins

So what happened to Sofie in the end? Well, I'd love to tell you that she went on to get full custody of her children and a wonderful property settlement, becoming the shining role model for all victims of narcissistic abuse. I would love to tell you that Justin disappeared for good. I would love to tell you that eventually Sofie was able to become the same woman she was before she was traumatised. I would love to tell you all these things, but that wouldn't be true.

What did happen was much more realistic: Sofie found a system that worked for her in parallel parenting the children with Justin, who had 50 per cent care. She eventually obtained a reasonable property settlement after a lengthy and painstaking court battle, she became very good at going 'grey rock'/minimal contact with both Justin and her mother, and it would only be every now and then that one of them would creep back with a proverbial prod or poke to see if she had let her guard down. Sofie slipped a couple of times in the beginning, but eventually her boundaries became rock-solid. Things were not perfect, but her healing journey had begun. And she became happy. She was no longer a victim, she was a survivor. Sofie was experiencing freedom and she was taking back her power.

Here are 13 steps to taking back your power and healing from narcissistic abuse. Sofie managed this process and I know they will also help you.

THE 13 STEPS TO TAKING BACK YOUR POWER

1. Validate your trauma
2. Talk about your trauma as much as you want
3. Prioritise self-care
4. Journalling
5. Grieve
6. Allow yourself to think freely about your trauma
7. Process your trauma
8. Go 'grey rock' with your abuser
9. Make your boundaries rock solid
10. Forget about revenge
11. Forgive yourself
12. Accept that you're going to be a different person
13. Give yourself closure

1. Validate your trauma

Sofie sought professional help and also joined a narcissistic abuse recovery support group on Facebook. She created an alias to begin with to super-protect her privacy. She now referred to herself as a survivor, not a victim.

One of the most important steps in the healing journey for every survivor of narcissistic abuse is to have their trauma validated. Like a record on repeat, you have been told again and again that your feelings are not valid. You've been told that *you're* the problem: you're crazy and oversensitive, you're a drama queen and all you want to do is start arguments.

However, through your research you have come to realise the problem was actually *not* with you and that you were gaslighted into believing this. But can you trust yourself? You have provided black and white evidence to the narcissist in the past, and have still been told that you're misinterpreting things. Your ability to trust your understanding of information has been compromised by the narcissist, and victims often still struggle with whether their ex-partner matches the definition of a narcissist.

This is the time to start trusting your instincts: *you* are the expert in your trauma. Narcissists rarely get diagnosed unless by court order. Don't listen to that little voice that may still be telling you you're imagining things: that's just your abuser who's still taking up space in your head rent-free. You are going to kick them out!

Once they understand what happened to them, and how crazy-making their trauma is, it is critical for survivors to have their trauma validated by others. It is normal to want to talk, talk, talk about it, and you will find yourself repeating the same story over and over again. This is you trying to make sense of the nonsensical. It's like watching a movie again and again, and picking up some tiny new detail every time you watch it.

Please don't think there's anything wrong with you in needing to talk about it so much. You are validating your trauma. You will, however, worry that friends will get sick of hearing about it, and the reality is that some friends will get sick of it. Even the most loving friend will eventually tire. This is why your trauma needs to be validated by the right people. Someone who understands implicitly the fog you have just emerged from, who will validate your experience with patience, and allow you free rein to take as long as you need.

The people who will have the most compassion and understanding of your experience, and who will be your greatest advocates, are your fellow survivors. Please search your social media platforms for narcissistic abuse recovery support groups. Most of them will be private groups, where you can speak freely, and there you can seek comfort from other humans who have walked in your shoes.

2. Talk about your trauma as much as you want

In the beginning Sofie found herself talking about her trauma constantly. Gradually, she reached a place where she knew she needed to prioritise her self-care. By processing her trauma, she didn't feel the need to talk about it so much. She joined a narcissistic abuse recovery group on Facebook so she could talk and read when she felt the need. Eventually, she found a healthy balance between her self-care and her need to talk about the abuse, which became less important to her over time.

When you've been traumatised by a narcissist, you must give yourself permission to talk about it as much as you need to. Talking about your abuse is different from the narcissist engaging in a smear campaign. The motivation of a narcissist is to punish; yours is to heal. Perhaps start a blog where you can connect with other victims and survivors to help each other. However, be mindful that one day you'll need to prioritise self-care.

It's easy to get stuck in a cycle of watching video after video online about narcissistic abuse because of the initial exhilaration you feel as your trauma is validated. Don't let this become your new addiction. I'm not telling you to stop; I'm simply asking you to look at the behaviour, and gauge whether it's having a negative impact on your life. Most victims know when they are becoming a little obsessed with gathering information. Again, trust your instincts. It is at this time I suggest that you look at whether it is taking up more time in your life than your passions and your self-care. If so, work towards ensuring that the things that bring you joy are taking precedence in your life, and any engagement in the narcissistic abuse recovery community is just a small interaction that keeps you grounded. It's all about balance.

3. Prioritise self-care

Sofie bought a self-care planner. She wrote up weekly blocks with a self-care activity for every day. At the end of each week, she would reward herself with a massage for sticking to her self-care commitments. She joined a gym, found a walking group with other single mothers, and took up dancing lessons, in which she found her passion. She got her nails done once a month even when the budget was a bit tight because this made her feel good.

So, what does self-care look like? Survivors understandably want to heal yesterday, and they want the handbook. Your self-care is about you and the things that bring you peace, joy and fulfillment. The essential self-care strategy I recommend to help process and heal from your trauma is therapy with a trauma-informed therapist. When you find the strategies that work for you, the most important thing to remember is that you have to commit to engaging in them. Your self-care needs to be a top priority and factored into your schedule before other commitments such as work. Get yourself a self-care planner and commit to putting at least one thing that relates to your self-care in it for every day. Perhaps write up your planner in one-week blocks as Sofie did. Every time you accomplish a self-care activity, put a line through it, and at the end of the week pride yourself on your commitment to healing, and reward yourself with something extra-special. Here are some suggestions for self-care activities.

+ **Daily exercise**: Start going for bike rides, join a gym, or go for a walk in your local park. Try yoga or Pilates. Get those endorphins flowing!
+ **Mind, body and spirit**: Visit your GP for a thorough check up. Address any physical ailments you have such as migraines, muscle tension or sleeping issues that relate directly to your abuse. Address any anxiety or depression you are experiencing and make a commitment to getting well.
+ **Meditation**: Empty your mind of anxious thoughts, break the spike in any impulsive behaviour and practise relaxation before trying to sleep.
+ **Diet**: Commit to a healthy diet and try to drink eight glasses of water a day.
+ **Personal care**: Get your hair done. Book in a regular massage. Buy yourself that new outfit you have been wanting for ages.

Every part of you has to be nurtured because it interacts with the other parts. Now is the time to spoil yourself and take care of yourself in every way. I can assure you the kids would rather get less for their birthday and have a happy, radiant mum or dad.

Don't make your self-care goals overwhelming, however, so that you set yourself up for failure. Baby steps. Small goals to begin with and bigger as you get stronger. Aim big too early, miss big. Aim small, win small – but you still win.

If you feel selfish for prioritising yourself, then try to negate those conditioned feelings by reasoning that you're doing it for someone else. Just to begin with. I want your self-care routine to eventually be something that comes naturally to you. Something you take for granted, for which you do not owe anyone an explanation, and you feel not one iota of guilt for engaging in. If you need a reason to prioritise yourself in your healing journey, then consider the following scenario.

You have boarded a plane and taken your seat and the flight attendant begins the pre-flight safety briefing. They inform passengers that masks will drop from above in case of emergency, and ask parents to secure their own mask before they secure the masks of their children. Isn't that the opposite of what you've been made to believe throughout your life? Shouldn't you make sure someone else is taken care of first, especially the children, before you can even think of looking after yourself?

But if you don't take care of yourself first, you will not be able to take care of others. Young children can't secure their own mask and they need an adult to help them. The positive repercussions of your self-care will filter out to every part of your life, especially to the people you love. By looking after yourself first, you benefit everyone.

4. Journalling

Sofie started to write about her feelings and her experiences. She found it very cathartic to offload the thoughts that were consuming her, and she was able to process them.

Journalling is another strategy that I always recommend. For those of you who hate writing, I'm not asking you to write *War and Peace*. Journalling is about emptying your head and putting those thoughts onto paper so you can process them. It can be simple sentences. It can be just bullet points. Whatever works for you. But please try it, even if you just start with five minutes each night. If you succeed in doing that, it's a win! Any more than five minutes then becomes a bonus.

Journalling allows you to slow things down and make sense of the jumble of thoughts in your head. You can look back at a later time and start to make connections with past and future behaviour, and you can see when patterns of behaviour start to develop.

When thinking, your brain works at a rate of up to 1400 words a minute. When we journal, we slow things down and our thoughts become more tangible. We can look at what we've written over time and say to ourselves, 'Wow! That really happened to me?'

We bring our experience to life – give it form. It's no longer a bunch of crazy thoughts that we can't make sense of.

Journalling is also cathartic. It's like releasing a pressure valve: you're emptying your mind and recording its contents so it doesn't have to worry about those thoughts anymore.

Journal about your abuse. Write down what this person did to you. Look at your notes when you're experiencing a craving to unblock the narcissist. Remind yourself just how evil the narcissist is. Cut that craving off at the pass.

5. Grieve

With the support of her therapist, Sofie grieved all the losses she endured because of her abuse. She grieved the loss of the family she wanted so badly, and the role of wife that she always dreamed of having. She grieved the image of the future that was wrapped up in being part of that family. She grieved the loss of her identity and the passion she once had for life. She grieved for the happy young woman she once was. She put her arms around that young woman and allowed her to cry.

When Sofie first realised she had been discarded it felt as if her whole world had imploded, and she had no idea how she was going to carry on. The feelings of betrayal were overwhelming and she felt as if she'd been body slammed into a brick wall. The pain of realising that her life with Justin was based on an illusion was immense. A pain different from any kind she'd experienced before, it permeated every part of her being.

Every victim of narcissistic abuse who has that lightbulb moment – when they discover the true identity of the person they've been in a relationship with – will experience loss. Immeasurable loss that must be processed. This requires grieving. Accepting that she needed to grieve was an essential part of Sofie's healing journey.

It is vital that you grieve the ending of the relationship. Sadness and anger are integral parts of that grieving process.

One of the issues that causes concern for Sofie and many other survivors is the anger they feel towards their ex-partner or family member. They've been betrayed at a soul level, and the person who betrayed them seems to be living their best life. Nothing has changed for them and if their social media pictures are any indication, they seem happier than ever.

Survivors feel almost consumed with an anger that affects every part of their lives and prevents them from moving forward. These angry thoughts come to them at night when they're trying to sleep or during work hours when they clearly should be thinking about something else. The survivor's hatred for their abusive ex is compounded by the fact that they still can't get them out of their head. They often get told by well-meaning individuals that they're not entitled to their anger and they should feel lucky that they made it out. They hear lines such as 'You just need to get over it' and they get even angrier with themselves because they *can't* seem to get over it. Once again, the notion that there is something wrong with the victim is reinforced.

Let me make it clear: you are 100 per cent entitled to your anger, and not allowing yourself to feel it is like plugging a hose then turning on the tap. Eventually that plug is going to come unstuck, and you will have about as much control over your emotions as you have over that exploding hose. This often brings feelings of resentment from survivors who would rather be shot out of a cannon with hot needles in their eyes than shed one more tear for the loss of their partner.

Let me put your mind to rest. When I say that grieving is imperative, I'm not talking about grieving the loss of your abuser. I'm talking about you. What did *you* lose in this relationship? You lost your hopes and dreams of being a happy family. You lost the future you'd planned and the person you planned to grow old with. You most probably lost money, assets and other things of a physical and sentimental nature. You lost friends. You lost time. You experienced the double whammy of losing a relationship, and losing a relationship that never was. But most of all? You lost yourself. It is all these things that you need to grieve. Not the toxic monster you now know the abuser to be.

You are allowed to feel the way you feel, and don't let anyone tell you differently. What happened to you was not fair. It was unjust and you did absolutely nothing to deserve what happened to you. Of course you're going to be angry. I would think there was something wrong if you weren't. It's what we do with that anger that makes all the difference. Now we've all heard the old saying 'Holding on to anger is like drinking poison and hoping the other person gets sick.'

I'm not asking you to hold on to your anger. I'm asking you to give yourself permission to feel it. Don't distract yourself from your feelings by trying to get busier at work, or by desperately trying to think about something else. Not only did you spend what feels like an eternity with the narcissist, where every second of your life was enmeshed with them, but they tried to destroy you. Of course you're going to be thinking about something that took up such a huge part of your life.

The only person who can turn their anger and fake love on and off like a light switch is a narcissist. Use your anger to propel you forward. Don't direct it at your abuser, because they would enjoy that, and certainly don't direct it at yourself. What you're feeling is normal, and you cannot go over, around or underneath this tunnel of grief. You have to hang on with all you've got and go straight through, allowing yourself to feel the feelings as they come. Everyone's tunnel is different and there is no time limit on grief. But at the of the grieving tunnel I hope you will find some acceptance and seek closure from the only person who can give it to you. That person is you.

Sadness at the unequivocal loss you've experienced is also a huge part of the grieving process, and once again, these emotions are not related to the monster you saw in the end. The monster you saw in the end is who the narcissist really is. Your sadness relates to the loss of the person you thought they were, and the way that imaginary person made you feel in the beginning. Allow yourself to feel these feelings of sadness and anger from the incredible losses in your life, and for the changes they have made in you.

If you're going to be angry, then be angry. Get yourself a punching bag and when you feel that anger brewing, give that punching bag all you've got. Go for a run, or scream into a pillow, but get it out.

If you're feeling sad, then let those tears flow. Work out your own strategy that will work for you and plan for these times. My only advice when you allow yourself to express these feelings is not to let them consume you. When you are feeling these emotions, put a timer on. Give yourself half an hour to express those feelings with gusto. When that timer goes off, wash your face, dry your eyes and stand tall like the king or queen that you are, and then do something that makes you happy. Replace the negative thoughts in your head with something positive. Say something like 'I'm so proud of myself. I survived all of that so I can survive anything. Bring on my future and watch me soar!'

6. Allow yourself to think freely about your trauma

Sofie stopped beating herself up for thinking about her trauma and her abuser, and eventually she started to think about him less and less until she hardly thought about him at all.

If you are thinking about your abuser constantly, ruminating about the good times, minimising the abuse and getting angry with yourself for doing so, I want you to remember the trauma bond that I discussed in Chapter 4. It's a very powerful connection to your abuser and you will need lots of support to break those invisible chains to your abuser. Over a long period of time, your soul was infiltrated by the insidious slow drip-feed of a toxic substance. It's going to take time. Considering the power of the trauma bond, your ruminating is normal. Irrational, but normal. Normal, because you are thinking about something that consumed your life. Irrational, because your brain is thinking about the infinitely small scraps of 'good times' but has rejected the mountains of abusive treatment. Our brains are wired for safety, not happiness. This is also why you hold onto those breadcrumbs of the good times. Your brain is keeping you 'safe' by discarding the thoughts that make you feel bad. Or maybe you're just constantly having conversations in your head with your abuser in which you finally get to feel heard. If you are driving yourself crazy with thoughts of this person you would do anything to forget, then I want you to engage in this little experiment.

I want you to completely empty your mind. Give yourself a minute or so to do this, and then I want you to think about anything else you possibly can, except ice cream. (I love ice cream so this works for me.) Think about your job, think about the fly crawling up the wall, but whatever you do, under any circumstances, don't. Think. About. Ice cream!

How hard was it to stop yourself from thinking about ice cream when you made such an important point of telling yourself that you mustn't think about it?

This is what you're trying to do every time you try to stop yourself from thinking about your abuser. Instead of beating yourself up for thinking regularly about a very 'topical issue' in your life, I want you to go with the flow and just allow the thoughts to come. Address them. Give them attention. You might be thinking about a time they gaslighted you, so instead of trying to stomp all over the thought, give it credence. You might say something like, 'Oh yes, I remember that time! Now I know I wasn't crazy and they were just trying to confuse me!'

To stop giving the thoughts so much power, stop doing everything you can not to think about them. When you stop making these thoughts such a bad thing and you just allow them to take place without resistance, they won't hold as much power over you. Without the power they once held, it will get relatively boring to think about what you were once consumed with, and those thoughts will get fewer and fewer over time. Just as it would be boring to sit around and think about ice cream all day, your brain will want to think about other things when it knows that thoughts about your abuse can come and go freely without you trying to fend them off.

7. Process your trauma

With the help of her therapist, Sofie processed what had happened to her, and realised it was not her fault in any way. She was no longer going to victim-blame herself. The processing helped her to give the feelings of ongoing anger and guilt away to the 'universe'.

Please also seek support with a counsellor. But not just any counsellor. Some therapy is not always better than none. Make sure that the therapist you choose is trauma-informed and experienced in supporting victims and survivors of narcissistic abuse. Ask your fellow survivors if they have recommendations. The wrong therapist will minimise your experience, and you will end up enlightening *them* about the dynamics of narcissistic abuse rather than the other way round.

Be aware of your triggers. A complex post-traumatic stress disorder trigger is something that reminds you of your trauma, such as a sound, a sight, a smell or even a feeling. It is normal to have symptoms of CPTSD because of the ongoing nature of your abuse. Perhaps your heart starts beating faster when you smell a cologne that your abuser used to wear, or perhaps you have a major anxiety attack every time you see a red car because your abuser used to drive a red car. You were conditioned to associate that cologne or red car with your abuser, and your fear is real. Your fear is real, just as it is real for the soldier home from war who breaks down every time they hear a car backfire or fireworks go off. They were conditioned to pair together loud bangs with the fear of death.

Work with your therapist to address your triggers and break these conditioned responses. Work with your therapist, too, to address any behaviours which are conditioned responses from your abuse that are negatively impacting your life. Perhaps you always feel under attack from your new partner because you had to constantly defend yourself from attack with your abuser. Perhaps you have trouble accepting any compliments from them because your abuser made you feel so ugly. Your therapist will help you to change your thought patterns and have more clarity when assessing incoming information.

Be aware that your healing journey will not be linear, and that you will be better on some days than others. If you know the trauma bond to your abuser is still strong, prepare for the days when you don't feel as strong. Like someone in Alcoholics Anonymous would, get yourself a sponsor, and when you feel you may break no-contact, call that trusted person to help you work through that craving.

8. Go 'grey rock' with your abuser

Sofie stopped engaging with Justin unless it was absolutely necessary. She blocked him everywhere except for one email address.

Taking your power back after narcissistic abuse is going to be so much harder if you're still engaging with your abuser in ways that are not 100 per cent necessary. If you have no ties with them at all, such as children, family or work, then going no-contact is the only answer.

No contact means no texting, no emails, no looking at their social media, and no asking friends about what your abuser is doing. This is not the same as the ending to a normal relationship. No contact is required to keep you free of the environment that made you sick in the first place. No contact gives you space to work on healing and to sever those powerful trauma bonds by essentially going cold turkey from the manipulative tactics of your abuser.

Any kind of contact, whether it be just having a sneak peek at their Instagram account, or maybe the Instagram account of their new target, keeps your abuser inside your head. Any kind of contact is the equivalent of the drug addict putting the needle back in their arm and reactivating the insidious cycle of addiction. You could have counselling every day of your life, but if your abuser still has access to your mind to manipulate you it's going to make healing so much harder. Much like pouring water into a bucket full of holes, the healing information will come in and your abuser will be doing their best to make sure that most of it goes straight back out, with little effect.

It may sound harsh, but I also recommend that you sever ties and go no-contact with anyone who knows your abuser. Seeing the narcissist's name pop up on your Facebook screen because they have been tagged in a mutual friend's post is contact. If you are still allowing this to happen then you may as well pick up the phone and call your abuser because it is just as damaging. Any friend of the abuser is a flying monkey and someone you will not be able to trust.

At this time in your life, it is imperative that you surround yourself with people you trust. Your circle will get smaller, that is inevitable. But you'll know that the people left are worth having in your life. In going no-contact, make sure you have thought of everything! Don't allow the narcissist the tiniest opportunity to hoover you back into the vortex of abuse. If you have to have some kind of contact with your abuser because you have children together or you work with them, ensure that you are using the 'grey rock' method in Chapter 9. Do not JADE (justify, argue, defend and explain) with them, and be as boring as possible so they go elsewhere for their supply.

If you are thinking that it's just too hard to change your email or your phone number because the narcissist is still contacting you, or that you would feel guilty by removing mutual friends from your social media, then please consider this. Imagine you've lived your whole life in an industrial area full of factories and traffic. This life is all you know. You've always suffered from hay fever, asthma and other allergies for which you take a slew of medications, and you put your ongoing tiredness down to the medication, or perhaps the busy lifestyle that you lead.

One day you decide you need a major change and you move from that area to an idyllic little town in the mountains. You breathe in the clean fresh air and after a while your energy levels increase dramatically and you no longer need your allergy medication. You look back to your life in the industrial area and think: 'I was really sick when I was living with all that smog and I just didn't know it!'

You didn't know until you had *contrast*. You had nothing to compare it to. Now imagine if you went back once a week to stay in that old house for a night or two. How long do you think you would remain feeling well? You might feel good for a while then have to repair the damage that occurred every time you went back.

It may be difficult to rearrange what seems like your whole life when you think about having to get a new email address, phone number and so on, but consider the alternative. Don't go back and breathe in those toxic fumes ever again.

9. Make your boundaries rock solid

Sofie worked through her guilt about feeling assertive and putting her own needs first, and learned to say no when she wanted to. The toxic people dropped off because they could no longer use her.

Your newfound boundaries are going to be your best friends. Having healthy boundaries is your right, and you will have to practise enforcing them. Boundaries are part of your self-care. They ward off people who want to treat you like a doormat, and encourage you to prioritise your own needs. To begin with, it may seem uncomfortable to say 'No' to someone when they ask you to do something you really don't want to do. But remember the feeling when you said yes when you really wanted to say no? You knew you were being taken advantage of, but you just couldn't say no, and it felt terrible. Remember how worried you were about what people would think if you said no, or, at the very least, if you didn't provide a ten page email outlining the reasons you were unable to do what they wanted?

Our boundaries are there to protect us, and the only people who will object to your boundaries are the people who benefited from you having none. Practise being assertive and replacing the negative thoughts of guilt such as 'I'm so mean. I really could have helped them out' or 'They're going to think I'm so selfish!' with 'It's perfectly okay to say no because I am very busy with my own schedule'.

You may wish to enforce a simple boundary, such as 'We would like it if you phoned first before you come over'. However, the feelings you have in telling, for example, a controlling mother-in-law that you want her to call first before coming over send you into a panic and you are racked with guilt.

I want you to journal about any 'irrational' guilt you may feel in setting up a boundary such as this. A boundary that really should be taken for granted. Why are you feeling so guilty? Is your request unreasonable? Of course it isn't. Calling before visiting is just manners. Or are you just used to the other person getting angry at you or sulking if you didn't give them free rein to do whatever suited them? In other words, you didn't let them control you and walk all over you. The people who love you will not have a problem with your boundaries. They won't make you feel bad for having them. The only people who will make you feel bad are the toxic people you either don't want in your life at all, or you wish to remain a healthy distance from.

10. Forget about revenge

Sofie knew karma would get Justin at some time in his life, and she was too busy with her new life to care. There were times in the beginning she wanted to see him hurt in some way, but then she realised that her happiness was the biggest 'stuff you' of all.

In going no-contact, it is important to also put aside any thoughts of seeking revenge against the narcissist for what they did to you. I don't think we would be human if there wasn't just some tiny part of us that wanted them to get a taste of their own medicine! You want them to feel just a little of what they dealt out to you on a regular basis. When you think of getting revenge, what springs to mind? Maybe thoughts of telling their new target what sort of person they are? Or perhaps calling their boss to inform them you have a restraining order against your ex? Or maybe it's getting ten pizzas delivered to their home using their credit card they forgot you had. Whatever you are thinking about doing to hurt them, it's actually going to have the opposite effect. Because when you do these things, you are continuing to reward the narcissist with your attention. You are handing yourself over to them on a platter, and all the narcissist thinks is: 'Wow. They're still thinking about me. That makes me feel pretty darn powerful.'

I'm not saying don't try to correct injustices through legal channels. If they owe you money then you have every right to get that back (as long as you've weighed up the probability that you might get it back against the impact on your emotional health). What I am saying is that you will never get them to hurt like you hurt, because for that to happen they would have to have the same feelings as you, which they don't. They will not be hurt, but they will get angry. And their actions resulting from that anger may be despicable. You will be no match for their anger because you have a conscience.

By trying to get revenge in these ways you are trying to beat the narcissist at their own game. They love it. So stop playing. However, please know this: you will get your revenge. Your revenge will come in the form of your healing and moving on with your life. It will come in the form of your happiness and success and in rendering them an insignificant part of your life. You will create the most egregious narcissistic wound to their ego by living happily ever after without them. And believe me, the narcissist will know. You won't have to 'accidentally' unblock them on Facebook so they can see how happy you are.

You will probably never see the impact of the wound you created, but just know the narcissist cares immensely whether their old source is happy or not. Your happiness is your revenge. Karma will not forget about them either, but once again, you're going to be too busy making new memories in your new life to care. Karma takes care of the narcissist by slowly eradicating the life-supplying fuel from their lives. They end up dying as lonely, bitter old people who still blame everyone else for their problems. Not even on their deathbed will they admit fault and seek your forgiveness.

11. Forgive yourself

Sofie forgave herself for not knowing then what she knows now, and staying too long in an abusive environment because she couldn't see a way out. She didn't feel any need to forgive Justin, but instead arrived at a place where he had absolutely no ability to impact on her life anymore. He was insignificant to her.

One question I regularly get asked by survivors who are trying to heal is about forgiveness. Survivors want to know if they have to forgive their abuser in order to heal. Most survivors breathe a huge sigh of relief when I give them my opinion, which is a resounding 'No!'

Of course, forgiveness is not about the abuser, it's about you. Many believe that withholding forgiveness keeps the anger and hurt alive and keeps you controlled by the person who harmed you. Their belief is that forgiveness sets you free. I would never seek to change your beliefs and values if this is how you feel. What I will say, however, is that forgiveness is a personal choice. If you want to forgive, that's up to you, but I would never tell anyone that they must forgive the person who tried to destroy them. I would never presume to tell them they must forgive the person who has never shown an ounce of remorse, and if they got their chance, would continue to abuse you.

If forgiveness is about freeing yourself from the hold of your abuser, you can do that without forgiving them. You free yourself from the control of your abuser when they have absolutely no capacity to affect your life anymore. You free yourself when you just don't think about them anymore, apart from occasional fleeting thoughts that hold no power over you. You get to this place of 'You can't hurt me anymore' through your self-care.

Don't let anybody tell you that you cannot move on without forgiving your abuser. It's not fair to place this burden on a survivor's shoulders, and much of the time it ends up having the opposite effect, by keeping their abuser stuck inside their heads.

If you do feel the need to forgive, then forgive yourself. Forgive yourself for not leaving sooner because you didn't know it was abuse or you just didn't know how to leave. Forgive yourself and let go of the shame you carry for loving someone who abused you. The shame is not yours to carry. It belongs to your abuser.

12. Accept that you're going to be a different person

Initially, Sofie wanted to believe that she could be exactly the same person she was before being abused. She grew to accept that this was not going to happen, but that the new Sofie would be happy, with a slightly different path in life than she had once planned.

Your healing journey is going to be the new story that you write about your life. You are not going to be the same person you were before you were traumatised. Expecting yourself to one day return to exactly the same individual you were before your trauma is going to set you up for failure. I am telling you this not to sabotage your healing, but to be your reality check. I do not believe it is helpful to imply to people that if they just do all the right 'work', one day they will be completely healed and will go on with their lives as if the trauma had never happened. This is unrealistic. You are going to be a different person in some ways, and maybe your life will take on a trajectory that you didn't envision. Your trauma happened. It is a part of who you are. However, what will happen as your healing journey continues is that it won't control your life anymore. It will no longer be a roadblock on your path forward or an impenetrable wall that confines you in a room full of painful memories. Your trauma is no longer going to control you. Your trauma will reside somewhere inside you, perhaps in a small part of your mind that you don't give too much attention to. A part of your mind you can draw thoughts from if you choose to, but these thoughts will not consume you as they once did.

No. You will not be exactly the same person, but you will be a person who has discovered just how strong they are. Your trauma did not make you stronger. You survived your trauma because of your strength. You were already strong. This is why the narcissist chose you.

There is strength in you because you are surviving. Draw on this strength. Recognise what you have accomplished, and use this strength to propel you forward in your healing journey, and your new life. The greater your commitment to your healing journey, the stronger you will feel. It might be terrifying to think about entering into another relationship, in case you meet another narcissist. You wonder how you will ever be able to trust another person again. Let me make it clear. You will meet another narcissist.

They are everywhere. However, it won't be a matter of whether you can trust someone else. It will be a matter of you trusting yourself. If a narcissist should cross your path again, any red flags will be deal-breakers and you will run a mile!

13. Give yourself closure

Sofie gave herself closure by doing something that symbolised closure for her. This was writing her abuser a letter that she never gave him, explaining that she had now given herself permission to move on from the past and be happy. She didn't need his validation anymore, and she would think of him no more. She then blocked Justin for good on all of her social media platforms and, together with her friend, tossed the cheap and nasty little engagement ring he had given her into the sea. The feelings of release this gave Sofie were indescribable.

You will never get closure from the narcissist. You will never get a sincere apology, and they will never take any level of responsibility or accountability for the pain they caused you. To do so would be for them to admit being flawed, and perhaps allow you the ability to move on.

Here are some ideas for finding closure:

+ Stop seeking closure from the person who benefits so much by you having none. Instead, seek to provide the closure you need to yourself. Wrap your arms around your wounded inner self and start loving her or him.
+ Don't compare your trauma with that of others and in doing so minimise your right to heal. Your trauma is valid to you.

+ Let go of the feeling that you might have changed the outcome if only you'd been more of something, or less of something else.

+ Do something symbolic that represents closure for you. Remove anything from your home that reminds you of your abuser. You wouldn't expect a heroin addict trying to go cold turkey to have empty syringes lying around, would you?

+ If you're having trouble removing that one final connection to your abuser, such as their number from your phone, then set yourself a quit date. Work towards that date and mentally prepare.

+ You may want to delete photos of yourself with your abuser, or have a yard sale and get rid of the last of any other reminders you have of them.

+ As Sofie did, consider writing your abuser a letter saying exactly what you've always wanted to say to them, but don't post it. Let them know in the letter that you are moving on and that you're giving yourself permission to be happy again, and that means saying goodbye to the part of your life they were involved in.

+ Perhaps write yourself some vows that equate to exactly the opposite of what you might say in a wedding ceremony. Words that symbolise an ending, but also new beginnings for yourself. Find what works for you. Something that makes your closure tangible.

CHAPTER THIRTEEN
Final thoughts

Everyone's journey to healing from narcissistic abuse is going to look different depending on their own unique circumstances, but in general we can see some commonalities in people who have healed and are *thriving* versus those who are simply *surviving*. We'll dive into what thriving looks like shortly.

Bear in mind that your healing journey is not going to be linear. It's unlikely you'll have a clear and predictable healing experience that takes you from point A to point B where each day you feel a little better than yesterday. Rather, your journey will be one where, every now and then, you find yourself stumbling over a pothole you didn't foresee, and you will have to dust yourself off and continue on your path. For example, you may unexpectedly run into your abuser, or someone who knows them, and be catapulted back to the traumatic experience of your former relationship. Try pre-empting these potholes and figuring out some coping strategies for when they inevitably crop up.

You'll also need to make your peace with the idea that you will sometimes find yourself taking two steps forward and one step back. You will experience setbacks that, at the time, will feel overwhelming. You will need to give yourself the grace, understanding and compassion that you freely give to others, when (not if) you hit a stumbling block that knocks the wind out of you. As time goes by, you will find those stumbling blocks crop up less frequently and your journey will become smoother and easier to navigate as you learn and grow. In other words, you will start to see that proverbial 'light at the end of the tunnel'. I know that there will be a day when you will look back and be proud at just how far you've come.

However, there will be no clear 'finishing line' that you bound over, triumphant, at the end of the forty-second kilometre of your own personal marathon. There will be no certificate declaring you healed for good from the trauma of narcissistic abuse.

So why won't your healing journey be straightforward?

+ Your healing will likely require constant routine maintenance. The abuse you've experienced leaves long-term psychological scars and you will need to check in with yourself every so often to ensure you're still functioning in a way that's normal for you.
+ The concrete positive changes in your life may not be noticeable initially while you heal slowly, subtly and gradually. Trust in the process anyway. In so many huge yet imperceptible ways, your brain and nervous system will be changing for the better as soon as you walk out that door never to look back.

You know you're healing from narcissistic abuse when ...

1. One day you wake up and realise it's been a few days, or even a week, since you ruminated about the narcissist or what they did to you. During this time, you've been busy getting on with your life and your mind hasn't been consumed with angry fantasy conversations with the narcissist where you've finally been able to put forward your side without interruption and gaslighting.

2. There was a time, not so very long ago, when you could never see the funny side, you were consumed with sadness and life was all doom and gloom. But now you're laughing and smiling more. You can enjoy a joke, and perhaps even have a giggle at the absurdity of some of the narcissist's crazy-making behaviours.

3. You feel physically better. You've noticed that you seem to be sleeping better and that the sleep you do have isn't plagued with nightmares. You have fewer headaches and less muscle tension, and you're not grinding your teeth in your sleep as much and waking up with a sore jaw as a result. You find yourself better able to concentrate, as your thoughts are not consumed by your abuser and your anger at the injustice of it all. You feel lighter in general, like a load you have been carrying has dropped away, and your energy levels have increased, allowing you to re-engage in the act of living.

4. Friends and loved ones tell you that you look different. There is a glow about you they haven't seen in a long time. They tell you that you look happy. You start to compare recent photos of yourself to those taken during the abuse, and, oh my goodness, they're right! The hollowness in your eyes is gone, and the smiles in the later pictures are genuine, not grimaces that mask your pain to the outside world.

5. Your circle of friends has become smaller, but that's because you've started to put boundaries in place, and you're no longer in touch with the toxic people you once settled for as friends. The people who remain are those you trust, who have your interests at heart and want you to thrive. You may even be starting to catch up with friends or family you were once isolated from, and developing new, healthy relationships with others.

6. You find yourself looking forward to things. You no longer fear that anything enjoyable will be sabotaged and you can start planning ahead for these activities. As a result, you have fulfilling and realistic goals to work towards. You are no longer obsessively watching videos about narcissism, and the bulk of your time is devoted to that which is important to you and your self-care.

7. You realise that you are now more confident in making decisions. There's no more second- (or third-, or fourth-) guessing yourself. No more panicking when someone asks you for your opinion. You're making choices without assuming they will be the wrong ones. You are starting to trust your intuition.

8. As your confidence increases and you start to reinstate your boundaries, you become aware that the feelings of guilt that consumed you before have eased or stopped. You no longer obsess about what other people think of you. You are not people-pleasing anymore. Far from feeling guilty about this, you feel empowered as you now know that your needs *are* important and the people that you want in your circle will respect and support those needs. Your fear of trusting others begins to dissipate as your ability to trust yourself increases. You view red flags for what they are, and you no longer override your intuition for the sake of making someone like you.

9. You are realising that situations or memories that were once extremely triggering for you do not elicit the same emotional responses. You can hear your abuser's name mentioned, or perhaps you are able to hear a song on the radio that was associated with your abuser, and you no longer freeze or relive the feelings associated with the abuse. Dates such as their birthday can come and go and while you may remember the date, it is just another day that does not hold the same significance for you that it once did.

10. You feel free, and it feels wonderful! You have more control over your life, and you don't feel the compulsion to apologise for having ordinary human needs or pretend that you don't have any. You are starting to call yourself a 'survivor' rather than a 'victim', and you realise the strength you had, and have, to not only endure the battle, but come out the other side and begin to thrive. You are learning to love yourself and you are establishing your value in this world as a person worthy, and deserving, of love.

11. You may be at the point where you want to help others. You know how incredibly painful the abuse was, and how much commitment and self-love your healing journey required. As a fellow survivor, you want to help others to heal with your knowledge, compassion and empathy.

12. You are starting to make new memories. Old, toxic routines that held historical significance for you are no longer important. Your new happy, healthy, non-toxic life is beckoning, and you are excited to start making it happen!

In closing, I must emphasise again that on your healing journey the most important thing to remember when trying to understand why and how you were abused by the narcissist is that the abuse was *not your fault*. It happened because someone chose to abuse you. You did nothing to deserve it.

However, while the abuse was never your fault, it is you and you alone who is responsible for your own healing. I believe in you. But you need to believe in yourself. The narcissist lied to you. You can, and will, not only survive without them, but thrive.

I hope this book has been helpful for you at whatever stage you're at in your journey, and there are two things in particular which I hope it will help you accomplish:

1. A deep knowledge that this abuse was never your fault.
2. Rediscovery of the strength that already exists within you.
   The strength that was always there.

In knowing your worth and taking your power back, you are no longer a victim of narcissistic abuse; you are a survivor. You are worth knowing, and the world is a better place because you are part of it.

Remember: you are worthy. You are worthy of so much love and happiness, and you are certainly worthy of a whole lot more than a lifetime of fake love.

USEFUL ACRONYMS

ACON: Adult children of narcissists

CPTSD: Complex post-traumatic stress disorder

DARVO: Deny, attack, reverse victim and offender

FOG: Fear, obligation and guilt

JADE: Justify, argue, defend and explain

NPD: Narcissistic Personality Disorder

PTSD: Post-traumatic stress disorder

ACKNOWLEDGEMENTS

I firstly want to thank my family, most importantly my six amazing children, Courtney, Mitchell, Tyler, Cooper, Brodie and Cruise (I love being your mum!). Thanks also to my grandbabies Ashton and Ariana for your gorgeous and often sloppy kisses and cuddles. To my sister Teri, my brother-in-law Keith, my nieces and nephews, my son-in-law George, and of course my own wonderful mum, Elizabeth, thank you all for your love and support. Your words of encouragement were a never-ending source of motivation for me to keep going and never give up working on this book.

The utmost love and gratitude to my amazing partner Brendan, whose tactfulness (maybe thoughts of self-preservation?) in not mentioning the state of my house while I was writing, namely the piles of unfolded washing that found its new home on the dining table, did not go unnoticed. I'm happy to say the dining room table is now being used for the purpose it was intended!

To my dad – when I first started to pen this book, I would send you each chapter as I wrote it seeking both your advice on how I could improve it, and your general words of wisdom. You were so proud of me! Sadly, you passed away unexpectedly before I could finish it. You never got to read the last two chapters that I finally got around to writing, knowing your spirit was with me the entire time. Thank you for being by my dad, my lifelong mentor, my biggest fan, and of course, the best father in the world.

I would also like to give my sincere thanks to my agent Catherine Wallace from High Spot Literary, for taking a newbie author like myself under her wing, and all the hard work she did to put my book in the hands of my publisher, HarperCollins.

My unequivocal thanks and gratitude to everyone at HarperCollins, most especially my publisher Roberta Ivers. Thank you for believing in me Roberta, for your recognition and understanding of narcissistic abuse and the importance of creating more awareness to help victims in need, but most of all, for your unwavering support and guidance along the way.

To my editors at HarperCollins, Lachlan McLaine and Katie Stackhouse – thank you! In particular, Katie's incredible initial editing shaped and moulded this book with such professionalism and insight, taking it to another level that I am so grateful for.

My sincere thanks to the sales team and the international rights team at HarperCollins headed up by Libby O'Donnell, for arranging international distribution, and placing this book in the hands of readers all over the world. And of course, to the award-winning design team, especially Hazel Lam and Darren Holt, for such an amazing cover, and to Kelli Lonergan for her work in laying out and typesetting.

And finally, thank you to each and every one of you who inspired me and played a part in helping me to create and write this book. (Except for the guy who yelled at me last year because I was too slow getting my groceries onto the conveyor belt.)

A narcissist no doubt! ☺

RESOURCES

AUSTRALIA

Emergency: 000

Lifeline Australia – crisis support, suicide prevention: 13 11 14

1800RESPECT – 24-hour national sexual assault, family and domestic violence counselling: 1800 737 732

DVConnect Womensline – domestic violence support for women: 1800 811 811

DVConnect Mensline – domestic violence support for men: 1800 600 636

Say it Out Loud – provides information and guidance relating to sexual, family and intimate partner violence in the LGBTQ+ community: website www.sayitoutloud.org.au

13YARN – A national Aboriginal and Torres Strait Islander crisis support line supported by Lifeline Australia providing a culturally safe space to yarn one-on-one about the caller's needs, worries or concerns: 13 92 76; website: www.13yarn.org.au

NEW ZEALAND
Emergency: 111

Shine domestic abuse services – provides support services to victims of domestic abuse and their families, 24-hour help line: 0508 744 633; website: www.2shine.org.nz

Lifeline New Zealand – confidential crisis support and counselling: 0800 543 354

Are You OK family violence information line – support and practical steps for individuals experiencing family violence: 0800 456 450; website: www.areyouok.org.nz

Canterbury Men's Centre – provides support and counselling to men who need help with their wellbeing as well as care for men who are living in abusive relationships: 03 365 9000; email: counsellor@canmen.org.nz; website: www.canmen.org.nz

Te Whare O Ngā Tūmanako Māori Women's Refuge – a not-for-profit organisation providing support for wāhine, their tamariki, rangatahi and whānau to live free from any form of violence and abuse, 24/7 helpline: (09) 834 5708 or 0800REFUGE (0800 733 843); website: www.womensrefuge.org.nz

UNITED KINGDOM

Emergency: 999

Lifeline – crisis support for people in distress and despair, a free and confidential helpline: 0808 808 8000; text phone users can contact; 18001 0808 808 8000

Refuge National Domestic Abuse Helpline – 24-hour confidential, non-judgemental support and information on your options: 0808 2000 247

Respect men's advice line – support for male victims of domestic abuse: 0808 8010327; email: info@mensadviceline.org.uk; website: www.mensadviceline.org.uk

Galop – emotional and practical support for LGBT people experiencing domestic abuse, helpline: 0800 999 5428; website: www.galop.org.uk

UNITED STATES

Emergency: 911

National Domestic Violence Hotline – crisis support and information for victims of abuse, concerned loved ones of abuse: 1800 799 7233

Lifeline – crisis support and suicide prevention: 988

Women in Distress – provides crisis intervention, advocacy services, counselling and information for women experiencing domestic violence, crisis hotline: 954 761 1133

LifeWire – supports all men, women and people in LGBTQIA2S+ relationships experiencing domestic abuse, 24-hour helpline: 425 746 1940 or 800 827 8840; website: www.lifewire.org

StrongHearts Native Helpline – a 24/7 safe, confidential and anonymous domestic and sexual violence helpline for Native Americans and Alaska Natives, offering culturally-appropriate support and advocacy: 1-844-7NATIVE (762-8483); website: www.strongheartshelpline.org

Other resources, services and foundations

AUSTRALIA

Brighter Outlook Narcissistic Abuse Counselling Service
Professional online counselling service for victims of narcissistic abuse all over the world. Nova Gibson is the principal counsellor at Brighter Outlook, where she supports victims to understand their abuse, to escape their abusive environment, and to heal.
Website: www.brighteroutlooknarcissisticabusecounselling.com.au
Email: nova.pollard123@gmail.com

Barton Family Lawyers

An experienced legal team of narcissistic abuse specialists who advocate on behalf of victims of narcissistic abuse who have separated from the narcissist to free themselves. Barton Family Lawyers ensure that their clients can negotiate with the narcissist on an equal playing field, free from coercion and control and without being re-victimised by the process.
Website: www.bartonfamilylaw.com.au
Email: reception@bartonfamilylaw.com.au

Small Steps 4 Hannah

In their quest to honour Hannah, Aaliyah, Laianah and Trey and ensure that no family should endure this pain again, the Clarke family have started a movement for change – Small Steps 4 Hannah. Through Small Steps 4 Hannah it is the hope of the Clarke family to harness the collective desire of us all to make positive changes required to HALT to the incidences and severity of domestic and family violence in Australia and take the steps required to do it; small steps that will eventually be giant leaps forward.
Website: www.smallsteps4hannah.com.au

NEW ZEALAND

Loves–Me–Not

Loves–Me–Not is a 'whole-school approach' to prevent relationship abuse and promote healthy relationships among senior secondary students. Loves–Me–Not includes a one-day workshop facilitated by police, school staff and relevant local non-governmental organisations. In 2019, Loves–Me–Not was implemented in 584 classes across 120 schools and educational institutions. Sophie Elliott, 22, was killed by her former boyfriend in 2008. The Sophie Elliott Foundation was then established by her mother Lesley with 'the sole intention of providing young people with knowledge and skills to enter safe and equal relationships', and to raise the awareness of all young women, their families and friends of the signs of partner abuse.

Rainbow Violence Prevention Network

Rainbow people experience disproportionately high rates of violence, with one in two rainbow people experiencing domestic, family and intimate partner violence and abuse in their lifetime. The RVPN's vision is that all rainbow people are free of family and sexual violence and all rainbow people who have experienced harm have access to safe supports.

Website: www.RVPN.nz

UNITED KINGDOM

Laura Richards

Criminal behavioural analyst and expert on stalking, domestic violence, sexual violence, risk assessment and homicide. Richards applies her psychology degrees and advanced training to all facets of these crimes from prevention and offender assessment to victim support and law reform. Richards led the campaign to make stalking a criminal offense and to criminalize coercive control in the UK. She is now focussed on similar processes for criminalizing coercive control in the US.

Website: www.thelaurarichards.com

The Joanna Simpson Foundation – Domestic abuse support for children

In 2010 at the age of 46 Joanna was battered to death by her husband in the vicinity of her children aged just 10 and 9 at the time. This was just one week before the finalisation of their divorce. The Joanna Simpson Foundation has been set up in her memory and their work is based on her beliefs, values and the love of her children. The Joanna Simpson Foundation charity transforms the care, support and protection of children affected by domestic abuse and homicide

Website: www.jsfoundation.org.uk

Email: Info@childrenheardandseen.co.uk

SUTDA (Stand Up to Domestic Abuse)

After 18 years in an abusive relationship, Rachel Williams was shot and severely injured by her violent partner in 2011. He then committed suicide, as did her 16-year-old son Jack, shortly after the attack. Rachel spent several weeks in hospital and now lives with life altering injuries. She campaigns tirelessly and is committed to ending domestic abuse. A qualified Independent Domestic Violence Advisor, Rachel also runs an online awareness Facebook page called Stand Up to Domestic Abuse.

Website: www.sutda.org

Muslim Women's Network Helpline

The helpline is a national specialist faith and culturally sensitive service that is confidential and non-judgmental, which offers information, support, guidance and referrals. Asian/Muslim women face additional cultural barriers that prevent them from seeking help such as fear of dishonouring family, shame, stigma, taboo and being rejected by the community. They are also usually blamed for any problem within the family including the violence and abuse they are subjected to. This fear of blame can also prevent women from coming forward and getting the help they need.

Phone: 0800 999 5786 (10am–4pm Monday to Friday)

Email: contact@mwnuk.co.uk

Website: www.mwnuk.co.uk

True Honour

True Honour was formed to offer support and assistance to all those suffering injustice. They provide confidential one-to-one victim support and training on how to deal with honour based violence and forced marriage. True Honour provides confidential one-to-one victim support and training on how to deal with honour-based violence, and forced marriage.

Phone: 07480 621711

Email: contact@truehonour.org.uk

Website: www.truehonour.org.uk

UNITED STATES

Dr Ramani Durvasula

A licensed clinical psychologist in private practice in Santa Monica and a professor of psychology at California State University in Los Angeles. Also a go-to media expert for a multitude of mental health topics – most notably: narcissism. She has also authored multiple books, including *Should I Stay or Should I Go: Surviving a Relationship With a Narcissist*. Doctor Ramani's YouTube channel provides helpful guidance for those suffering from narcissism, narcissistic abuse, and related personality disorders.

Website: www.doctor-ramani.com

Gabby Petito Foundation

Our story: In September 2021, tragedy struck our family and friends. Our daughter Gabby was missing, and we would soon find out that she was murdered by her boyfriend while on a cross country road trip. In the wake of Gabby's murder, Gabby Petito Foundation was born. Our Foundation is rooted in the belief that we all have an inherent responsibility to make a meaningful difference in our communities. We are honoured to be assisting organizations that provide immediate tangible help to survivors of domestic violence, and we are proud to work with organizations that assist with locating missing persons.

Website: www.gabbypetitofoundation.org

Books

See What You Made Me Do: Power, Control and Domestic Violence by Jess Hill (Black Inc, 2019). A searing investigation that challenges everything you thought you knew about domestic abuse, now an SBS documentary series.

Should I Stay or Should I Go: Surviving a Relationship With a Narcissist by Ramani Durvasula, PhD (Permuted Press, 2017).

Becoming the Narcissist's Nightmare: How to Devalue and Discard the Narcissist While Supplying Yourself by Shahida Arabi (CreateSpace, 2016).

A Mother's Story by Rosie Batty with Bryce Corbett (HarperCollins Publishers, 2015).